Year 6C

A Guide to Teaching for Mastery

Series Editor: Tony Staneff

Contents

Introduction   page 4
What is *Power Maths*?   page 5
Introduction to the author team   page 6
Your *Power Maths* resources   page 7
The *Power Maths* teaching model   page 10
The *Power Maths* lesson sequence   page 12
Using the *Power Maths* Teacher Guide   page 15
Power Maths Year 6, yearly overview   page 16
Mindset: an introduction   page 20
The *Power Maths* characters   page 21
Mathematical language   page 22
The role of talk and discussion   page 23
Assessment strategies   page 24
Power Maths unit assessment grid   page 26
Keeping the class together   page 27
Depth and breadth   page 28
Same-day intervention   page 29
The role of practice   page 30
Structures and representations   page 31
Practical aspects of *Power Maths*   page 32
List of practical resources   page 34
Variation helps visualisation   page 36
Getting started with *Power Maths*   page 37

Unit 13 – Geometry – properties of shapes   page 38
Lesson 1 – Measuring with a protractor   page 40
Lesson 2 – Drawing shapes accurately   page 44
Lesson 3 – Angles in triangles (1)   page 48
Lesson 4 – Angles in triangles (2)   page 52
Lesson 5 – Angles in triangles (3)   page 56
Lesson 6 – Angles in polygons (1)   page 60
Lesson 7 – Angles in polygons (2)   page 64
Lesson 8 – Vertically opposite angles   page 68
Lesson 9 – Equal distance   page 72
Lesson 10 – Parts of a circle   page 76
Lesson 11 – Nets (1)   page 80
Lesson 12 – Nets (2)   page 84
End of unit check   page 88

Unit 14 – Problem solving   page 90
Lesson 1 – Problem solving – place value   page 92
Lesson 2 – Problem solving – negative numbers   page 96
Lesson 3 – Problem solving – addition and subtraction   page 100
Lesson 4 – Problem solving – four operations (1)   page 104
Lesson 5 – Problem solving – four operations (2)   page 108
Lesson 6 – Problem solving – fractions   page 112
Lesson 7 – Problem solving – decimals   page 116
Lesson 8 – Problem solving – percentages   page 120
Lesson 9 – Problem solving – ratio and proportion   page 124
Lesson 10 – Problem solving – time (1)   page 128
Lesson 11 – Problem solving – time (2)   page 132
Lesson 12 – Problem solving – position and direction   page 136
Lesson 13 – Problem solving – properties of shapes (1)   page 140
Lesson 14 – Problem solving – properties of shapes (2)   page 144
End of unit check   page 148

Unit 15 – Statistics   page 152
Lesson 1 – The mean (1)   page 154
Lesson 2 – The mean (2)   page 158
Lesson 3 – The mean (3)   page 162
Lesson 4 – Introducing pie charts   page 166
Lesson 5 – Reading and interpreting pie charts   page 170
Lesson 6 – Fractions and pie charts (1)   page 174
Lesson 7 – Fractions and pie charts (2)   page 178
Lesson 8 – Percentages and pie charts   page 182
Lesson 9 – Interpreting line graphs   page 186
Lesson 10 – Constructing line graphs   page 190
End of unit check   page 194

Introduction

Foreword by the series editor and author, Tony Staneff

For far too long in the UK, maths has been feared by learners – and by many teachers, too. As a result, most learners consistently underachieve. More crucially, negative beliefs about ability, aptitude and the nature of maths are entrenched in children's thinking from an early age.

Yet, as someone who has loved maths all my life, I've always believed that every child has the capacity to succeed in maths. I've also had the great pleasure of leading teams and departments who share that belief and passion. Teaching for mastery, as practised in China and other South-East Asian jurisdictions since the 1980s, has confirmed my conviction that maths really is for everyone and not just those who have a special talent. In recent years, my team and I at Trinity Academy, Halifax, have had the privilege of researching with and working alongside some of the finest mastery practitioners from the UK and beyond, whose impact on learners' confidence, achievement and attitude is an inspiration.

The mastery approach recognises the value of developing the power to think rather than just do. It also recognises the value of making a coherent journey in which whole-class groups tackle concepts in very small steps, one by one. You cannot build securely on loose foundations – and it is just the same with maths: by creating a solid foundation of deep understanding, our children's skills and confidence will be strong and secure. What's more, the mindset of learner and teacher alike is fundamental: everyone can do maths … EVERYONE CAN!

I am proud to have been part of the extensive team responsible for turning the best of the world's practice, research, insights, and shared experiences into *Power Maths*, a unique teaching and learning resource developed especially for UK classrooms. *Power Maths* embodies our vision to help and support primary maths teachers to transform every child's mathematical and personal development. 'Everyone can!' has become our mantra and our passion, and we hope it will be yours, too.

Now, explore and enjoy all the resources you need to teach for mastery, and please get back to us with your *Power Maths* experiences and stories!

What is *Power Maths*?

Created especially for UK primary schools, and aligned with the new National Curriculum, *Power Maths* is a whole-class, textbook-based mastery resource that empowers every child to understand and succeed. *Power Maths* rejects the notion that some people simply 'can't do' maths. Instead, it develops growth mindsets and encourages hard work, practice and a willingness to see mistakes as learning tools.

Best practice consistently shows that mastery of small, cumulative steps builds a solid foundation of deep mathematical understanding. *Power Maths* combines interactive teaching tools, high-quality textbooks and continuing professional development (CPD) to help you equip children with a deep and long lasting understanding. Based on extensive evidence, and developed in partnership with practising teachers, *Power Maths* ensures that it meets the needs of children in the UK.

Power Maths and Mastery

Power Maths makes mastery practical and achievable by providing the structures, pathways, content, tools and support you need to make it happen in your classroom.

To develop mastery in maths children need to be enabled to acquire a deep understanding of maths concepts, structures and procedures, step by step. Complex mathematical concepts are built on simpler conceptual components and when children understand every step in the learning sequence, maths becomes transparent and makes logical sense. Interactive lessons establish deep understanding in small steps, as well as effortless fluency in key facts such as tables and number bonds. The whole class works on the same content and no child is left behind.

Power Maths

- ⚡ Builds every concept in small, progressive steps.
- ⚡ Is built with interactive, whole-class teaching in mind.
- ⚡ Provides the tools you need to develop growth mindsets.
- ⚡ Helps you check understanding and ensure that every child is keeping up.
- ⚡ Establishes core elements such as intelligent practice and reflection.

The *Power Maths* approach

Everyone can!

Founded on the conviction that every child can achieve, *Power Maths* enables children to build number fluency, confidence and understanding, step by step.

Child-centred learning

Children master concepts one step at a time in lessons that embrace a Concrete-Pictorial-Abstract (C-P-A) approach, avoid overload, build on prior learning and help them see patterns and connections. Same-day intervention ensures sustained progress.

Continuing professional development

Embedded teacher support and development offer every teacher the opportunity to continually improve their subject knowledge and manage whole-class teaching for mastery.

Whole-class teaching

An interactive, whole-class teaching model encourages thinking and precise mathematical language and allows children to deepen their understanding as far as they can.

Introduction to the author team

Power Maths arises from the work of maths mastery experts who are committed to proving that, given the right mastery mindset and approach, **everyone can do maths**. Based on robust research and best practice from around the world, *Power Maths* was developed in partnership with a group of UK teachers to make sure that it not only meets our children's wide-ranging needs but also aligns with the National Curriculum in England.

Tony Staneff, Series Editor and author

Vice Principal at Trinity Academy, Halifax, Tony also leads a team of mastery experts who help schools across the UK to develop teaching for mastery via nationally recognised CPD courses, problem-solving and reasoning resources, schemes of work, assessment materials and other tools.

 A team of experienced authors, including:

- ⚡ **Josh Lury** – a specialist maths teacher, author and maths consultant with a passion for innovative and effective maths education

- ⚡ **Trinity Academy, Halifax** (Michael Gosling CEO, Tony Staneff, Emily Fox, Kate Henshall, Rebecca Holland, Stephanie Kirk, Stephen Monaghan, Beth Smith and Rachel Webster)

- ⚡ **David Board, Belle Cottingham, Jonathan East, Tim Handley, Derek Huby, Neil Jarrett, Timothy Weal, Paul Wrangles** – skilled maths teachers and mastery experts

- ⚡ **Cherri Moseley** – a maths author, former teacher and professional development provider

 Professors Liu Jian and Zhang Dan, Series Consultants and authors, and their team of mastery expert authors:

- ⚡ **Wei Huinv, Huang Lihua, Zhu Dejiang, Zhu Yuhong, Hou Huiying, Yin Lili, Zhang Jing, Zhou Da and Liu Qimeng**

Used by over 20 million children, Professor Liu Jian's textbook programme is one of the most popular in China. He and his author team are highly experienced in intelligent practice and in embedding key maths concepts using a C-P-A approach.

 A group of 15 teachers and maths co-ordinators

We have consulted our teacher group throughout the development of *Power Maths* to ensure we are meeting their real needs in the classroom.

Your *Power Maths* resources

To help you teach for mastery, *Power Maths* comprises a variety of high-quality resources.

Pupil Textbooks

Discover, Share, and Think together sections promote discussion and introduce mathematical ideas logically, so that children understand more easily.

Using a Concrete-Pictorial-Abstract approach, clear mathematical models help children to make connections and grasp concepts.

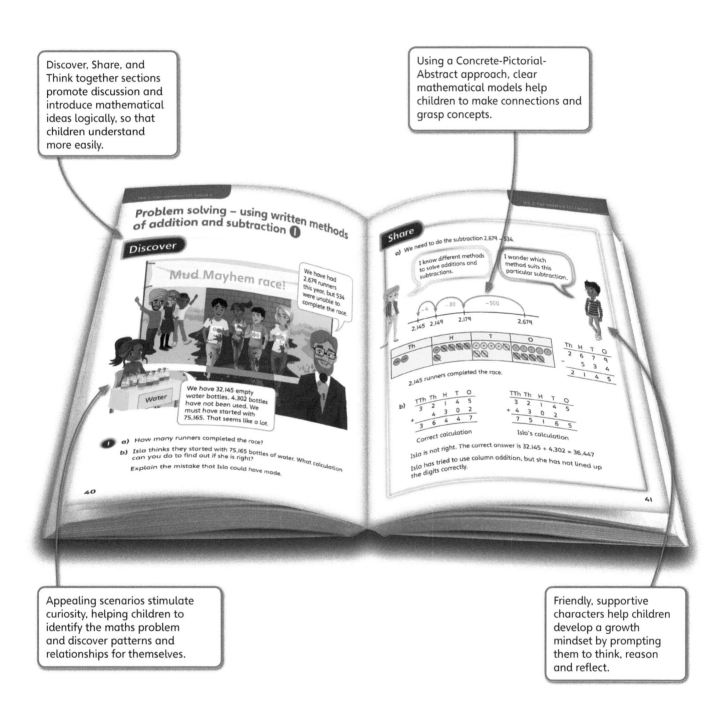

Appealing scenarios stimulate curiosity, helping children to identify the maths problem and discover patterns and relationships for themselves.

Friendly, supportive characters help children develop a growth mindset by prompting them to think, reason and reflect.

The coherent *Power Maths* lesson structure carries through into the vibrant, high-quality textbooks. Setting out the core learning objectives for each class, the lesson structure follows a carefully mapped journey through the curriculum and supports children on their journey to deeper understanding.

Pupil Practice Books

The Practice Books offer just the right amount of intelligent practice for children to complete independently in the final section of each lesson.

The practice questions are for everyone – each question varies one small element to move children on in their thinking. Look at the different parts in question ❶!

Calculations are connected so that children think about the underlying concept. In question ❸, children have to write out the calculation to find the answer. Concepts are presented differently again in question ❹ to challenge children.

Practice questions are finely tuned to move children forward in their thinking and to reveal misconceptions.

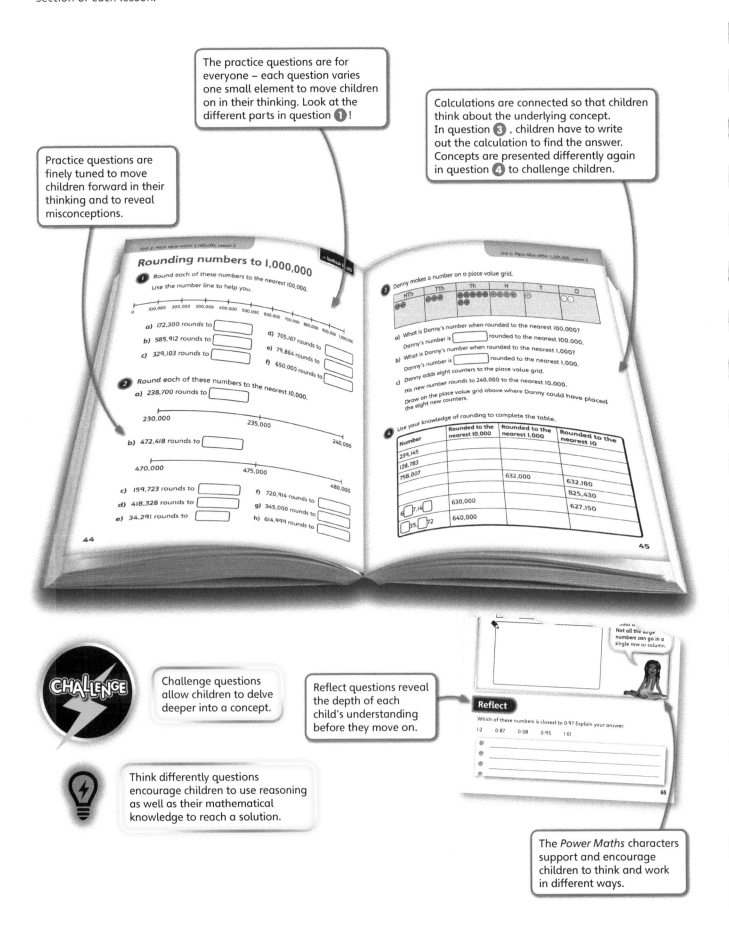

Challenge questions allow children to delve deeper into a concept.

Reflect questions reveal the depth of each child's understanding before they move on.

Think differently questions encourage children to use reasoning as well as their mathematical knowledge to reach a solution.

The *Power Maths* characters support and encourage children to think and work in different ways.

Online subscriptions

The online subscription will give you access to additional resources.

eTextbooks

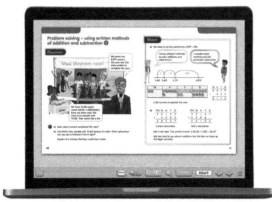

Digital versions of *Power Maths* Textbooks allow class groups to share and discuss questions, solutions and strategies. They allow you to project key structures and representations at the front of the class, to ensure all children are focusing on the same concept.

Teaching tools

Here you will find interactive versions of key *Power Maths* structures and representations.

Power Ups

Use this series of daily activities to promote and check number fluency.

Online versions of Teacher Guide pages

PDF pages give support at both unit and lesson levels. You will also find help with key strategies and templates for tracking progress.

Unit videos

Watch the professional development videos at the start of each unit to help you teach with confidence. The videos explore common misconceptions in the unit, and include intervention suggestions as well as suggestions on what to look out for when assessing mastery in your children.

End of unit Strengthen and Deepen materials

Each Strengthen activity at the end of every unit addresses a key misconception and can be used to support children who need it. The Deepen activities are designed to be 'Low Threshold High Ceiling' and will challenge those children who can understand more deeply. These resources will help you ensure that every child understands and will help you keep the class moving forward together. These printable activities provide an optional resource bank for use after the assessment stage.

Underpinning all of these resources, *Power Maths* is infused throughout with continual professional development, supporting you at every step.

The *Power Maths* teaching model

At the heart of *Power Maths* is a clearly structured teaching and learning process that helps you make certain that every child masters each maths concept securely and deeply. For each year group, the curriculum is broken down into core concepts, taught in units. A unit divides into smaller learning steps – lessons. Step by step, strong foundations of cumulative knowledge and understanding are built.

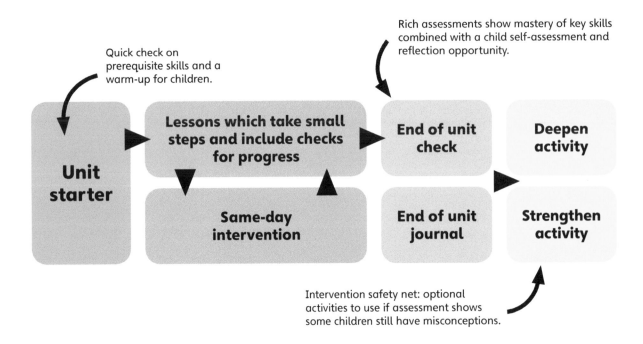

Quick check on prerequisite skills and a warm-up for children.

Rich assessments show mastery of key skills combined with a child self-assessment and reflection opportunity.

Intervention safety net: optional activities to use if assessment shows some children still have misconceptions.

Unit starter

Each unit begins with a unit starter, which introduces the learning context along with key mathematical vocabulary, structures and representations.

- The Textbooks include a check on readiness and a warm-up task for children to complete.

- Your Teacher Guide gives support right from the start on important structures and representations, mathematical language, common misconceptions and intervention strategies.

- Unit-specific videos develop your subject knowledge and insights so you feel confident and fully equipped to teach each new unit. These are available via the online subscription.

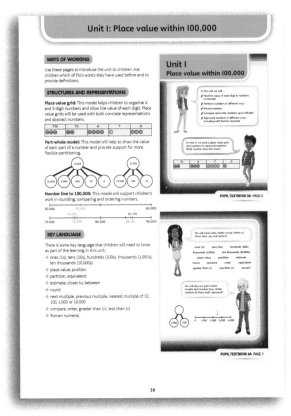

Lesson

Once a unit has been introduced, it is time to start teaching the series of lessons.

- Each lesson is scaffolded with Textbook and Practice Book activities and always begins with a Power Up activity (available via online subscription).

- *Power Maths* identifies lesson by lesson what concepts are to be taught.

- Your Teacher Guide offers lots of support for you to get the most from every child in every lesson. As well as highlighting key points, tricky areas and how to handle them, you will also find question prompts to check on understanding and clarification on why particular activities and questions are used.

Same-day intervention

Same-day interventions are vital in order to keep the class progressing together. Therefore, *Power Maths* provides plenty of support throughout the journey.

- Intervention is focused on keeping up now, not catching up later, so interventions should happen as soon as they are needed.

- Practice questions are designed to bring misconceptions to the surface, allowing you to identify these easily as you circulate during independent practice time.

- Child-friendly assessment questions in the Teacher Guide help you identify easily which children need to strengthen their understanding.

End of unit check and journal

At the end of a unit, summative assessment tasks reveal essential information on each child's understanding. An End of unit check in the Pupil Textbook lets you see which children have mastered the key concepts, which children have not and where their misconceptions lie. The Practice Book includes an End of unit journal in which children can reflect on what they have learnt.
Each unit also offers Strengthen and Deepen activities, available via the online subscription.

The Teacher Guide offers support with handling misconceptions.

The End of unit check presents six to nine multiple-choice questions. These questions are designed to reveal misconceptions and help you target areas that need strengthening.

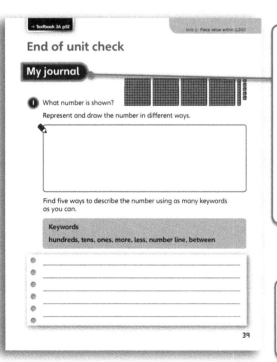

→ Textbook 3A p52
Unit 1: Place value within 1,000

End of unit check

My journal

1. What number is shown?
Represent and draw the number in different ways.

Find five ways to describe the number using as many keywords as you can.

Keywords
hundreds, tens, ones, more, less, number line, between

39

The End of unit journal is an opportunity for children to test out their learning and reflect on how they feel about it. Tackling the 'journal' problem reveals whether a child understands the concept deeply enough to move on to the next unit.

In KS2, the End of unit assessment will also include at least one SATs-style question.

Unit 1: Place value within 100,000

End of unit check

1. What is the value of the 9 in the number 8,898?
   A 9   B 90   C 900   D 9,000

2. Round 53,609 to the nearest 1,000.
   A 53,000   B 52,000   C 50,000   D 54,000

3. Which number is represented on the place value grid?

TTh	Th	H	T	O

   A 8,436   B 84,036   C 84,306   D 80,436

4. Which partitioning sentence is incorrect for the number 33,575?
   A 33,575 = 20,000 + 13,000 + 500 + 75
   B 33,575 = 20,000 + 10,000 + 500 + 70 + 5
   C 33,575 = 30,000 + 2,000 + 1,500 + 70 + 5
   D 33,575 = 30,000 + 3,000 + 500 + 70 + 5

40

The *Power Maths* lesson sequence

At the heart of *Power Maths* is a unique lesson sequence designed to empower children to understand core concepts and grow in confidence. Embracing the National Centre for Excellence in the Teaching of Mathematics' (NCETM's) definition of mastery, the sequence guides and shapes every *Power Maths* lesson you teach.

Flexibility is built into the *Power Maths* programme so there is no one-to-one mapping of lessons and concepts meaning you can pace your teaching according to your class. While some children will need to spend longer on a particular concept (through interventions or additional lessons), others will reach deeper levels of understanding. However, it is important that the class moves forward together through the termly schedules.

Power Up 🕐 5 minutes

Each lesson begins with a Power Up activity (available via the online subscription) which supports fluency in key number facts.

The whole-class approach depends on fluency, so the Power Up is a powerful and essential activity.

TOP TIP
If the class is struggling with the task, revisit it later and check understanding.

Power Ups reinforce key skills such as times-tables, number bonds and working with place value.

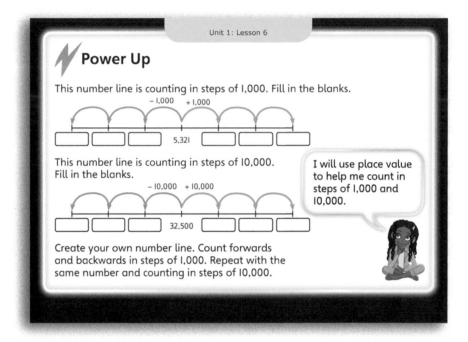

Discover 🕐 10 minutes

A practical, real-life problem arouses curiosity. Children find the maths through story-telling.

A real-life scenario is provided for the Discover section but feel free to build upon these with your own examples that are more relevant to your class.

TOP TIP
Discover works best when run at tables, in pairs with concrete objects.

Question ❶ a) tackles the key concept and question ❶ b) digs a little deeper. Children have time to explore, play and discuss possible strategies.

Share ⏱ 10 minutes

Teacher-led, this interactive section follows the Discover activity and highlights the variety of methods that can be used to solve a single problem.

TOP TIP
Ask children to discuss their methods. Pairs sharing a textbook is a great format for this!

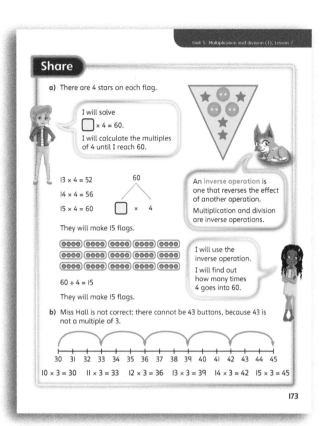

Your Teacher Guide gives target questions for children. The online toolkit provides interactive structures and representations to link concrete and pictorial to abstract concepts.

TOP TIP
Bring children to the front to share and celebrate their solutions and strategies.

Think together

⏱ 10 minutes

Children work in groups on the carpet or at tables, using their textbooks or eBooks.

TOP TIP
Make sure children have mini whiteboards or pads to write on if they are not at their tables.

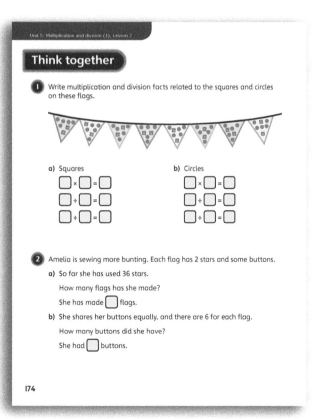

Using the Teacher Guide, model question 1 for your class.

Question 2 is less structured. Children will need to think together in their groups, then discuss their methods and solutions as a class.

In questions 3 and 4 children try working out the answer independently. The openness of the challenge question helps to check depth of understanding.

Practice ⏱ 15 minutes

Using their Practice Books, children work independently while you circulate and check on progress.

Questions follow small steps of progression to deepen learning.

TOP TIP
Some children could work separately with a teacher or assistant.

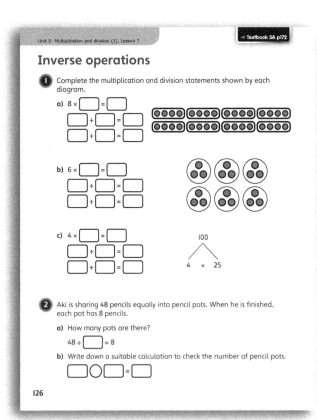

→ Textbook 5A p172

Inverse operations

1 Complete the multiplication and division statements shown by each diagram.

a) 8 × ☐ = ☐
☐ ÷ ☐ = ☐
☐ ÷ ☐ = ☐

b) 6 × ☐ = ☐
☐ ÷ ☐ = ☐
☐ ÷ ☐ = ☐

c) 4 × ☐ = ☐
☐ ÷ ☐ = ☐
☐ ÷ ☐ = ☐

100
4 × 25

2 Aki is sharing 48 pencils equally into pencil pots. When he is finished, each pot has 8 pencils.

a) How many pots are there?
48 ÷ ☐ = 8

b) Write down a suitable calculation to check the number of pencil pots.
☐ ◯ ☐ = ☐

126

Are some children struggling? If so, work with them as a group, using mathematical structures and representations to support understanding as necessary.

There are no set routines: for real understanding, children need to think about the problem in different ways.

Reflect ⏱ 5 minutes

'Spot the mistake' questions are great for checking misconceptions.

The Reflect section is your opportunity to check how deeply children understand the target concept.

6 a) What number did Reena start with?

Reena

CHALLENGE

I divide my number by 8 and get the answer 2 remainder 7.

Reena started with ☐ .

b) What number did Andy divide by?

Andy

I start with 69. I divide by a number and get the answer 9 remainder 6.

Andy divided by ☐ .

c) What numbers could Jamie have started with?

Jamie

I am thinking of a prime number between 50 and 100. I divide by 6 and get a remainder of 1.

Jamie could have started with ☐ or ☐ .

Reflect

Show the different strategies required to find the missing values of the following calculations.

18 ÷ ☐ = 3   ☐ ÷ 3 = 18

128

The Practice Books use various approaches to check that children have fully understood each concept.

Looking like they understand is not enough! It is essential that children can show they have grasped the concept.

14

Using the *Power Maths* Teacher Guide

Think of your Teacher Guides as *Power Maths* handbooks that will guide, support and inspire your day-to-day teaching. Clear and concise, and illustrated with helpful examples, your Teacher Guides will help you make the best possible use of every individual lesson. They also provide wrap-around professional development, enhancing your own subject knowledge and helping you to grow in confidence about moving your children forward together.

There is a Teacher Guide per year group for every term with unit and lesson level guidance and support.

Tips and advice on key elements such as C-P-A approaches, misconceptions, language, modelling growth mindsets and same-day intervention.

Annotations for every Pupil Textbook and Practice Book page, providing prompts for key questions to ask to expose understanding and explanations as to why key questions have been chosen.

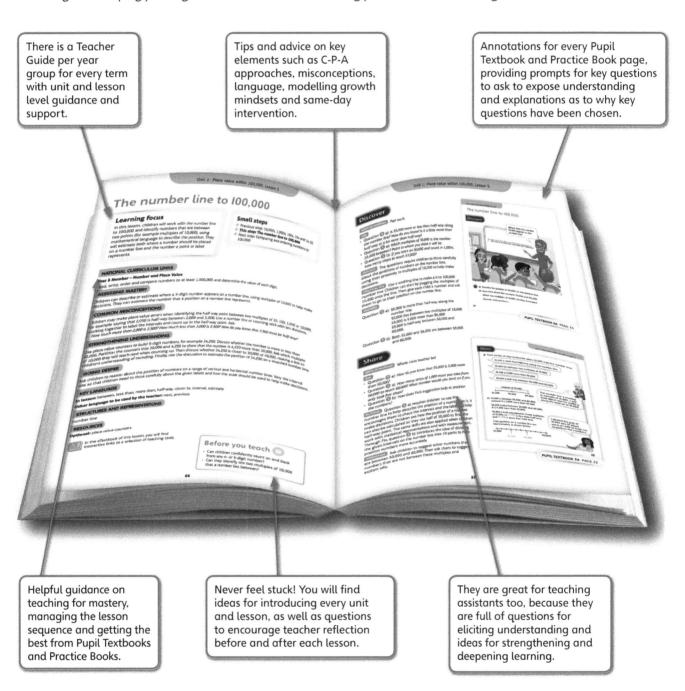

Helpful guidance on teaching for mastery, managing the lesson sequence and getting the best from Pupil Textbooks and Practice Books.

Never feel stuck! You will find ideas for introducing every unit and lesson, as well as questions to encourage teacher reflection before and after each lesson.

They are great for teaching assistants too, because they are full of questions for eliciting understanding and ideas for strengthening and deepening learning.

At the end of each unit, your Teacher Guide helps you identify who has fully grasped the concept, who has not and how to move every child forward. This is covered later in the Assessment strategies section.

Power Maths Year 6, yearly overview

Textbook	Strand	Unit		Number of Lessons
Textbook A / Practice Workbook A (Term 1)	Number – number and place value	1	Place value within 10,000,000	7
	Number – addition, subtraction, multiplication and division	2	Four operations (1)	10
	Number – addition, subtraction, multiplication and division	3	Four operations (2)	9
	Number – fractions	4	Fractions (1)	11
	Number – fractions	5	Fractions (2)	9
	Geometry – position and direction	6	Geometry – position and direction	4
Textbook B / Practice Workbook B (Term 2)	Number – fractions (including decimals and percentages)	7	Decimals	9
	Number – fractions (including decimals and percentages)	8	Percentages	9
	Algebra	9	Algebra	11
	Measurement	10	Measure – imperial and metric measures	5
	Measurement	11	Measure – perimeter, area and volume	11
	Ratio and proportion	12	Ratio and proportion	9
Textbook C / Practice Workbook C (Term 3)	Geometry – properties of shapes	Unit 13	Geometry – properties of shapes	12
	Number – number and place value	Unit 14	Problem solving	14
	Statistics	Unit 15	Statistics	10

Power Maths Year 6, Textbook 6C (Term 3) Overview

Strand 1	Strand 2	Unit		Lesson number	Lesson title	NC Objective 1	NC Objective 2	NC Objective 3
Geometry – properties of shapes		Unit 13	Geometry – properties of shapes	1	Measuring with a protractor	Draw 2-D shapes using given dimensions and angles		
Geometry – properties of shapes		Unit 13	Geometry – properties of shapes	2	Drawing shapes accurately	Draw 2-D shapes using given dimensions and angles		
Geometry – properties of shapes		Unit 13	Geometry – properties of shapes	3	Angles in triangles (1)	Compare and classify geometric shapes based on their properties and sizes and find unknown angles in any triangles, quadrilaterals, and regular polygons		
Geometry – properties of shapes		Unit 13	Geometry – properties of shapes	4	Angles in triangles (2)	Compare and classify geometric shapes based on their properties and sizes and find unknown angles in any triangles, quadrilaterals, and regular polygons		

Strand 1	Strand 2	Unit		Lesson number	Lesson title	NC Objective 1	NC Objective 2	NC Objective 3
Geometry – properties of shapes		Unit 13	Geometry – properties of shapes	5	Angles in triangles (3)	Compare and classify geometric shapes based on their properties and sizes and find unknown angles in any triangles, quadrilaterals, and regular polygons		
Geometry – properties of shapes		Unit 13	Geometry – properties of shapes	6	Angles in polygons (1)	Compare and classify geometric shapes based on their properties and sizes and find unknown angles in any triangles, quadrilaterals, and regular polygons		
Geometry – properties of shapes		Unit 13	Geometry – properties of shapes	7	Angles in polygons (2)	Compare and classify geometric shapes based on their properties and sizes and find unknown angles in any triangles, quadrilaterals, and regular polygons		
Geometry – properties of shapes		Unit 13	Geometry – properties of shapes	8	Vertically opposite angles	Recognise angles where they meet at a point, are on a straight line, or are vertically opposite, and find missing angles		
Geometry – properties of shapes		Unit 13	Geometry – properties of shapes	9	Equal distance	Illustrate and name parts of circles, including radius, diameter and circumference and know that the diameter is twice the radius		
Geometry – properties of shapes		Unit 13	Geometry – properties of shapes	10	Parts of a circle	Illustrate and name parts of circles, including radius, diameter and circumference and know that the diameter is twice the radius		
Geometry – properties of shapes	Year 5 – Geometry – properties of shapes	Unit 13	Geometry – properties of shapes	11	Nets (1)	Recognise, describe and build simple 3-D shapes, including making nets	Identify 3-D shapes, including cubes and other cuboids, from 2-D representations	
Geometry – properties of shapes	Year 5 – Geometry – properties of shapes	Unit 13	Geometry – properties of shapes	12	Nets (2)	Recognise, describe and build simple 3-D shapes, including making nets	Identify 3-D shapes, including cubes and other cuboids, from 2-D representations	
Number – number and place value		Unit 14	Problem solving	1	Problem solving – place value	Solve number and practical problems that involve all of the above		
Number – number and place value		Unit 14	Problem solving	2	Problem solving – negative numbers	Solve number and practical problems that involve all of the above		
Number – addition, subtraction, multiplication and division		Unit 14	Problem solving	3	Problem solving – addition and subtraction	Use estimation to check answers to calculations and determine, in the context of a problem, an appropriate degree of accuracy	Solve addition and subtraction multi-step problems in contexts, deciding which operations and methods to use and why	Solve problems involving addition, subtraction, multiplication and division

Strand 1	Strand 2	Unit		Lesson number	Lesson title	NC Objective 1	NC Objective 2	NC Objective 3
Number – addition, subtraction, multiplication and division		Unit 14	Problem solving	4	Problem solving – four operations (1)	Solve problems involving addition, subtraction, multiplication and division	Use their knowledge of the order of operations to carry out calculations involving the four operations	Use estimation to check answers to calculations and determine, in the context of a problem, an appropriate degree of accuracy
Number – addition, subtraction, multiplication and division		Unit 14	Problem solving	5	Problem solving – four operations (2)	Solve problems involving addition, subtraction, multiplication and division		
Number – fractions (including decimals and percentages)		Unit 14	Problem solving	6	Problem solving – fractions	Recall and use equivalences between simple fractions, decimals and percentages, including in different contexts		
Number – fractions (including decimals and percentages)		Unit 14	Problem solving	7	Problem solving – decimals	Recall and use equivalences between simple fractions, decimals and percentages, including in different contexts		
Number – fractions (including decimals and percentages)		Unit 14	Problem solving	8	Problem solving – percentages	Recall and use equivalences between simple fractions, decimals and percentages, including in different contexts		
Ratio and proportion		Unit 14	Problem solving	9	Problem solving – ratio and proportion	Solve problems involving unequal sharing and grouping using knowledge of fractions and multiples	Solve problems involving the relative sizes of two quantities where missing values can be found by using integer multiplication and division facts	
Measurement		Unit 14	Problem solving	10	Problem solving – time (1)	Use, read, write and convert between standard units, converting measurements of length, mass, volume and time from a smaller unit of measure to a larger unit, and vice versa, using decimal notation to up to three decimal places		
Measurement		Unit 14	Problem solving	11	Problem solving – time (2)	Use, read, write and convert between standard units, converting measurements of length, mass, volume and time from a smaller unit of measure to a larger unit, and vice versa, using decimal notation to up to three decimal places		

Strand 1	Strand 2	Unit		Lesson number	Lesson title	NC Objective 1	NC Objective 2	NC Objective 3
Geometry – position and direction		Unit 14	Problem solving	12	Problem solving – position and direction	Describe positions on the full coordinate grid (all four quadrants)		
Geometry – properties of shapes		Unit 14	Problem solving	13	Problem solving – properties of shapes (1)	Recognise angles where they meet at a point, are on a straight line, or are vertically opposite, and find missing angles	Compare and classify geometric shapes based on their properties and sizes and find unknown angles in any triangles, quadrilaterals, and regular polygons	
Geometry – properties of shapes		Unit 14	Problem solving	14	Problem solving – properties of shapes (2)	Recognise angles where they meet at a point, are on a straight line, or are vertically opposite, and find missing angles	Compare and classify geometric shapes based on their properties and sizes and find unknown angles in any triangles, quadrilaterals, and regular polygons	
Statistics		Unit 15	Statistics	1	The mean (1)	Calculate and interpret the mean as an average		
Statistics		Unit 15	Statistics	2	The mean (2)	Calculate and interpret the mean as an average		
Statistics		Unit 15	Statistics	3	The mean (3)	Calculate and interpret the mean as an average		
Statistics		Unit 15	Statistics	4	Introducing pie charts	Interpret and construct pie charts and line graphs and use these to solve problems		
Statistics		Unit 15	Statistics	5	Reading and interpreting pie charts	Interpret and construct pie charts and line graphs and use these to solve problems		
Statistics		Unit 15	Statistics	6	Fractions and pie charts (1)	Interpret and construct pie charts and line graphs and use these to solve problems		
Statistics		Unit 15	Statistics	7	Fractions and pie charts (2)	Interpret and construct pie charts and line graphs and use these to solve problems		
Statistics	Ratio and proportion	Unit 15	Statistics	8	Percentages and pie charts	Interpret and construct pie charts and line graphs and use these to solve problems	Solve problems involving the calculation of percentages [for example, of measures, and such as 15% of 360] and the use of percentages for comparison	
Statistics		Unit 15	Statistics	9	Interpreting line graphs	Interpret and construct pie charts and line graphs and use these to solve problems		
Statistics		Unit 15	Statistics	10	Constructing line graphs	Interpret and construct pie charts and line graphs and use these to solve problems		

Mindset: an introduction

Global research and best practice deliver the same message: learning is greatly affected by what learners perceive they can or cannot do. What is more, it is also shaped by what their parents, carers and teachers perceive they can do. Mindset – the thinking that determines our beliefs and behaviours – therefore has a fundamental impact on teaching and learning.

Everyone can!

Power Maths and mastery methods focus on the distinction between 'fixed' and 'growth' mindsets (Dweck, 2007).[1] Those with a fixed mindset believe that their basic qualities (for example, intelligence, talent and ability to learn) are pre-wired or fixed: 'If you have a talent for maths, you will succeed at it. If not, too bad!' By contrast, those with a growth mindset believe that hard work, effort and commitment drive success and that 'smart' is not something you are or are not, but something you become. In short, everyone can do maths!

Key mindset strategies

A growth mindset needs to be actively nurtured and developed. *Power Maths* offers some key strategies for fostering healthy growth mindsets in your classroom.

It is okay to get it wrong

Mistakes are valuable opportunities to re-think and understand more deeply. Learning is richer when children and teachers alike focus on spotting and sharing mistakes as well as solutions.

Praise hard work

Praise is a great motivator, and by focusing on praising effort and learning rather than success, children will be more willing to try harder, take risks and persist for longer.

Mind your language!

The language we use around learners has a profound effect on their mindsets. Make a habit of using growth phrases, such as, 'Everyone can!', 'Mistakes can help you learn' and 'Just try for a little longer'. The king of them all is one little word, 'yet …
I cannot solve this … yet!'
Encourage parents and carers to use the right language too.

Build in opportunities for success

The step-by-small-step approach enables children to enjoy the experience of success. In addition, avoid ability grouping and encourage every child to answer questions and explain or demonstrate their methods to others.

[1] Dweck, C (2007) *The New Psychology of Success*, Ballantine Books: New York

The *Power Maths* characters

The *Power Maths* characters model the traits of growth mindset learners and encourage resilience by prompting and questioning children as they work. Appearing frequently in the Textbooks and Practice Books, they are your allies in teaching and discussion, helping to model methods, alternatives and misconceptions, and to pose questions. They encourage and support your children, too: they are all hardworking, enthusiastic and unafraid of making and talking about mistakes.

Meet the team!

Flexible Flo is open-minded and sometimes indecisive. She likes to think differently and come up with a variety of methods or ideas.

Determined Dexter is resolute, resilient and systematic. He concentrates hard, always tries his best and he'll never give up – even though he doesn't always choose the most efficient methods!

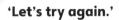

'Let's try again.'

'Mistakes are cool!'

'Have I found all of the solutions?'

'Let's try it this way …'

'Can we do it differently?'

'I've got another way of doing this!'

'I'm going to try this!'

'I know how to do that!'

'Want to share my ideas?'

Curious Ash is eager, interested and inquisitive, and he loves solving puzzles and problems. Ash asks lots of questions but sometimes gets distracted.

'What if we tried this …?'

'I wonder …'

'Is there a pattern here?'

Miaow! Sparks the Cat

Brave Astrid is confident, willing to take risks and unafraid of failure. She is never scared to jump straight into a problem or question, and although she often makes simple mistakes she is happy to talk them through with others.

Mathematical language

Traditionally, we in the UK have tended to try simplifying mathematical language to make it easier for young children to understand. By contrast, evidence and experience show that by diluting the correct language, we actually mask concepts and meanings for children. We then wonder why they are confused by new and different terminology later down the line! *Power Maths* is not afraid of 'hard' words and avoids placing any barriers between children and their understanding of mathematical concepts. As a result, we need to be planned, precise and thorough in building every child's understanding of the language of maths. Throughout the Teacher Guides you will find support and guidance on how to deliver this, as well as individual explanations throughout the Pupil Textbooks.

Use the following key strategies to build children's mathematical vocabulary, understanding and confidence.

Precise and consistent

Everyone in the classroom should use the correct mathematical terms in full, every time. For example, refer to 'equal parts', not 'parts'. Used consistently, precise maths language will be a familiar and non-threatening part of children's everyday experience.

Full sentences

Teachers and children alike need to use full sentences to explain or respond. When children use complete sentences, it both reveals their understanding and embeds their knowledge.

Stem sentences

These important sentences help children express mathematical concepts accurately, and are used throughout the *Power Maths* books. Encourage children to repeat them frequently, whether working independently or with others. Examples of stem sentences are:

'4 is a part, 5 is a part, 9 is the whole.'

'There are ... groups. There are ... in each group.'

Key vocabulary

The unit starters highlight essential vocabulary for every lesson. In the Pupil Textbooks, characters flag new terminology and the Teacher Guide lists important mathematical language for every unit and lesson. New terms are never introduced without a clear explanation.

Mathematical signs

Mathematical signs are used early on so that children quickly become familiar with them and their meaning. Often, the *Power Maths* characters will highlight the connection between language and particular signs.

The role of talk and discussion

When children learn to talk purposefully together about maths, barriers of fear and anxiety are broken down and they grow in confidence, skills and understanding. Building a healthy culture of 'maths talk' empowers their learning from day one.

Explanation and discussion are integral to the *Power Maths* structure, so by simply following the books your lessons will stimulate structured talk. The following key 'maths talk' strategies will help you strengthen that culture and ensure that every child is included.

Sentences, not words

Encourage children to use full sentences when reasoning, explaining or discussing maths. This helps both speaker and listeners to clarify their own understanding. It also reveals whether or not the speaker truly understands, enabling you to address misconceptions as they arise.

Working together

Working with others in pairs, groups or as a whole class is a great way to support maths talk and discussion. Use different group structures to add variety and challenge. For example, children could take timed turns for talking, work independently alongside a 'discussion buddy', or perhaps play different *Power Maths* character roles within their group.

Think first – then talk

Provide clear opportunities within each lesson for children to think and reflect, so that their talk is purposeful, relevant and focused.

Give every child a voice

Where the 'hands up' model allows only the more confident child to shine, *Power Maths* involves everyone. Make sure that no child dominates and that even the shyest child is encouraged to contribute – and is praised when they do.

Assessment strategies

Teaching for mastery demands that you are confident about what each child knows and where their misconceptions lie: therefore, practical and effective assessment is vitally important.

Formative assessment within lessons

The Think together section will often reveal any confusions or insecurities: try ironing these out by doing the first Think together question as a class. For children who continue to struggle, you or your teaching assistant should provide support and enable them to move on.

Performance in Practice can be very revealing: check Practice Books and listen out both during and after practice to identify misconceptions.

The Reflect section is designed to check on the all-important depth of understanding. Be sure to review how children performed in this final stage before you teach the next lesson.

End of unit check – Textbook

Each unit concludes with a summative check to help you assess quickly and clearly each child's understanding, fluency, reasoning and problem-solving skills. In KS2 this check also contains a SATs-style question to help children become familiar with answering this type of question.

In KS2 we would suggest the End of unit check is completed independently in children's exercise books, but you can adapt this to suit the needs of your class.

End of unit check – Practice Book

The Practice Book contains further opportunities for assessment, and can be completed by children independently whilst you are carrying out diagnostic assessment with small groups. Your Teacher Guide will advise you on what to do if children struggle to articulate an explanation – or perhaps encourage you to write down something they have explained well. It will also offer insights into children's answers and their implications for the next learning steps. It is split into three main sections, outlined below.

My journal

My journal is designed to allow children to show their depth of understanding of the unit. It can also serve as a way of checking that children have grasped key mathematical vocabulary. Children should have some time to think about how they want to answer the question, and you could ask them to talk to a partner about their ideas. Then children should write their answer in their Practice Book.

Power check

The Power check allows children to self-assess their level of confidence on the topic by colouring in different smiley faces. You may want to introduce the faces as follows:

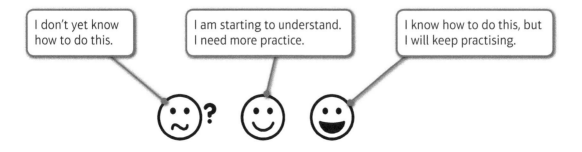

I don't yet know how to do this.

I am starting to understand. I need more practice.

I know how to do this, but I will keep practising.

Power play or Power puzzle

Each unit ends with either a Power play or a Power puzzle. This is an activity, puzzle or game that allows children to use their new knowledge in a fun, informal way. In Key Stage 2 we have also included a deeper level to each game to help challenge those children who have grasped a concept quickly.

How to use diagnostic questions

The diagnostic questions provided in *Power Maths* Textbooks are carefully structured to identify both understanding and misconceptions (if children answer in a particular way, you will know why). The simple procedure below may be helpful:

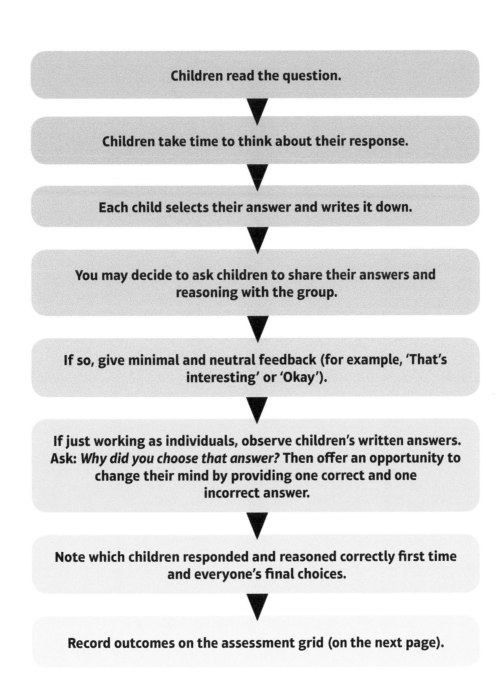

Children read the question.

Children take time to think about their response.

Each child selects their answer and writes it down.

You may decide to ask children to share their answers and reasoning with the group.

If so, give minimal and neutral feedback (for example, 'That's interesting' or 'Okay').

If just working as individuals, observe children's written answers. Ask: *Why did you choose that answer?* Then offer an opportunity to change their mind by providing one correct and one incorrect answer.

Note which children responded and reasoned correctly first time and everyone's final choices.

Record outcomes on the assessment grid (on the next page).

Power Maths unit assessment grid

Year ___   Unit ___ _____

Record only as much information as you judge appropriate for your assessment of each child's mastery of the unit and any steps needed for intervention.

Name	Diagnostic questions	SATs-style question	My journal	Power check	Power play/puzzle	Mastery	Intervention/ Strengthen

Keeping the class together

Traditionally, children who learn quickly have been accelerated through the curriculum. As a consequence, their learning may be superficial and will lack the many benefits of enabling children to learn with and from each other.

By contrast, *Power Maths'* mastery approach values real understanding and richer, deeper learning above speed. It sees all children learning the same concept in small, cumulative steps, each finding and mastering challenge at their own level. Remember that when you teach for mastery, EVERYONE can do maths! Those who grasp a concept easily have time to explore and understand that concept at a deeper level. The whole class therefore moves through the curriculum at broadly the same pace via individual learning journeys.

For some teachers, the idea that a whole class can move forward together is revolutionary and challenging. However, the evidence of global good practice clearly shows that this approach drives engagement, confidence, motivation and success for all learners, and not just the high flyers. The strategies below will help you keep your class together on their maths journey.

Mix it up

Do not stick to set groups at each table. Every child should be working on the same concept, and mixing up the groupings widens children's opportunities for exploring, discussing and sharing their understanding with others.

Recycling questions

Reuse the Pupil Textbook and Practice Book questions with concrete materials to allow children to explore concepts and relationships and deepen their understanding. This strategy is especially useful for reinforcing learning in same-day interventions.

Strengthen at every opportunity

The next lesson in a *Power Maths* sequence always revises and builds on the previous step to help embed learning. These activities provide golden opportunities for individual children to strengthen their learning with the support of teaching assistants.

Prepare to be surprised!

Children may grasp a concept quickly or more slowly. The 'fast graspers' won't always be the same individuals, nor does the speed at which a child understands a concept predict their success in maths. Are they struggling or just working more slowly?

Depth and breadth

Just as prescribed in the National Curriculum, the goal of *Power Maths* is never to accelerate through a topic but rather to gain a clear, deep and broad understanding.

"Pupils who grasp concepts rapidly should be challenged through being offered rich and sophisticated problems before any acceleration through new content. Those who are not sufficiently fluent with earlier material should consolidate their understanding, including through additional practice, before moving on."

National Curriculum: Mathematics programmes of study: KS1 & 2, 2013

The lesson sequence offers many opportunities for you to deepen and broaden children's learning, some of which are suggested below.

Discover

As well as using the questions in the Teacher Guide, check that children are really delving into why something is true. It is not enough to simply recite facts, such as '6 + 3 = 9'. They need to be able to see why, explain it, and to demonstrate the solution in several ways.

Share

Make sure that every child is given chances to offer answers and expand their knowledge and not just those with the greatest confidence.

Think together

Encourage children to think about how they found the solution and explain it to their partner. Be sure to make concrete materials available on group tables throughout the lesson to support and reinforce learning.

Practice

Avoid any temptation to select questions according to your assessment of ability: practice questions are presented in a logical sequence and it is important that each child works through every question.

Reflect

Open-ended questions allow children to deepen their understanding as far as they can by discovering new ways of finding answers. For example, *Give me another way of working out how high the wall is … And another way?*

Online materials

For each unit you will find additional strengthening activities to support those children who need it and to deepen the understanding of those who need the additional challenge.

Same-day intervention

Since maths competence depends on mastering concepts one-by-one in a logical progression, it is important that no gaps in understanding are ever left unfilled. Same-day interventions – either within or after a lesson – are a crucial safety net for any child who has not fully made the small step covered that day. In other words, intervention is always about keeping up, not catching up, so that every child has the skills and understanding they need to tackle the next lesson. That means presenting the same problems used in the lesson, with a variety of concrete materials to help children model their solutions.

We offer two intervention strategies below, but you should feel free to choose others if they work better for your class.

Within-lesson intervention

The Think together activity will reveal those who are struggling, so when it is time for Practice, bring these children together to work with you on the first Practice questions. Observe these children carefully, ask questions, encourage them to use concrete models and check that they reach and can demonstrate their understanding.

After-lesson intervention

You might like to use Think together before an assembly, giving you or teaching assistants time to recap and expand with slow graspers during assembly time. Teaching assistants could also work with strugglers at other convenient points in the school day.

The role of practice

Practice plays a pivotal role in the *Power Maths* approach. It takes place in class groups, smaller groups, pairs and independently, so that children always have the opportunities for thinking as well as the models and support they need to practise meaningfully and with understanding.

Intelligent practice

In *Power Maths*, practice never equates to the simple repetition of a process. Instead we embrace the concept of intelligent practice, in which all children become fluent in maths through varied, frequent and thoughtful practice that deepens and embeds conceptual understanding in a logical, planned sequence. To see the difference, take a look at the following examples.

Traditional practice

- Repetition can be rote – no need for a child to think hard about what they are doing.

- Praise may be misplaced.

- Does this prove understanding?

Intelligent practice

- Varied methods – concrete, pictorial and abstract.

- Calculations expressed in different ways, requiring thought and understanding.

- Constructive feedback.

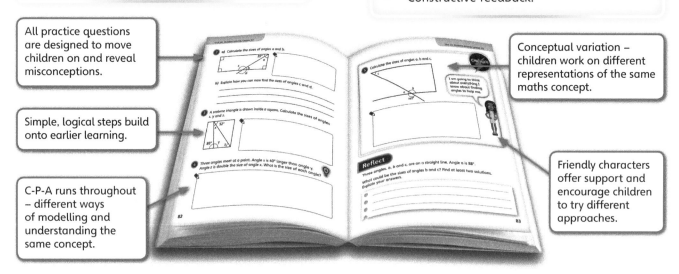

All practice questions are designed to move children on and reveal misconceptions.

Simple, logical steps build onto earlier learning.

C-P-A runs throughout – different ways of modelling and understanding the same concept.

Conceptual variation – children work on different representations of the same maths concept.

Friendly characters offer support and encourage children to try different approaches.

A carefully designed progression

The Practice Books provide just the right amount of intelligent practice for children to complete independently in the final sections of each lesson. It is really important that all children are exposed to the Practice questions, and that children are not directed to complete different sections. That is because each question is different and has been designed to challenge children to think about the maths they are doing. The questions become more challenging so children grasping concepts more quickly will start to slow down as they progress. Meanwhile, you have the chance to circulate and spot any misconceptions before they become barriers to further learning.

Homework and the role of carers

While *Power Maths* does not prescribe any particular homework structure, we acknowledge the potential value of practice at home. For example, practising fluency in key facts, such as number bonds and times-tables, is an ideal homework task, and carers could work through uncompleted Practice Book questions with children at either primary stage.

However, it is important to recognise that many parents and carers may themselves lack confidence in maths, and few, if any, will be familiar with mastery methods. A Parents' and Carers' Evening that helps them understand the basics of mindsets, mastery and mathematical language is a great way to ensure that children benefit from their homework. It could be a fun opportunity for children to teach their families that everyone can do maths!

Structures and representations

Unlike most other subjects, maths comprises a wide array of abstract concepts – and that is why children and adults so often find it difficult. By taking a Concrete-Pictorial-Abstract (C-P-A) approach, *Power Maths* allows children to tackle concepts in a tangible and more comfortable way.

Non-linear stages

Concrete

Replacing the traditional approach of a teacher working through a problem in front of the class, the concrete stage introduces real objects that children can use to 'do' the maths – any familiar object that a child can manipulate and move to help bring the maths to life. It is important to appreciate, however, that children must always understand the link between models and the objects they represent. For example, children need to first understand that three cakes could be represented by three pretend cakes, and then by three counters or bricks. Frequent practice helps consolidate this essential insight. Although they can be used at any time, good concrete models are an essential first step in understanding.

Pictorial

This stage uses pictorial representations of objects to let children 'see' what particular maths problems look like. It helps them make connections between the concrete and pictorial representations and the abstract maths concept. Children can also create or view a pictorial representation together, enabling discussion and comparisons. The *Power Maths* teaching tools are fantastic for this learning stage, and bar modelling is invaluable for problem solving throughout the primary curriculum.

Abstract

Our ultimate goal is for children to understand abstract mathematical concepts, signs and notation and, of course, some children will reach this stage far more quickly than others. To work with abstract concepts, a child needs to be comfortable with the meaning of, and relationships between, concrete, pictorial and abstract models and representations. The C-P-A approach is not linear, and children may need different types of models at different times. However, when a child demonstrates with concrete models and pictorial representations that they have grasped a concept, we can be confident that they are ready to explore or model it with abstract signs such as numbers and notation.

Use at any time and with any age to support understanding.

Practical aspects of *Power Maths*

One of the key underlying elements of *Power Maths* is its practical approach, allowing you to make maths real and relevant to your children, no matter their age.

Manipulatives are essential resources for both key stages and *Power Maths* encourages teachers to use these at every opportunity, and to continue the Concrete-Pictorial-Abstract approach right through to Year 6.

The Textbooks and Teacher Guides include lots of opportunities for teaching in a practical way to show children what maths means in real life.

Discover and Share

The Discover and Share sections of the Textbook give you scope to turn a real-life scenario into a practical and hands-on section of the lesson. Use these sections as inspiration to get active in the classroom. Where appropriate, use the Discover contexts as a springboard for your own examples that have particular resonance for your children – and allow them to get their hands dirty trying out the mathematics for themselves.

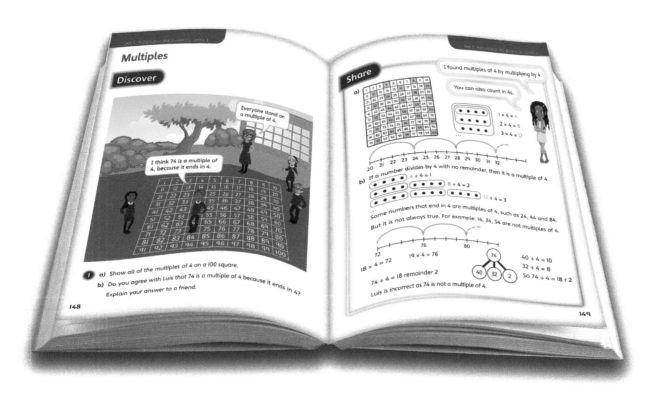

Unit videos

Every unit has a video which incorporates real-life classroom sequences.

These videos show you how the reasoning behind mathematics can be carried out in a practical manner by showing real children using various concrete and pictorial methods to come to the solution. You can see how using these practical models, such as part-whole and bar models, helps them to find and articulate their answer.

Mastery tips

Mastery Experts give anecdotal advice on where they have used hands-on and real-life elements to inspire their children.

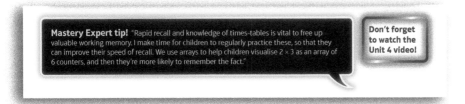

Concrete-Pictorial-Abstract (C-P-A) approach

Each Share section uses various methods to explain an answer, helping children to access abstract concepts by using concrete tools, such as counters. Remember this isn't a linear process, so even children who appear confident using the more abstract method can deepen their knowledge by exploring the concrete representations. Encourage children to use all three methods to really solidify their understanding of a concept.

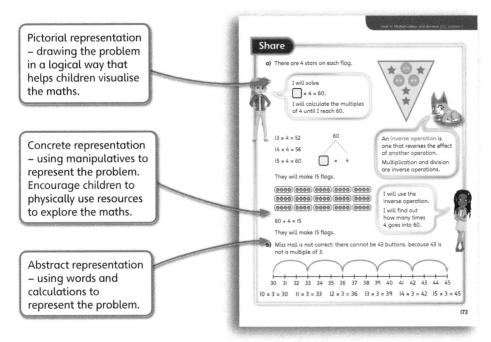

Practical tips

Every lesson suggests how to draw out the practical side of the Discover context.

You'll find these in the Discover section of the Teacher Guide for each lesson.

> **PRACTICAL TIPS** You could use balls, counters or cubes under plastic cups to re-enact the artwork and help children get a feel for this activity.

Resources

Every lesson lists the practical resources you will need or might want to use. There is also a summary of all of the resources used throughout the term on page 34 to help you be prepared.

> **RESOURCES**
>
> **Mandatory:** cubes, counters, number lines
> **Optional:** balls, plastic cups

List of practical resources

Year 6C Mandatory resources

Resource	Lesson
Coloured paper	**Unit 13** lessons 6, 7, 8
Counters	**Unit 15** lessons 1, 2, 3, 4, 5, 6, 7
Cubes	**Unit 15** lessons 1, 2, 3, 4, 5, 6, 7
Highlighter pens	**Unit 13** lesson 8
Pair of compasses	**Unit 13** lesson 9
Pin	**Unit 13** lessons 9, 10
Plain paper	**Unit 13** lessons 2, 5, 8, 9, 11, 12
Protractor	**Unit 13** lessons 1, 2, 3, 4, 5, 6, 7, 8, 11
Ruler	**Unit 13** lessons 2, 3, 4, 5, 7, 8, 9, 10, 11, 12
Scissors	**Unit 13** lessons 6, 7, 8, 11, 12
String	**Unit 13** lessons 9, 10
Squared paper/graph paper	**Unit 15** lessons 9, 10

Year 6C Optional resources

Resource	Lesson
2D shapes	**Unit 14** lesson 14
2p coins	**Unit 13** lesson 9
5p coins	**Unit 13** lesson 9
Adhesive tape	**Unit 13** lesson 4
Calendar	**Unit 14** lesson 10 **Unit 15** lesson 7
Circles split into segments	**Unit 15** lessons 6, 7, 8
Coloured paper	**Unit 13** lesson 3
Copies of diagrams for children to annotate	**Unit 14** lesson 5
Counters	**Unit 14** lesson 9 **Unit 15** lesson 4, 5, 6, 8
Cubes	**Unit 13** lesson 12 **Unit 14** lesson 9 **Unit 15** lesson 4, 5, 6, 8
Dice	**Unit 13** lesson 12 **Unit 15** lesson 2
Digit cards	**Unit 14** lesson 6
Dry-wipe pens	**Unit 13** lesson 4
Examples of products, prices and discounts	**Unit 14** lesson 8
Geared clock	**Unit 14** lesson 10
Geometric construction set	**Unit 13** lesson 12
Hexagonal paper	**Unit 13** lesson 2
Images of pie charts	**Unit 15** lessons 5, 7, 8
Individual whiteboards	**Unit 15** lesson 8
Isometric paper	**Unit 13** lesson 2
Large whiteboard protractor	**Unit 13** lesson 1
Lollipop sticks	**Unit 13** lesson 5
Marshmallows	**Unit 15** lesson 1

Resource	Lesson
Mini whiteboards	**Unit 13** lesson 4
Multiplication grid	**Unit 14** lesson 6
Pair of compasses	**Unit 13** lesson 10
Paper nets	**Unit 13** lesson 11
Pictures of puzzle books, computer games and boxes of coloured pencils	**Unit 14** lesson 4
Place value counters	**Unit 14** lessons 1, 7
Play coins	**Unit 14** lesson 7
Protractors	**Unit 14** lessons 12, 13, 14
Rope	**Unit 13** lesson 10
Ruler	**Unit 15** lessons 9, 10
Set squares	**Unit 14** lesson 12
Sticky notes	**Unit 14** lesson 3
String or ribbon	**Unit 15** lesson 3
Squared paper	**Unit 13** lesson 10 **Unit 14** lesson 12
Square dotted paper	**Unit 13** lesson 2
Straws	**Unit 13** lesson 5
Templates of pie charts	**Unit 15** lesson 5
Tracing paper	**Unit 13** lesson 8 **Unit 14** lesson 12 **Unit 15** lessons 9, 10

Variation helps visualisation

Children find it much easier to visualise and grasp concepts if they see them presented in a number of ways, so be prepared to offer and encourage many different representations.

For example, the number six could be represented in various ways:

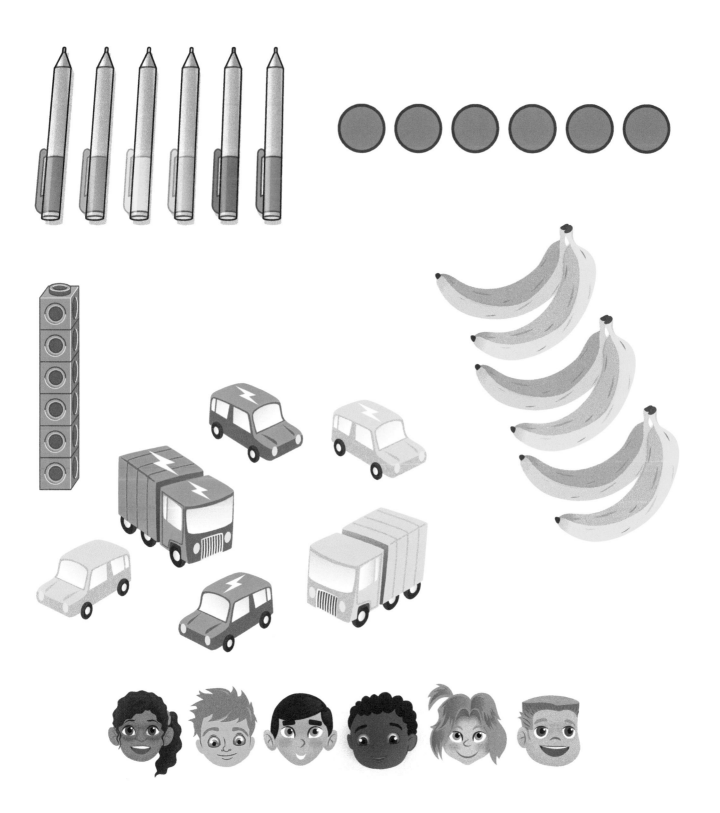

Getting started with *Power Maths*

As you prepare to put *Power Maths* into action, you might find the tips and advice below helpful.

STEP 1: Train up!

A practical, up-front, full-day professional development course will give you and your team a brilliant head-start as you begin your *Power Maths* journey. You will learn more about the ethos, how it works and why.

▼

STEP 2: Check out the progression

Take a look at the yearly and termly overviews. Next take a look at the unit overview for the unit you are about to teach in your Teacher Guide, remembering that you can match your lessons and pacing to your class.

▼

STEP 3: Explore the context

Take a little time to look at the context for this unit: what are the implications for the unit ahead? (Think about key language, common misunderstandings and intervention strategies, for example.) If you have the online subscription, don't forget to watch the corresponding unit video.

▼

STEP 4: Prepare for your first lesson

Familiarise yourself with the objectives, essential questions to ask and the resources you will need. The Teacher Guide offers tips, ideas and guidance on individual lessons to help you anticipate children's misconceptions and challenge those who are ready to think more deeply.

▼

STEP 5: Teach and reflect

Deliver your lesson – and enjoy!

Afterwards, reflect on how it went … Did you cover all five stages?
Does the lesson need more time? How could you improve it?
What percentage of your class do you think mastered the concept?
How can you help those that didn't?

Unit 13
Geometry – properties of shapes

Mastery Expert tip! "To develop confidence in properties of shape create opportunities for children to explore geometry in practical settings. For example, in art, children could use shapes to make pictures or make nets of shapes to form 3D shapes, or children could investigate shapes found in nature (such as hexagons in honeycomb)."

Don't forget to watch the Unit 13 video!

WHY THIS UNIT IS IMPORTANT

This unit is important since it further develops children's understanding of properties of shapes drawing on a range of skills including using a protractor, angles in shapes, and applying knowledge of shape properties to accurately draw them. It encourages reasoning with shapes while also exploring different methods.

WHERE THIS UNIT FITS

→ Unit 12: Ratio and proportion
→ **Unit 13: Geometry – properties of shapes**
→ Unit 14: Problem solving

In this unit children extend their understanding of measuring angles to draw shapes accurately and explore the interior angles of shapes, building on prior knowledge of angles on a straight line. Children will continue to develop their reasoning skills by interpreting properties of shapes formed from a centre and will focus on exploring 3D shapes given 2D representations.

Before they start this unit, it is expected that children:
- can identify types of angle and use angle facts, such as angles around a point total 360° and angles on a straight line total 180°
- can measure lines using a ruler and know the properties of 2D and 3D shapes
- can multiply, divide, add and subtract numbers, and use a part-whole model and a bar model.

ASSESSING MASTERY

Children who have mastered this unit are able to measure angles, draw accurately, calculate missing angles confidently using angle facts, solve multi-step problems and explore properties of shapes.

COMMON MISCONCEPTIONS	STRENGTHENING UNDERSTANDING	GOING DEEPER
When using a protractor children may incorrectly line it up or look at the wrong scale.	Encourage children to rotate their paper, so the baseline is horizontal and to ensure the crosshairs are at the vertex. Identifying the angle type can help them decide if the answer seems reasonable.	Ask children to explore and explain different ways of measuring angles using both scales on the protractor. Give children angles to measure which involve using angle facts, such as measuring a reflex angle.
When calculating a missing angle, children may not know which operation to use.	Showing the numbers on a bar model will help children understand which operations are needed.	Encourage children to further explore missing angle problems which include other angle facts, such as angles on a straight line or angles around a point.
Children may struggle to recognise 3D shapes from 2D representations.	Encourage children to use paper versions of the shapes, so they can manipulate them in a concrete way.	Encourage children to explore all possible ways of representing a 3D shape using a 2D form.

Unit 13: Geometry – properties of shapes

Introduce this unit using teacher-led discussion. Allow children time to discuss questions in small groups or pairs and then share ideas as a whole class. Children should be encouraged to use concrete resources where possible to make and explore multiple representations of shapes.

STRUCTURES AND REPRESENTATIONS

Bar model: Allows children to translate problems into calculations and interpret the correct operation.

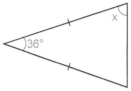 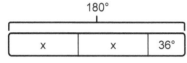

Polygons: Divide polygons into triangles so children can see how the sum of the interior angles of a polygon is always a multiple of 180°. This can help them to calculate the value of one interior angle.

Circles: Children will be introduced to parts of a circle: circumference, radius and diameter.

Nets: Children will explore 2D representations of 3D shapes to further consolidate their understanding of the properties of shapes.

KEY LANGUAGE

There is some key language that children will need to know as part of the learning in this unit.

- degrees, measurement, length
- angle, obtuse, acute, reflex, right angle, interior
- protractor, baseline, crosshairs, scale
- vertex, edge, face
- parallel
- properties
- triangle, isosceles, equilateral, scalene
- regular, polygon, quadrilateral, parallelogram, kite, rhombus, trapezium
- diameter, radius, circumference, concentric, centre
- perimeter
- pyramid, tetrahedron, cylinder, prism, cuboid, cube

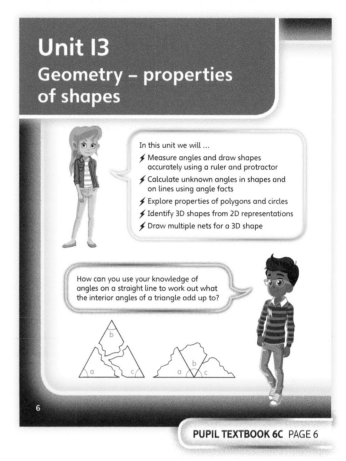

PUPIL TEXTBOOK 6C PAGE 6

PUPIL TEXTBOOK 6C PAGE 7

Measuring with a protractor

Learning focus

In this lesson, children reinforce prior knowledge of angle types and understand how to measure angles using a protractor.

Small steps

→ Previous step: Problem solving – ratio and proportion (2)
→ **This step: Measuring with a protractor**
→ Next step: Drawing shapes accurately

NATIONAL CURRICULUM LINKS

Year 6 Geometry – Properties of Shapes

Draw 2D shapes using given dimensions and angles.

ASSESSING MASTERY

Children can confidently measure angles using a protractor, demonstrating an understanding of angle types. They can read the correct scale and give an accurate measurement while showing fluency in using known angle facts.

COMMON MISCONCEPTIONS

Children may incorrectly line up the protractor to measure the angle, especially when the angle is oriented so that the baseline is not horizontal. Ask:

• *Have you positioned the baseline on top of the line that contains the angle and ensured the crosshairs are aligned at the vertex?*

Children may look at the wrong scale on the protractor and so read the incorrect measurement. Encourage them to draw an arrow between the baseline and the other line to help them see which scale to look at. Ask:

• *What type of angle do you think it is? Is your answer logical?*

STRENGTHENING UNDERSTANDING

Show children incorrect and correct ways of lining up a protractor to measure an angle. Begin with angles that have a horizontal baseline and allow children to practise positioning the protractor on several different angles before they attempt to measure them. Next, move on to angles that are easy to measure, such as 60°; this is neither too small nor too big and is a multiple of 10. Once children are confident with this move on to angles that are multiples of 5.

GOING DEEPER

Ask children to explore and explain different ways of measuring angles using both scales on the protractor. For example, they could use one line as the baseline and use one scale to measure the angle or they could use the other line as the baseline and use the other scale on the protractor.

Ask children to measure angles that are in different orientations (i.e. the baseline is not horizontal). Give children irregular shapes and ask them to measure the interior and exterior angles.

KEY LANGUAGE

In lesson: measurement, angle, obtuse, protractor, baseline, crosshairs, scale, interior, regular, vertex

Other language to be used by the teacher: align, rotate, line up, accurate, degrees, acute, reflex

STRUCTURES AND REPRESENTATIONS

angles represented in lines and shapes

RESOURCES

Mandatory: protractor

Optional: large whiteboard, protractor

 In the eTextbook of this lesson, you will find interactive links to a selection of teaching tools.

Before you teach

• Can children identify types of angle?
• Do children know that angles around a point add to 360°?
• Can children identify interior angles?

Discover

Measuring with a protractor

WAYS OF WORKING Pair work

ASK

- Question ❶ a): *How can you work out which angle is which?*
- Question ❶ b): *Why do you think Max got these answers? What mistake has he made?*

IN FOCUS Question ❶ a) introduces the concept of measuring angles using a protractor. Children also use their knowledge of types of angle to match the obtuse angle.

Question ❶ b) addresses the common misconception of reading from the wrong scale when measuring angles with a protractor.

PRACTICAL TIPS You could introduce this topic using a whiteboard activity (similar to Jamilla's activity) and a large protractor, or ask children to measure angles around the classroom, possibly as part of a 'Scavenger Hunt' activity. It will be important for children to understand that a right angle is 90° and to get a 'feel' for angles that are less than or more than 90°, labelling them as acute and obtuse, respectively.

ANSWERS

Question ❶ a):

Question ❶ b): Max has read the wrong scale on the protractor.

Discover

> I measured these angles: 50°, 45° and 110°.

Jamilla

❶ a) Match the angles to Jamilla's measurements.

b) Max measured the angles and his measurements were 130°, 70° and 135°.

What mistake did he make?

8

PUPIL TEXTBOOK 6C PAGE 8

Share

WAYS OF WORKING Whole class teacher led

ASK

- Question ❶ a): *What types of angles are these? Can you match any without measuring the angle? How can you measure the other angles? What equipment can you use? How do you line up the protractor? Where are the crosshairs? What is the baseline? How do you know which scale to look at?*
- Question ❶ b): *What do you notice about the protractor? How do you know which scale to look at?*

IN FOCUS Question ❶ a) requires children to match the measurements to the diagrams. Encourage children to categorise the angles as obtuse and acute. Children should recognise that 110° is the only obtuse angle, so they can match this without measuring it. Watch out for children who try to guess the other angles. Discuss how to line up the protractor correctly, introducing key words such as baseline and crosshairs. Explain how to read from the correct scale as this is a common misconception. Ensure children are confident with the unit of degrees and the notation for this.

In question ❶ b), discuss the diagrams and ensure children understand which scale measures which angle.

Share

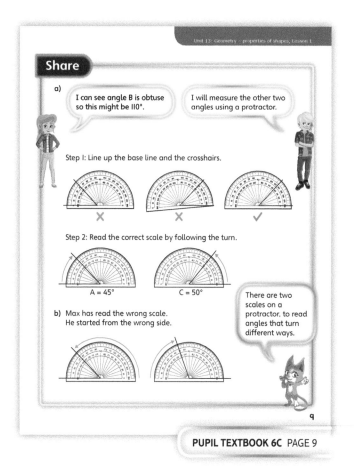

PUPIL TEXTBOOK 6C PAGE 9

Think together

WAYS OF WORKING Whole class teacher led (I do, We do, You do)

ASK

- Question **1**: *How can you measure the angles? Which scale do you need to read? What number does the scale show? Is your answer accurate?*
- Question **2**: *Can you sort the angles into angle types? What is different about how the angles are drawn? How can you measure them?*
- Question **3**: *What does interior angle mean? How can you check if the pentagon is regular? What is special about a regular pentagon? How can you measure the interior angles?*

IN FOCUS Question **1** requires children to measure the given angles. They will need to use a protractor for the third angle. Encourage children to read the scales accurately and watch out for children who round their answers.

Question **2** asks children to sort angles into size order. It may be useful to encourage children to rotate the paper, so the baseline of each angle is horizontal.

Question **3** presents children with angles in a different representation. It may be necessary to discuss the definition of interior angle and regular. Encourage children to identify the line they are going to use as a baseline first, then line up the protractor with the scale on top of the angle. In Shape B, the interior angle at vertex C is 90°; remind children that this is known as a right angle. Watch out for children who measure the exterior angle at vertex E on Shape B and remind them that this is a reflex angle. Children will need to use knowledge of angles around a point.

STRENGTHEN Encourage children to draw the angle on to the shape if it is not shown. Children can draw an arrow to help them identify which scale to read.

DEEPEN To deepen learning in question **3**, children could work out the exterior angles of each shape. Extend by asking children to draw their own angles, measure them and categorise them as acute, obtuse, reflex and right angles.

ASSESSMENT CHECKPOINT In questions **1** and **2**, look for children who are confident in lining up the baseline and the crosshairs and those who give an accurate reading, demonstrating understanding of which scale to read.

In question **3**, look for children who are confident in using the correct lines to measure the angles while fluently using associated angle facts to measure reflex angles.

ANSWERS

Question **1**: a) 34°; b) 103°; c) 178° ± 2°

Question **2**: C (55°); A (60°); D (120°); B (135°)

Question **3**: Shape A: A = B = C = D = E = 108°
Shape B: A = 55°, B = 102°, C = 90°, D = 61°, E = 232°

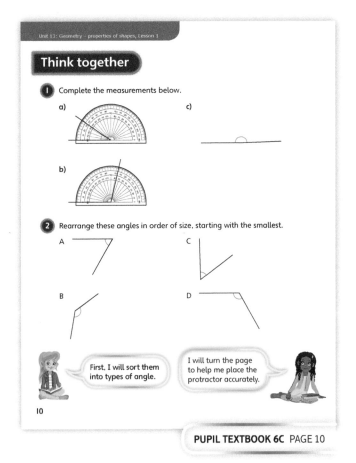

PUPIL TEXTBOOK 6C PAGE 10

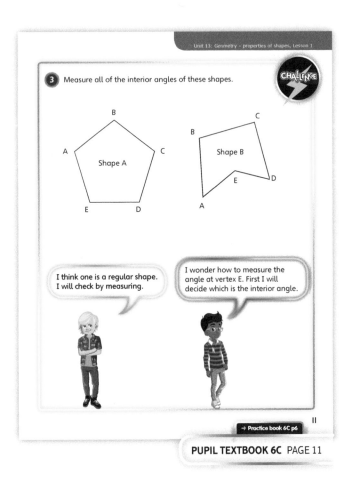

PUPIL TEXTBOOK 6C PAGE 11

Practice

WAYS OF WORKING Independent thinking

IN FOCUS Questions **1** and **2** consolidate children's understanding of measuring angles using a protractor. Encourage children to rotate the page if necessary when the baseline is not horizontal.

In question **3**, children measure interior angles. Watch out for children who measure the exterior angle rather than the interior angle when it is a reflex angle. In part b), children may assume shape A is regular because the lengths are the same. Encourage children to measure all the interior angles and use their knowledge of angles in a regular shape.

In question **5**, children use their knowledge of symmetry and then measure the interior angles, noticing that some of the angles are the same.

STRENGTHEN To strengthen understanding, encourage children to identify and draw each angle on to the diagram before measuring and to rotate the page so the baseline is horizontal.

DEEPEN Question **5** can be extended by giving children squared paper and asking them to create their own symmetric shapes and to measure the interior angles. Deepen further by asking children to include an acute, obtuse and reflex angle in their shapes.

THINK DIFFERENTLY In question **4**, children may believe the angles are different because the lines are different lengths. Encourage children to measure each angle and explain their reasoning.

ASSESSMENT CHECKPOINT In questions **1** and **2**, look for children confidently lining up the protractor, using the correct scale and taking accurate measurements.

In questions **3** and **5**, look for children who can use the correct units in their measurements, show understanding of regular shapes and symmetry and deal with reflex angles.

In question **4**, look for children who can confidently explain why the angles are equivalent.

ANSWERS Answers for the **Practice** part of the lesson appear in the separate **Practice and Reflect answer guide**.

Reflect

WAYS OF WORKING Pair work

IN FOCUS Encourage children to discuss the misconceptions arising from the mistakes that have occurred in the lesson.

ASSESSMENT CHECKPOINT Look for children who are able to confidently explain mistakes, even if they did not make the mistake themselves, such as not lining up the protractor correctly or not reading the correct scale on the protractor.

ANSWERS Answers for the **Reflect** part of the lesson appear in the separate **Practice and Reflect answer guide**.

After the lesson

- Can children identify angle types and measure angles accurately?
- Can children accurately measure angles between two lines, interior angles of a shape and reflex angles?

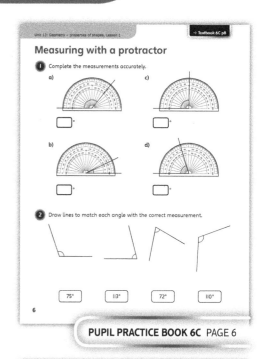

PUPIL PRACTICE BOOK 6C PAGE 6

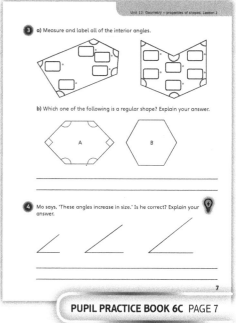

PUPIL PRACTICE BOOK 6C PAGE 7

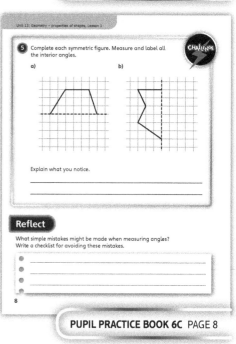

PUPIL PRACTICE BOOK 6C PAGE 8

Drawing shapes accurately

Learning focus

In this lesson, children will understand how to draw shapes accurately using a ruler and a protractor. Children also explore drawing shapes on dotted paper.

Small steps

→ Previous step: Measuring with a protractor
→ **This step: Drawing shapes accurately**
→ Next step: Angles in triangles (1)

NATIONAL CURRICULUM LINKS

Year 6 Geometry – Properties of Shapes

Draw 2D shapes using given dimensions and angles.

ASSESSING MASTERY

Children can accurately draw shapes to scale, measuring and drawing straight lines to the nearest millimetre and drawing angles to the nearest degree, demonstrating an understanding of right angles.

COMMON MISCONCEPTIONS

Children may incorrectly draw the length of a line or the size of an angle because they do not know how to use a ruler or protractor correctly. Remind them how to use a ruler and protractor to measure lines and angles before looking at drawing shapes accurately. Ask:

• *Can you copy this shape accurately?*

Children may draw the lines or angles the wrong way around (for example, if a shape has a length of 8 cm on the left-hand side and 9 cm on the right-hand side, this needs to be the same on the scale drawing). Ask:

• *What type of angle have you drawn? Does the shape look accurate?*

STRENGTHENING UNDERSTANDING

Start by asking children to construct accurate copies of angles between two lines where the baseline is horizontal, the lengths of the lines are rounded to the nearest centimetre and the angles are multiples of 10. It may be useful to provide the baseline so children only need to draw the angle and the other line.

GOING DEEPER

Give children diagrams of shapes that are not accurately drawn and that have missing lengths and ask them to accurately draw the shapes and find the actual lengths of the unknown sides. Provide descriptions of shapes and ask children to draw them from the words rather than from a diagram.

Ask children to draw an irregular polygon on a blank piece of paper then measure the size of the angles and the length of the sides. Children can then swap with a partner and make an accurate copy of their shape.

KEY LANGUAGE

In lesson: protractor, midpoint, right angle, parallelogram, extend, length

Other language to be used by the teacher: accurate, halving, isometric, degrees, baseline, crosshairs, scale, interior, kite, rhombus

STRUCTURES AND REPRESENTATIONS

angles represented in lines and shapes

RESOURCES

Mandatory: protractor, ruler, blank paper

Optional: dotted paper

 In the eTextbook of this lesson, you will find interactive links to a selection of teaching tools.

Before you teach

• Can children draw and measure lines and angles?
• Do children know the definition of midpoint and can they find a midpoint by dividing by 2?
• Do children know the properties of a square, rectangle, parallelogram, kite and rhombus?

Discover

WAYS OF WORKING Pair work

ASK

- Question **1** a): *How can you accurately draw the square? What equipment will you need?*
- Question **1** b): *How can you find the midpoint of each side?*

IN FOCUS Question **1** introduces the concept of drawing a shape accurately using a ruler and a protractor. Children will need to use their knowledge of right angles, midpoints and halving numbers.

PRACTICAL TIPS Encourage children to experiment with finding midpoints and using this to draw shapes within shapes, perhaps using coloured paper to demonstrate the different shapes they can make.

ANSWERS

Question **1** a): Ensure children have drawn an accurate square, with sides measuring 12 cm and a 90° angle at each corner.

Question **1** b): Refer to the completed diagram in the **Share** section of the **Textbook**.

Share

WAYS OF WORKING Whole class teacher led

ASK

- Question **1** a): *Where could you start when drawing the square? What are the interior angles of a square? What can you use to make sure each angle is accurate? What do you know about the lengths of the sides? Can you check your square is correct by measuring?*
- Question **1** b): *What does midpoint mean? How can you find the midpoint? Can you draw another square?*

IN FOCUS Question **1** a) requires children to accurately draw a square, starting with a 12 cm horizontal line. (Make sure they leave enough room above to draw the vertical lines.) Children are required to use blank paper so they have to use a protractor to measure and draw the angles; remind them that the interior angles of a square are right angles (90°). Encourage children to follow the steps described in **Share**, rotating the paper if necessary so the baseline is horizontal when measuring and drawing the angles. Encourage children to check their square is accurate by measuring the length of each line and the size of each angle.

For question **1** b) children are required to complete the logo. Discuss the definition of midpoint and ensure children are confident with dividing numbers by 2 using a suitable method. Encourage children to accurately measure the midpoint of each line using a ruler, then to join up these points. Children should realise that it is not necessary to use a protractor for this part. Encourage children to measure accurately, to the nearest millimetre, and to check the sides of each square are the same.

DEEPEN Encourage children to draw other shapes within shapes using midpoints, for example parallelograms inside rectangles.

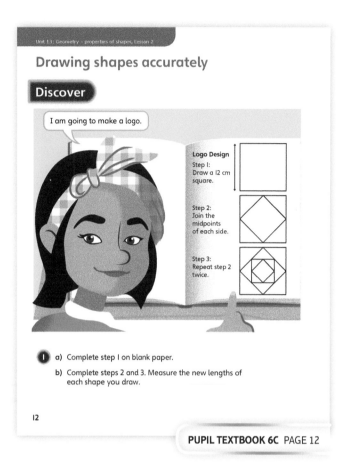

PUPIL TEXTBOOK 6C PAGE 12

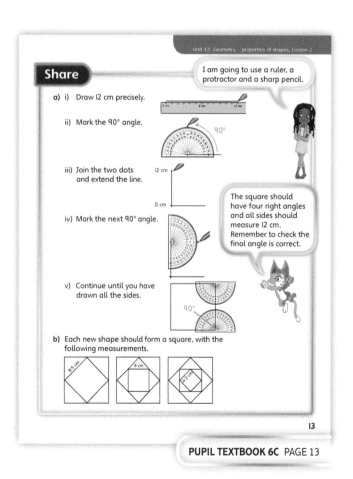

PUPIL TEXTBOOK 6C PAGE 13

Think together

WAYS OF WORKING Whole class teacher led (I do, We do, You do)

ASK

• Question **1**: *How can you draw these angles? How can you use your ruler accurately? How can you line up your protractor? How can you check your drawing is accurate?*
• Question **2**: *Where will you begin? Which sides and angles can you draw? Can you extend the lines until they meet? What are the lengths of the missing sides? How can you check your drawings are accurate?*
• Question **3**: *What are the properties of parallelograms? How can you complete the shapes to make parallelograms? Can you use the dots and lines to help? How can you check your drawings are accurate?*

IN FOCUS Question **1** requires children to draw angles and lines accurately using a ruler and protractor. Encourage children to try to draw the angles in a similar orientation, but explain that as long as the lengths and angle sizes are correct then they have completed an accurate copy. Encourage children to check their drawings by measuring all lines and angles when finished.

Question **2** asks children to draw an accurate quadrilateral. They will need to draw lines and angles in a particular order to find the lengths of the unknown sides; the lines will need to be extended until they cross. Crossed lines do not need to be rubbed out.

Question **3** requires children to complete the drawings of parallelograms. It may be necessary to discuss the definition and properties of a parallelogram.

STRENGTHEN To support understanding of drawing shapes, give children a starting line and guide them through the steps needed to complete the shapes accurately.

DEEPEN The final part of question **3** allows children to explore multiple solutions, so encourage them to suggest several different parallelograms.

ASSESSMENT CHECKPOINT In question **1**, look for children confidently measuring to the nearest millimetre and using a protractor correctly and accurately.

In questions **2** and **3**, look for children who can identify where to start and can work through the steps to draw the shapes in a logical order.

ANSWERS

Question **1**: Each angle should be drawn accurately to match the original.

Question **2**: Check children have reproduced the figure accurately. The missing side lengths should be 11·3 cm and 18 cm.

Question **3**: Check children have completed their diagrams accurately. Note that there are various possible answers to part c).

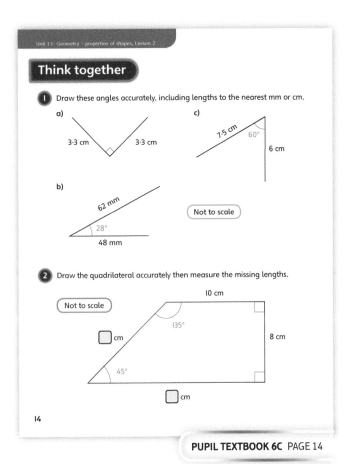

PUPIL TEXTBOOK 6C PAGE 14

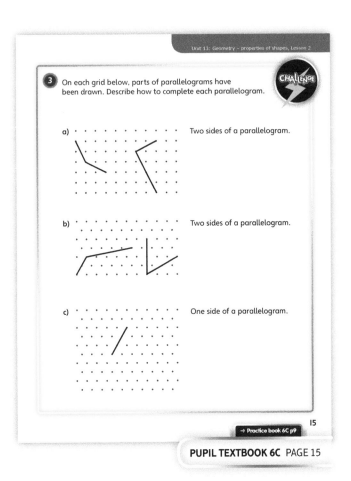

PUPIL TEXTBOOK 6C PAGE 15

Practice

WAYS OF WORKING Independent thinking

IN FOCUS Question ① aims to consolidate children's understanding of drawing angles using a protractor.

Question ② builds on the **Think together** question. Watch out for children who try to measure the lengths and angles on the diagram given and those who copy the diagram in the wrong order and guess the length of the top line.

In question ⑥, children are required to use their knowledge of the area and interior angles of rectangles to make accurate scale drawings. Encourage them to use a suitable written method, such as short division, to find the length of the missing sides. Ensure children use a protractor to accurately draw the interior right angles and encourage them to label all lengths and angles on their diagrams.

STRENGTHEN To strengthen learning, remind children to rotate the page so baselines are horizontal when drawing shapes.

DEEPEN Extend question ⑤ by encouraging children to explore the different ways they can make the shapes using isometric paper.

Deepen learning with question ⑥ by asking children to make accurate drawings of different shapes that have a certain area. This could include triangles as well as rectangles.

ASSESSMENT CHECKPOINT In questions ① and ②, look for children confidently drawing lines using a ruler, lining up the protractor, using the correct scale and taking accurate measurements.

In questions ③, ④ and ⑤, look for children who can confidently use known properties of shapes to complete the diagrams.

In question ⑥, look for children who can confidently divide with decimal answers and can draw accurate rectangles, demonstrating understanding of the size of the interior angles.

ANSWERS Answers for the **Practice** part of the lesson appear in the separate **Practice and Reflect answer guide**.

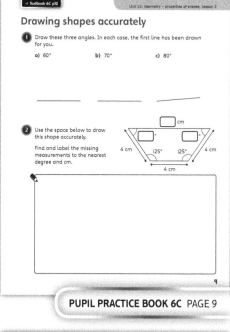

PUPIL PRACTICE BOOK 6C PAGE 9

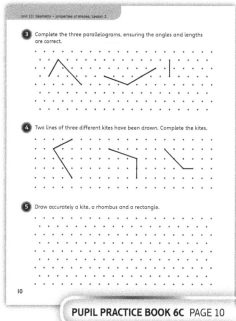

PUPIL PRACTICE BOOK 6C PAGE 10

Reflect

WAYS OF WORKING Pair work

IN FOCUS This reflection gives an opportunity for children to describe how to draw an angle and what are the mistakes to avoid. Encourage them to reflect on the lesson and recall any mistakes or misconceptions.

ASSESSMENT CHECKPOINT Look for children who are able to confidently explain the steps needed to draw the angle accurately and who can highlight the mistakes to avoid.

ANSWERS Answers for the **Reflect** part of the lesson appear in the separate **Practice and Reflect answer guide**.

After the lesson

- Can children accurately draw angles, lines and shapes, and measure missing lines and angles?
- Can children complete drawings of shapes on dotted paper?

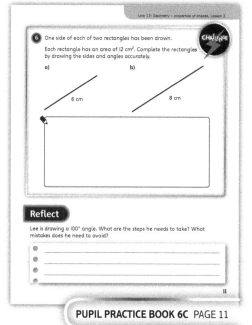

PUPIL PRACTICE BOOK 6C PAGE 11

Angles in triangles

Learning focus

In this lesson, children will apply their knowledge of accurately drawing shapes and measuring angles to understand that angles in a triangle total 180°.

Small steps

→ Previous step: Drawing shapes accurately
→ **This step: Angles in triangles (1)**
→ Next step: Angles in triangles (2)

NATIONAL CURRICULUM LINKS

Year 6 Geometry – Properties of Shapes

Compare and classify geometric shapes based on their properties and sizes and find unknown angles in any triangles, quadrilaterals, and regular polygons.

ASSESSING MASTERY

Children can understand that the interior angles of a triangle total 180° showing fluency in measuring angles, accurately drawing shapes and demonstrating an understanding of the sum of the angles on a straight line.

COMMON MISCONCEPTIONS

Children may incorrectly measure the interior angles of a triangle because they do not know how to use a protractor correctly. Develop competency by asking:
• *Which line are you going to use as the baseline? Where do you need to put the crosshairs? Which scale will you use?*

Another common misconception occurs when rearranging the interior angles of a triangle to form a straight line. This is important since it aids children's understanding of the sum of the angles in a triangle. Ensure children split the triangle into three sections (i.e none is left behind) and then put the angles together, so all the straight lines meet together and the cut or torn edges are at the top and sides. Ask:
• *How can you position the angles to form a straight line?*

STRENGTHENING UNDERSTANDING

Start by asking children to add the interior angles of a range of triangles, to help them discover the total of 180°. Then move on to children measuring the angles and finally constructing the triangles themselves.

GOING DEEPER

Encourage children to draw their own triangles that are not to scale and label the interior angles, emphasising that they must total 180°. Give children triangles that are not accurately drawn and that have one unknown angle and ask them to use their new learning about the interior angles in a triangle to work out the missing angle.

KEY LANGUAGE

In lesson: angle, obtuse, acute, right angle

Other language to be used by the teacher: extend, accurate, sum, scale, rotate, degrees, protractor, baseline, crosshairs

STRUCTURES AND REPRESENTATIONS

angles represented in triangles, angles on a straight line

RESOURCES

Mandatory: protractor, ruler

Optional: coloured paper to make into triangles to tear up

 In the eTextbook of this lesson, you will find interactive links to a selection of teaching tools.

Before you teach

• Can children accurately draw and measure shapes using a ruler and protractor?
• Do children know simple properties and the different types of triangle?
• Do children know angles on a straight line add to 180°?

Discover

WAYS OF WORKING Pair work

ASK

- Question **1** a): *How can you accurately draw a triangle like this? What equipment do you need?*
- Question **1** b): *How can you check Kate's solution?*

IN FOCUS Question **1** a) encourages children to discover how the challenge cannot be completed by using their knowledge of obtuse angles and properties of triangles. Question **1** b) develops this, requiring children to assess Kate's solution using their knowledge of types of angle. This is a good opportunity to assess children's confidence with identifying angle types within a triangle.

PRACTICAL TIPS The concept of angles in a triangle is introduced via an 'impossible' triangle. Explain to children that they will be attempting the challenge and encourage them to use their knowledge of angle types.

ANSWERS

Question **1** a): It is impossible to draw a triangle with two obtuse angles.

Question **1** b): The right angle is correct, but both of the other angles are acute, so they cannot be 130° and 140°. Kate has not solved the challenge.

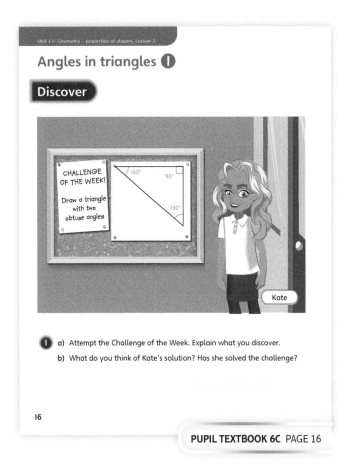

Angles in triangles ❶

Discover

1 a) Attempt the Challenge of the Week. Explain what you discover.

b) What do you think of Kate's solution? Has she solved the challenge?

16

PUPIL TEXTBOOK 6C PAGE 16

Share

WAYS OF WORKING Whole class teacher led

ASK

- Question **1** a): *How many sides does a triangle have? How many angles? Where can you start when drawing the triangle? What does it need to look like? What is an obtuse angle? Can you draw an obtuse angle? Can you draw another obtuse angle? Can you make a triangle? Could you complete this in a different way?*
- Question **1** b): *How can you check Kate's solution? What could you use?*

IN FOCUS Question **1** a) requires children to attempt the challenge. Discuss the properties of a triangle, ensuring children know how a triangle might look. Encourage children to start by drawing a horizontal baseline, ensuring they leave enough room above. Check they understand the definition of an obtuse angle. Encourage children to draw an obtuse angle at each end of the line, then ask them to explain why it is impossible to create a triangle from these lines, reinforcing the properties of a triangle. Children could attempt the challenge again using different obtuse angles to confirm that it is impossible.

Question **1** b) requires children to assess Kate's solution. This is important as it creates an opportunity to further explore types of angle in a triangle. Encourage children to use a protractor to check the 90-degree angle.

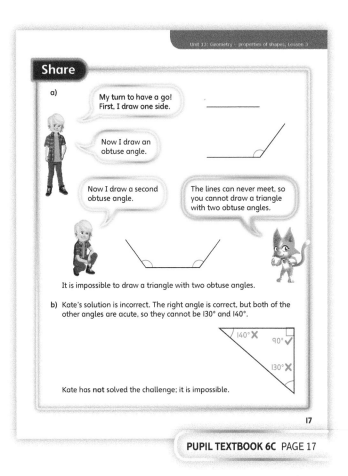

Share

a)

My turn to have a go! First, I draw one side.

Now I draw an obtuse angle.

Now I draw a second obtuse angle.

The lines can never meet, so you cannot draw a triangle with two obtuse angles.

It is impossible to draw a triangle with two obtuse angles.

b) Kate's solution is incorrect. The right angle is correct, but both of the other angles are acute, so they cannot be 130° and 140°.

Kate has **not** solved the challenge; it is impossible.

17

PUPIL TEXTBOOK 6C PAGE 17

Think together

WAYS OF WORKING Whole class teacher led (I do, We do, You do)

ASK

- Question ❶: *How can you check the angle measurements? Which line will you use as the baseline?*
- Question ❷: *Where will you begin? Which sides can you draw? Which angles can you draw? Can you extend the lines until they meet? What is the size of the missing angle? How can you check your drawing is accurate?*
- Question ❸: *What different triangles can you draw? How can you put the angles together? Do they always form a straight line? What do you know about angles on a straight line? What can you say about angles in a triangle?*

IN FOCUS Question ❶ requires children to measure the interior angles in a triangle. Watch out for children who find the orientation of the triangles and angles challenging.

Question ❷ asks children to independently draw an accurate triangle in order to measure the unknown angle. Only one length is given so children will need to measure the angles then extend the lines until they cross.

Question ❸ gives children an opportunity to discover the sum of the interior angles of a triangle. Children are encouraged to use a range of triangles to investigate this, using their knowledge of angles on a straight line.

STRENGTHEN Encourage children to choose a line as a baseline and rotate the paper so this line is horizontal, ensuring they line up the crosshairs.

DEEPEN Question ❶ can be deepened by asking children to identify the types of triangle based on the correct angles.

Extend question ❸ by encouraging children to look back at the previous questions and check if they follow their theories about angles in a triangle. Give children a triangle with one unknown angle and ask them to work out what it is by calculation, before measuring to check their answer.

ASSESSMENT CHECKPOINT Questions ❶ and ❷ will assess children's ability to measure angles within a triangle. Look for children confidently using a protractor, measuring angles accurately using the correct scale.

In question ❸, look for children who can draw different types of triangle and deduce that angles in a triangle add to 180°.

ANSWERS

Question ❶ a): All angles in the equilateral triangle are correct.

Question ❶ b): The right-angled triangle has an incorrect angle of 60°, which should be 40°.

Question ❶ c): The isosceles triangle has an incorrect angle of 60°, which should be 40°.

Question ❷: The unknown angle is 90°.

Question ❸: Angles in a triangle add to 180°. The order in which the angles make up the straight line does not matter.

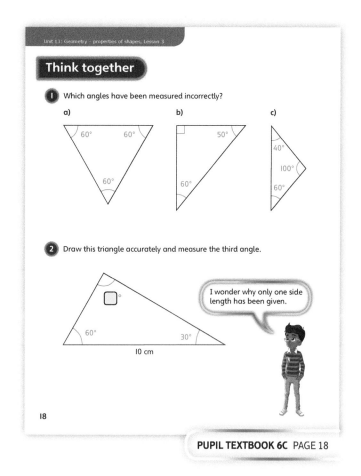

PUPIL TEXTBOOK 6C PAGE 18

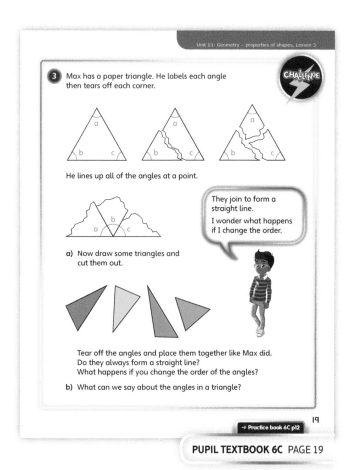

PUPIL TEXTBOOK 6C PAGE 19

Practice

WAYS OF WORKING Independent thinking

IN FOCUS Question ❶ a) aims to consolidate children's understanding of measuring angles in a triangle. Encourage children to also consider the total of the interior angles. Question ❶ b) develops this, requiring children to accurately draw a triangle before measuring an unknown angle.

Question ❷ reinforces children's understanding of angles in a triangle forming a straight line and therefore summing to 180°.

Question ❸ requires children to analyse generalised statements about angles in triangles. Encourage them to experiment by drawing triangles to support the options they choose.

Question ❹ develops abstract thinking. Encourage children to use a ruler to join the dots, so that the lines are straight. Children then need to measure and label the angles in their triangles and add them using a suitable method.

STRENGTHEN Encourage children to rotate the page so the baseline is horizontal when measuring the interior angles of the triangles.

DEEPEN Extend question ❸ by encouraging children to make other statements that are sometimes true, always true or never true, and get them to prove them using examples.

ASSESSMENT CHECKPOINT In questions ❶ and ❷, look for children confidently drawing lines using a ruler, measuring angles using a protractor, using the correct scale and taking accurate measurements.

In question ❸, look for children who are confident in explaining the statements using examples to support their reasoning.

ANSWERS Answers for the **Practice** part of the lesson appear in the separate **Practice and Reflect answer guide**.

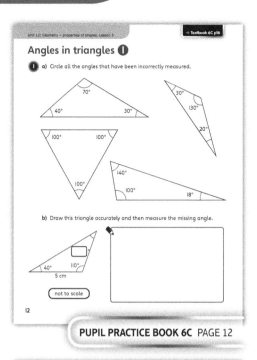

PUPIL PRACTICE BOOK 6C PAGE 12

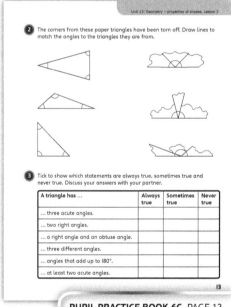

PUPIL PRACTICE BOOK 6C PAGE 13

Reflect

WAYS OF WORKING Pair work

IN FOCUS This question checks children's understanding of angles in a triangle summing to 180°. Encourage children to explain how they know the total of the interior angles in a triangle.

ASSESSMENT CHECKPOINT Children should be able to explain that the angles sum to 180°, using their understanding of angles on a straight line.

ANSWERS Answers for the **Reflect** part of the lesson appear in the separate **Practice and Reflect answer guide**.

After the lesson ⏸

- Can children measure interior angles of triangles?
- Can children accurately draw shapes and measure missing angles?
- Can children take the three interior angles of a triangle and form a straight line, linking this to understanding that the angles in a triangle sum to 180°?

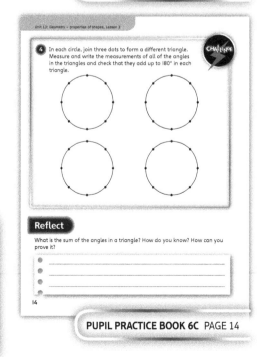

PUPIL PRACTICE BOOK 6C PAGE 14

Angles in triangles ②

Learning focus

In this lesson, children will extend their understanding of angles in a triangle and will apply their knowledge to calculate missing angles without using a protractor.

Small steps

→ Previous step: Angles in triangles (1)
→ **This step: Angles in triangles (2)**
→ Next step: Angles in triangles (3)

NATIONAL CURRICULUM LINKS

Year 6 Geometry – Properties of Shapes

Compare and classify geometric shapes based on their properties and sizes and find unknown angles in any triangles, quadrilaterals, and regular polygons.

ASSESSING MASTERY

Children can confidently calculate missing angles in a triangle without using a protractor, showing fluency in addition and subtraction and demonstrating an understanding of angle facts (such as angles around a point and angles on a straight line).

COMMON MISCONCEPTIONS

Children may try to use a protractor to measure all the angles, rather than calculating the angles using angle rules. Ensure children understand that not all diagrams are drawn to scale and that it would be time consuming to redraw all diagrams accurately, so it is more efficient to use the rule for angles in a triangle. Ask:
• *Can you check the angles given to see if the diagram is to scale? What do the three angles in a triangle always add up to?*

Children may not know which operation to use to calculate the missing angle. Showing the angles on a bar model will help children to understand which operations are needed. Ask:
• *What does this bar model show? How can you work out what is missing?*

STRENGTHENING UNDERSTANDING

To strengthen understanding, encourage children to use bar models for pictorial support. Children who need help with addition and subtraction could be encouraged to use a written method, such as the column method.

GOING DEEPER

Deepen learning by asking children to write down three angles that could be the three interior angles of a triangle, then ask them to draw the triangle. Encourage children to use other angle facts, such as angles on a straight line, by giving them missing angle problems that incorporate these facts.

KEY LANGUAGE

In lesson: angle, scale

Other language to be used by the teacher: degrees, protractor, right angle, efficient method, crosshairs, baseline

STRUCTURES AND REPRESENTATIONS

triangles, part-whole model, bar model, angles on a straight line, angles around a point

RESOURCES

Mandatory: protractor, ruler

Optional: adhesive tape, dry-wipe pens, mini whiteboards

 In the eTextbook of this lesson, you will find interactive links to a selection of teaching tools.

Before you teach ⏸

• Can children measure angles using a protractor?
• Can children use a part-whole model and a bar model?
• Do children know the angle rules for angles on a straight line and angles around a point?

Discover

Pair work

ASK

- Question **1** a): *How can you work out the size of the angles? Do you need to measure both of them?*
- Question **1** b): *How can you work out the size of the angles? Do you need to measure them all?*

IN FOCUS Both parts of this question focus on the interior angles of a triangle. Children will use a protractor, but will also develop their understanding of using the sum of the interior angles of a triangle.

PRACTICAL TIPS Recap learning from the previous lesson with a practical activity creating triangles using adhesive tape and dry-wipe pens on mini whiteboards or even desks. Encourage children to use known angle facts to work out the missing angles in the triangles.

ANSWERS

Question **1** a): Angle b = 70°, Angle c = 60°

Question **1** b): Angle x = 15°, Angle y = 85°, Angle z = 80°

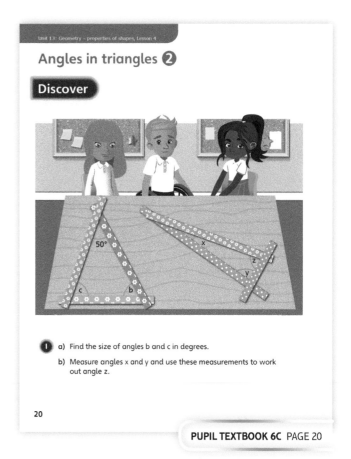

PUPIL TEXTBOOK 6C PAGE 20

Share

WAYS OF WORKING Whole class teacher led

ASK

- Question **1** a): *How can you find the size of angle c? What do the angles in a triangle add up to? If you know two of the angles how can you work out the third angle? What do the diagrams show you? Do both methods give the same answer? How can you check your answers?*
- Question **1** b): *How many angles do you need to measure? What is the size of angle x? What is the size of angle y? How can you now work out the size of angle z?*

IN FOCUS Question **1** a) encourages children to use a protractor to measure one unknown angle, then use the angles in a triangle rule to calculate the third. Ensure children realise that they only need to measure one of the angles. Discuss the two possible methods for finding the other angle, using the part-whole model and bar model for pictorial support. Encourage children to check the answers by adding together 50°, 60° and 70°; they should recognise that the total should be 180°.

In question **1** b), none of the interior angles are labelled. Emphasise that it is only necessary to measure two angles, then the third can be calculated. Encourage discussion of the different methods for calculating the size of the third angle (i.e. adding then subtracting or just subtracting).

STRENGTHEN Encourage children to use a bar model for pictorial support.

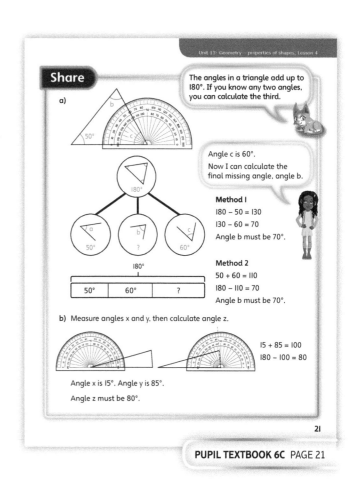

PUPIL TEXTBOOK 6C PAGE 21

Think together

WAYS OF WORKING **WAYS OF WORKING** Whole class teacher led (I do, We do, You do)

ASK

- Question **1**: *How can you work out the missing angles? Do you need to use a protractor? Could you use a more efficient method? How can you check your answers?*
- Question **2**: *What do you know about the sum of angles a, b and c? Can you draw a bar model to help?*
- Question **3**: *How can you calculate the missing angles? What other angle rules do you know that could help?*

IN FOCUS Question **1** reinforces calculating a missing angle in a triangle when given two of the angles. Encourage children to use their knowledge of the sum of the interior angles of a triangle and watch out for children who try to measure the angles with a protractor – encourage them to use a more efficient method. With the third triangle, ensure children recognise the right angle as 90°. Encourage them to check their answers using inverse operations (i.e. by adding the three angles together).

Question **2** is more complex and children are encouraged to use trial and error or a bar model to set up the problem.

Question **3** gives children an opportunity to explore angles in a triangle using other known angle facts, requiring multiple steps for a solution. It will be beneficial to discuss the order in which the missing angles can be found. It may be necessary to reinforce the angle rules that are needed to calculate the missing angles.

STRENGTHEN Strengthen learning by encouraging children to draw a bar model to show the angles given, the missing angle and the total. This should help them to identify the operations needed to calculate the missing angles.

DEEPEN Question **2** can be explored further by giving children similar problems where all the angles are missing.

Question **3** can be deepened by asking children to explore the different methods for calculating angle c.

ASSESSMENT CHECKPOINT In question **1**, look for children who understand how to use the rule for angles in a triangle to find an unknown angle. Children who try to measure the angles using a protractor are likely to need more support with this concept.

In question **3**, look for children who can confidently work through the problems in a logical order using known angle facts, demonstrating fluency in addition and subtraction.

ANSWERS

Question **1** a): 80°

Question **1** b): 15°

Question **1** c): 52°

Question **2**: a = 60°, b = 30°, c = 90°

Question **3**: a = 110°, b = 305°, c = 50°

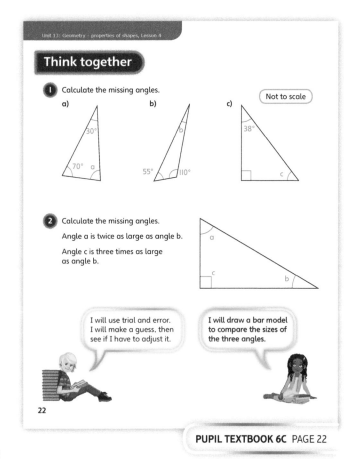

PUPIL TEXTBOOK 6C PAGE 22

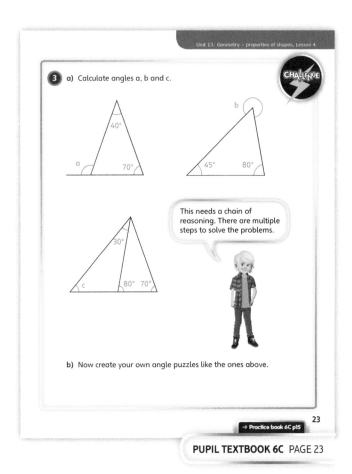

PUPIL TEXTBOOK 6C PAGE 23

Practice

WAYS OF WORKING Independent thinking

IN FOCUS Questions ❶ and ❷ aim to consolidate children's understanding of calculating a missing angle in a triangle. Watch out for children who find it challenging to measure the angles in question ❷ due to the orientation of the triangle – encourage them to rotate the paper, if necessary. Ensure children calculate the third angle rather than measuring it by encouraging them to show their working.

Question ❸ involves problem solving with angles in a triangle. Encourage children to use and complete the bar model and ensure they do not try to measure the angles since the diagram is not to scale.

Question ❹ requires children to match three angles that could form the interior angles of a triangle. Encourage them to explore different possibilities.

In question ❺, children need to use other angle facts to calculate the missing angles. Watch out for children who assume that angle y is 75°. Reinforce angle rules and the interior angles of a rectangle and encourage children to work through the questions in a logical order, showing their reasoning for each angle they calculate.

STRENGTHEN Strengthen learning by encouraging children to work out the missing angles in multiple steps (i.e. add the two known angles together, then subtract from 180°). Encourage children to draw bar models as this will help them to identify the required calculations.

DEEPEN Extend question ❺ by asking children to create their own missing angle problems using other known angle facts.

ASSESSMENT CHECKPOINT In questions ❶ and ❷, look for children confidently using the angles in a triangle rule to find the unknown angle.

In question ❸, look for children who can confidently complete the bar model, demonstrating an understanding of equal parts and division.

In question ❺, look for children who can explain their working using known angle facts, showing fluency in addition and subtraction.

ANSWERS Answers for the **Practice** part of the lesson appear in the separate **Practice and Reflect answer guide**.

Reflect

WAYS OF WORKING Pair work

IN FOCUS This reflection question involves children drawing two different triangles that contain an interior angle of 50°, while explaining how they chose them. Encourage children to label all angles, and explain that clearly labelled diagrams do not need to be to scale.

ASSESSMENT CHECKPOINT Look for children confidently explaining that the other two angles need to total 130°, reliably using subtraction and confidently drawing triangles to represent their solutions.

ANSWERS Answers for the **Reflect** part of the lesson appear in the separate **Practice and Reflect answer guide**.

After the lesson

- Can children calculate the missing angle of a triangle when given two angles, without measuring?
- Do children understand that angles in a triangle add to 180°?
- Can children use known angle facts to solve missing angle problems?

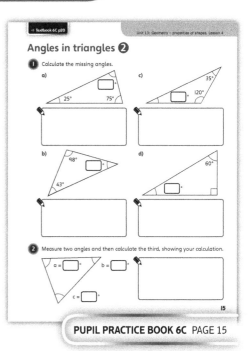

PUPIL PRACTICE BOOK 6C PAGE 15

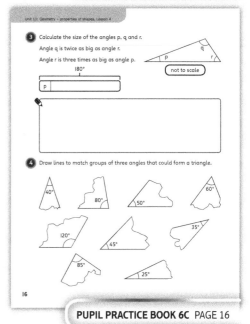

PUPIL PRACTICE BOOK 6C PAGE 16

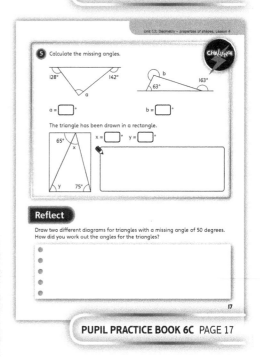

PUPIL PRACTICE BOOK 6C PAGE 17

Angles in triangles ③

Learning focus

In this lesson, children will understand how to calculate missing angles in an isosceles triangle given one of the other angles. Children will also solve problems that incorporate this.

Small steps

→ Previous step: Angles in triangles (2)
→ **This step: Angles in triangles (3)**
→ Next step: Angles in polygons (1)

NATIONAL CURRICULUM LINKS

Year 6 Geometry – Properties of Shapes

Compare and classify geometric shapes based on their properties and sizes and find unknown angles in any triangles, quadrilaterals, and regular polygons.

ASSESSING MASTERY

Children can fluently find missing angles in isosceles and equilateral triangles using the sum of the interior angles of a triangle by adding, subtracting and dividing, showing understanding of other associated angle facts.

COMMON MISCONCEPTIONS

Children may assume that the one given angle in an isosceles triangle is always the independent angle, particularly if it is at the top of the triangle. Before carrying out any calculations, ask:
• *Can you identify the lines that are the same length and the angles that are equal?*

Children may add or subtract the numbers without dividing, or vice versa. Use a bar model to address this misconception, to secure understanding and to encourage children to break down the method into steps. Ask:
• *What is shown in the bar model? What steps need to be taken?*

STRENGTHENING UNDERSTANDING

Children who find it a challenge to calculate missing angles in isosceles triangles and equilateral triangles should be encouraged to revisit finding angles in scalene triangles by adding and subtracting. When solving missing angles problems, encourage children to use a bar model so they can visualise why they add or subtract and divide to find the unknown angles.

GOING DEEPER

Encourage children to reason with angles in an isosceles triangle, for example by asking: *Is it possible to draw two different isosceles triangles that contain an angle of 40°? Can you draw two different isosceles triangles that contain an angle of 100°?*

KEY LANGUAGE

In lesson: isosceles, equal, length, angle, degrees
Other language to be used by the teacher: equilateral

STRUCTURES AND REPRESENTATIONS

triangles, bar model

RESOURCES

Mandatory: ruler, protractor, plain paper

Optional: straws or lollipop sticks (to make isosceles triangles)

 In the eTextbook of this lesson, you will find interactive links to a selection of teaching tools.

Before you teach

• Do children know the properties of isosceles triangles?
• Can children divide by a single digit, including finding half of a number?
• Do children know the angle rules for angles on a straight line and angles around a point?

Discover

Angles in triangles ③

WAYS OF WORKING Pair work

ASK

- Question ① a): *What types of triangle have been formed? How can you work out the missing angles?*
- Question ① b): *Can you draw a diagram to help? Which angle could be 80°?*

IN FOCUS Question ① a) introduces the concept of finding angles in isosceles triangles when given one of the angles.

Question ① b) develops the concept of finding missing angles in an isosceles triangle and looks at the different angles that can be found.

PRACTICAL TIPS The context of making triangular frames could be introduced in a practical way, perhaps in an art lesson using straws or lollipop sticks of equal length, encouraging children to think about the angles formed in the triangles.

ANSWERS

Question ① a): a = 75°, b = 75°, c = 40°, d = 40°

Question ① b): The other angles could be 80° and 20° or
the other angles could both be 50°.

Discover

① a) Kate and Ebo use equal lengths of wood to form these triangle frames. Find the angles a, b, c and d.

b) They form a new triangle frame with the two equal lengths. One of the angles is 80°. What could the other two angles be?

24

PUPIL TEXTBOOK 6C PAGE 24

Share

WAYS OF WORKING Whole class teacher led

ASK

- Question ① a): *Why are the triangles isosceles? What do you know about angles in an isosceles triangle? What do angles in a triangle add up to? What do the bar models show? How can you calculate the missing angles? How can you check your answers?*
- Question ① b): *What do you need to find? How do the diagrams help? How can you calculate the other angles? What operation do you need to use? Why are there two solutions?*

IN FOCUS Question ① a) requires children to use knowledge of isosceles triangles to calculate the missing angles. Discuss the small marks that are used to indicate a triangle is isosceles and explain that two of the angles will also be equal. Encourage children to use the bar models to reason that to find the missing angles they need to subtract from 180 and divide by 2. Ensure children understand that dividing by 2 and finding half of a number give the same answer. Use the bar model to support this concept. Encourage children to check their answers by adding them to find the total.

Question ① b) only describes the triangle with missing angles. Explore with children the different possibilities and encourage them to draw diagrams to identify what they are looking for. Ensure children are confident with the operations needed to calculate the answers. Some children may need help with this, so use a bar model to represent the problem and strengthen understanding.

STRENGTHEN Strengthen learning by encouraging children to revisit finding angles in scalene triangles by adding and subtracting. Allow the use of a bar model for pictorial support, so children can visualise why they add or subtract and divide to find the unknown angles.

Share

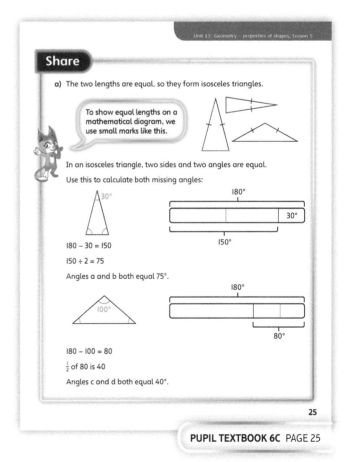

a) The two lengths are equal, so they form isosceles triangles.

To show equal lengths on a mathematical diagram, we use small marks like this.

In an isosceles triangle, two sides and two angles are equal.

Use this to calculate both missing angles:

180 – 30 = 150

150 ÷ 2 = 75

Angles a and b both equal 75°.

180 – 100 = 80

½ of 80 is 40

Angles c and d both equal 40°.

25

PUPIL TEXTBOOK 6C PAGE 25

Think together

WAYS OF WORKING Whole class teacher led (I do, We do, You do)

ASK

- Question **1**: *Which angles are the same? How do you know? How can you calculate the missing angles? Could you draw a bar model to help?*
- Question **2**: *How can you draw an isosceles triangle? How can you measure one of the angles? Does it matter which one? How can you calculate the other angles?*
- Question **3**: *What other angle facts could help solve this?*

IN FOCUS Question **1** requires children to calculate the missing angles when given one angle in an isosceles triangle. Watch out for children who assume 70° is the independent angle in part c) since it is at the top of the triangle; this can be a common misconception.

In question **2**, children are required to independently draw a triangle and calculate angles. Look out for children who think they have to measure the angle between the two equal lengths. Encourage children to compare their answers with others.

Question **3** incorporates other angle facts. In the second problem, watch out for children who assume that the angles are the same because the lengths are the same. In the third problem, use a bar model to help children understand why they need to divide 180° by 3. Encourage children to complete each question in steps and show their reasoning.

STRENGTHEN To support understanding, encourage children to represent the calculations on a bar model. When solving question **3** encourage children to decipher the diagrams and consider other angle facts.

DEEPEN Question **3** can be explored further by giving children other problems that incorporate other angle facts.

ASSESSMENT CHECKPOINT Questions **1** and **2** assess children's ability to calculate missing angles in isosceles triangles. Look for children clearly explaining the steps needed and confidently using addition, subtraction and division to find the answers.

Question **3** assesses children's ability to find missing angles in a problem-solving context with no support or structure. If children can fluently use associated angle facts and then complete the calculations, while clearly explaining the steps, they are likely to have mastered this topic.

ANSWERS

Question **1** a): The other two angles are 76°.

Question **1** b): The other two angles are 34°.

Question **1** c): The other angles are 70° and 40°.

Question **2**: Range of answers. Ensure two angles are the same and all three angles add up to 180°.

Question **3**: a = 75°, b = 75°, c = 72°, d = 54°, e = 130°, f = 30°

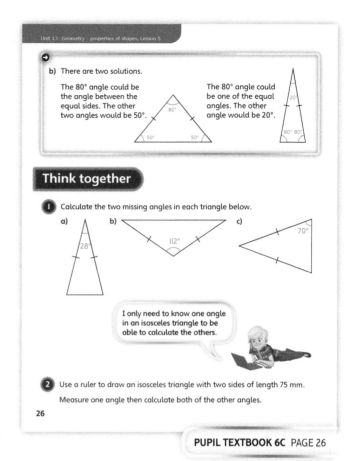

PUPIL TEXTBOOK 6C PAGE 26

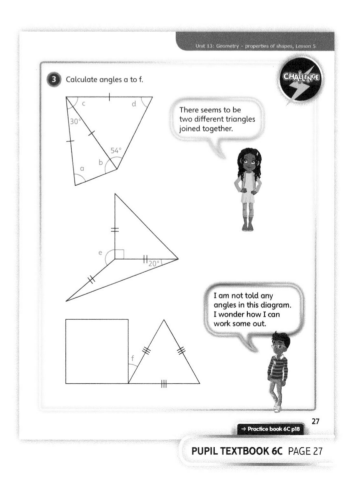

PUPIL TEXTBOOK 6C PAGE 27

Practice

WAYS OF WORKING Independent thinking

IN FOCUS Question ① aims to consolidate children's understanding of the notation for equal lengths in isosceles triangles.

In question ②, children practise calculating two unknown angles. Encourage them to write down their calculations and explain their steps.

Question ③ develops children's understanding of identifying an isosceles triangle. Encourage them to use a ruler to measure the lengths, if necessary.

Question ④ develops children's reasoning skills and encourages them to explore the different angles within an isosceles triangle. Watch out for children who believe there are two solutions to Bella's triangle. Encourage children to draw accurate diagrams to support their reasoning.

Question ⑤ requires children to problem solve and use a range of angle facts to calculate the unknown angles.

STRENGTHEN To strengthen understanding, encourage children to represent the numbers on a bar model to help them identify the correct calculations.

DEEPEN Question ④ can be explored further by asking: *What other triangles can you find where one angle is given and can only be drawn in one way? What is the smallest or biggest angle this could be?*

ASSESSMENT CHECKPOINT Questions ① and ③ assess children's ability to identify isosceles triangles and mark equivalent lengths and angles, using the correct notation.

Question ② assesses children's ability to calculate missing angles in isosceles triangles. Look for children clearly explaining the steps needed and confidently using addition, subtraction and division and showing fluency when working abstractly.

Question ④ assesses children's ability to reason. Look for children who can explain that there is only one solution for Bella's triangle.

In question ⑤, children should be able to complete the calculations, recognising when to add, subtract or divide and demonstrating understanding of known angle facts.

ANSWERS Answers for the **Practice** part of the lesson appear in the separate **Practice and Reflect answer guide**.

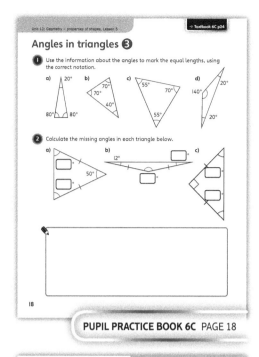

PUPIL PRACTICE BOOK 6C PAGE 18

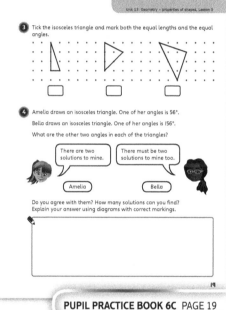

PUPIL PRACTICE BOOK 6C PAGE 19

Reflect

WAYS OF WORKING Pair work

IN FOCUS This reflection gives children an opportunity to create a missing angle problem. Encourage them to draw on known angle facts.

ASSESSMENT CHECKPOINT Children should be able to confidently explain how to solve their problem, showing the steps required to reach the answer.

ANSWERS Answers for the **Reflect** part of the lesson appear in the separate **Practice and Reflect answer guide**.

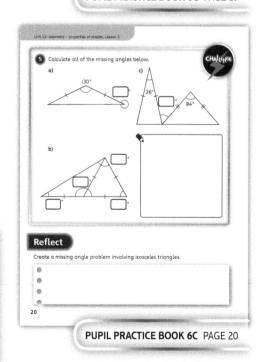

PUPIL PRACTICE BOOK 6C PAGE 20

After the lesson ⏸

- Can children label isosceles triangles using the correct notation and calculate missing angles without measuring?
- Can children draw isosceles triangles and measure the interior angles?
- Can children use known angle facts to solve missing angle problems?

Angles in polygons ❶

Learning focus

In this lesson, children will reinforce prior knowledge of properties of shapes and extend their learning to understand the interior angles of a quadrilateral sum to 360°.

Small steps

→ Previous step: Angles in triangles (3)
→ **This step: Angles in polygons (1)**
→ Next step: Angles in polygons (2)

NATIONAL CURRICULUM LINKS

Year 6 Geometry – Properties of Shapes

Compare and classify geometric shapes based on their properties and sizes and find unknown angles in any triangles, quadrilaterals, and regular polygons.

ASSESSING MASTERY

Children can confidently describe properties of shapes and use these to discover that the interior angles of quadrilaterals add to 360°, demonstrating an understanding of other angle facts and showing fluency in addition, subtraction and division.

COMMON MISCONCEPTIONS

Children may not know the properties of shapes and so cannot apply this knowledge when exploring the interior angles of quadrilaterals. Children may not know the notation for properties of shapes (for example, they think that a small dash on two lines means that the lines are parallel and therefore identify the wrong shape). Ensure children are confident with properties of shapes by discussing these before completing the lesson. Ask:
• *What are the properties of this shape? What does this dash mean?*

STRENGTHENING UNDERSTANDING

Begin by revisiting properties of shapes and encourage children to describe the properties, focusing particularly on the interior angles. A matching activity could be useful. When exploring angles, encourage children to use paper versions of the shapes, so they can manipulate them to help strengthen understanding.

GOING DEEPER

Ask children to explore and explain different ways in which they can calculate a missing angle, discussing and deciding which is more efficient. Encourage children to reason and problem solve with angles in quadrilaterals asking: *Is it possible to have three obtuse angles in a quadrilateral?*

KEY LANGUAGE

In lesson: quadrilateral, isosceles, angle, degrees, shape, right angle, trapezium, scalene, equal, length, parallel, relationship

Other language to be used by the teacher: properties, interior, sum, parallelogram, calculate

STRUCTURES AND REPRESENTATIONS

triangles, quadrilaterals

RESOURCES

Mandatory: coloured paper, scissors, protractors

 In the eTextbook of this lesson, you will find interactive links to a selection of teaching tools.

Before you teach ⏸

• Do children know the properties of trapeziums and parallelograms?
• Can children add, subtract and divide numbers?
• Do children know the angle rules for angles on a straight line, angles around a point and the sum of the interior angles of a triangle?

Discover

WAYS OF WORKING Pair work

ASK

- Question ① a): *How can you describe the shapes left over? What properties could you describe?*
- Question ① b): *What do you notice about the two triangles? What is the size of each angle in the triangle?*

IN FOCUS This question asks children to describe the properties of shapes while introducing the concept of the sum of the interior angles in a quadrilateral.

PRACTICAL TIPS The concept of angles in a quadrilateral could be introduced in a practical way using paper. Encourage children to explore the different shapes that can be formed, describing their properties.

ANSWERS

Question ① a): At step 1 the shape is a rectangle. After step 2, the shape is a right-angled trapezium. It has one pair of parallel sides, two right angles and sides of different lengths. The interior angles add to 360°. After step 3, the shape is an isosceles trapezium. It has two pairs of equal angles, one pair of parallel sides.

Question ① b): The left-over triangles can form two other triangles and three quadrilaterals.

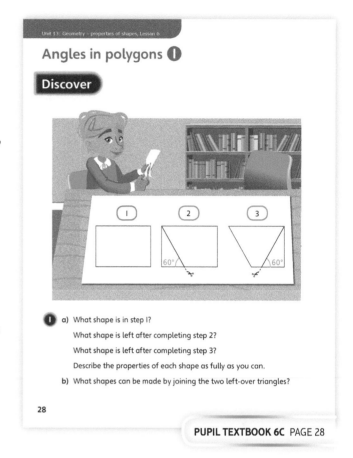

Angles in polygons ①

Discover

① a) What shape is in step 1?

What shape is left after completing step 2?

What shape is left after completing step 3?

Describe the properties of each shape as fully as you can.

b) What shapes can be made by joining the two left-over triangles?

28

PUPIL TEXTBOOK 6C PAGE 28

Share

WAYS OF WORKING Whole class teacher led

ASK

- Question ① a): *What are the properties of the shapes? How do you show sides are parallel? The same length? What makes a shape a trapezium? What is the same about the shapes? What do you notice about the total of the interior angles?*
- Question ① b): *What do you notice about the total of the interior angles?*

IN FOCUS Question ① a) helps children to discover the sum of the interior angles of a quadrilateral. Encourage children to describe the properties of the shapes, using the diagrams to support this. Ensure children are confident with the different markings used for parallel sides and sides that are equal length. Encourage children to discuss what is the same about the shapes (i.e. they are quadrilaterals and the sum of the interior angles is 360°).

Question ① b) requires children to form shapes from the two identical triangles. Reinforce previous learning by discussing the interior angles of the triangles that are formed and develop the new concept of angles in a quadrilateral.

STRENGTHEN It may be useful to begin by revisiting properties of shapes, focusing particularly on the interior angles.

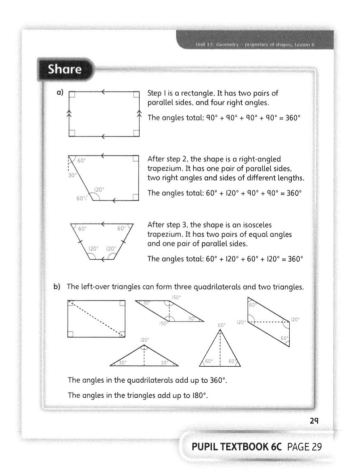

Share

a) Step 1 is a rectangle. It has two pairs of parallel sides, and four right angles.

The angles total: 90° + 90° + 90° + 90° = 360°

After step 2, the shape is a right-angled trapezium. It has one pair of parallel sides, two right angles and sides of different lengths.

The angles total: 60° + 120° + 90° + 90° = 360°

After step 3, the shape is an isosceles trapezium. It has two pairs of equal angles and one pair of parallel sides.

The angles total: 60° + 120° + 60° + 120° = 360°

b) The left-over triangles can form three quadrilaterals and two triangles.

The angles in the quadrilaterals add up to 360°.

The angles in the triangles add up to 180°.

29

PUPIL TEXTBOOK 6C PAGE 29

Think together

WAYS OF WORKING Whole class teacher led (I do, We do, You do)

ASK

• Question ❶: *How has the shape been formed? What shape is left over? What are the properties of the shape? What do you notice about the sum of the interior angles?*
• Question ❷: *What are the properties of the shapes? What do the markings on the shapes tell you?*
• Question ❸: *What shapes are shown? What are the properties of each shape? How can you work out the answers?*

IN FOCUS Question ❶ requires children to identify the shape left over and describe the properties given the pictorial representations. Encourage them to explore and discuss if the angles always total to the same number.

In question ❷, encourage children to use the properties of the shapes to calculate the angles, rather than trying to measure them with a protractor.

Question ❸ presents children with some quadrilaterals where the angles are not numerical. Encourage children to make their own versions and manipulate the angles to explore the relationships between them. For example, they will be able to see that some of the angles are equal by placing one on top of the other.

STRENGTHEN To support understanding, encourage children to make paper versions of each shape to help them describe the properties and explore the interior angles.

DEEPEN For question ❸, children could be encouraged to draw their own quadrilaterals and explore other relationships between the angles.

ASSESSMENT CHECKPOINT In question ❶, look for children who are able to describe the properties of the parallelogram and find the total of the interior angles.

In questions ❷ and ❸, look for children who are confident using properties of shapes and angle facts to find the missing angles. Watch out for children who try to measure the angles with a protractor as they are likely to need more support with this concept.

ANSWERS

Question ❶: The shape that is left is a parallelogram. It has two pairs of parallel sides and opposite angles are equal. The interior angles are 120°, 60°, 120°, 60° and total 360°.

Question ❷: Interior angles, clockwise from bottom left:
a) 75°, 105°, 75°, 105°; b) 65°, 115°, 115°, 65°;
c) 90°, 73°, 107°, 90°; d) 101°, 79°, 101°, 79°

Question ❸: $a + b = c + d = 180°$; $b + c = a + d = 180°$;
$a + b + c + d = 360°$; $f + e = 180°$;
$f + e + \square + \square = 360°$; $g + i = h + j = 180°$;
$g + j = h + i = 180°$; $g + i + h + j = 360°$

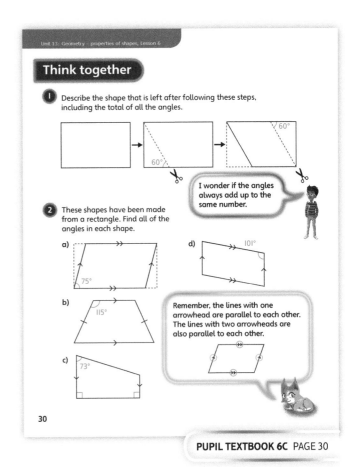

PUPIL TEXTBOOK 6C PAGE 30

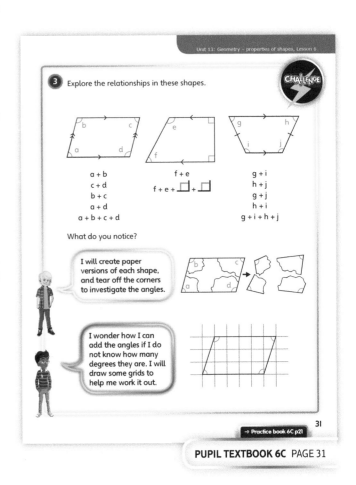

PUPIL TEXTBOOK 6C PAGE 31

Practice

WAYS OF WORKING Independent thinking

IN FOCUS Question ❷ asks children to find missing angles using the sum of the interior angles of a quadrilateral. Encourage them to work through the calculations in steps and show their working.

Question ❻ focuses on two quadrilaterals in particular and asks children to explore the different ways they can create them. Encourage children to think about the different types of trapezium they could draw and to focus on the total of the interior angles.

STRENGTHEN To strengthen understanding encourage children to use bar models to represent the numbers and identify the calculations needed to find missing angles. Children may find it helpful to make shapes out of paper to help them explore the properties.

DEEPEN Extend question ❺ by asking children to write other statements about shapes that are always true, sometimes true and never true.

THINK DIFFERENTLY Question ❺ aims to develop children's reasoning with angles in quadrilaterals. There is no prompting or visual representation so encourage children to explain their answers using diagrams.

ASSESSMENT CHECKPOINT Questions ❶ and ❸ give an opportunity to assess children's ability to name and label shapes. Look for children confidently using properties of shapes.

In questions ❷ and ❹, look for children who demonstrate understanding of the sum of the interior angles of quadrilaterals, while showing fluency in selecting the correct operations to find the unknown.

Question ❺ assesses children's ability to reason with quadrilaterals by focusing on the interior angles. Look for children who can confidently reason, justifying their answers with diagrams.

Question ❻ assesses children's ability to draw parallelograms and trapeziums. Look for children who can confidently draw a variety of these shapes demonstrating an understanding of the properties of shapes.

ANSWERS Answers for the **Practice** part of the lesson appear in the separate **Practice and Reflect answer guide**.

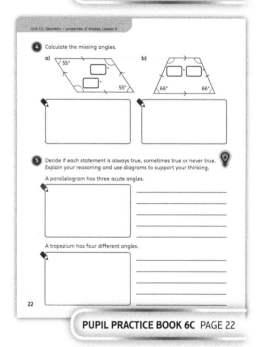

PUPIL PRACTICE BOOK 6C PAGE 21

PUPIL PRACTICE BOOK 6C PAGE 22

Reflect

WAYS OF WORKING Pair work

IN FOCUS This reflection gives children an opportunity to show their understanding of the total of the angles in quadrilaterals. Encourage children to explain the sum of the angles as well as drawing a diagram.

ASSESSMENT CHECKPOINT Children should be able to explain that the interior angles sum to 360°.

ANSWERS Answers for the **Reflect** part of the lesson appear in the separate **Practice and Reflect answer guide**.

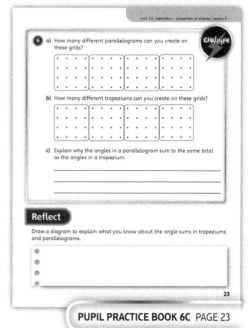

PUPIL PRACTICE BOOK 6C PAGE 23

After the lesson ⏸

- Can children name and describe quadrilaterals and their properties?
- Can children correctly label the properties of quadrilaterals?
- Can children understand why angles in a quadrilateral sum to 360° and use this fact to calculate missing angles in quadrilaterals?

Angles in polygons ②

Learning focus

In this lesson, children will develop their understanding of the sum of the angles in quadrilaterals and extend this to calculate the sum of the interior angles in other polygons, then use these to find missing angles.

Small steps

→ Previous step: Angles in polygons (1)
→ **This step: Angles in polygons (2)**
→ Next step: Vertically opposite angles

NATIONAL CURRICULUM LINKS

Year 6 Geometry – Properties of Shapes

Compare and classify geometric shapes based on their properties and sizes and find unknown angles in any triangles, quadrilaterals, and regular polygons.

ASSESSING MASTERY

Children understand that angles in a quadrilateral total 360° and can find the total of the angles in polygons. They can confidently use this learning to calculate missing angles in shapes showing fluency in addition, subtraction, multiplication and division, while demonstrating knowledge of associated angle facts.

COMMON MISCONCEPTIONS

Children may focus on the numbers given in a shape and ignore right angles when they are labelled with a square. Encourage children to identify all angles before carrying out any calculations. Ask:
• *What does labelling an angle with a square mean?*

Another misconception may occur when the shape is not regular, for example, children may mistake arrowheads for triangles and use 180° as the total of the interior angles rather than 360°. Ask:
• *Is this a triangle or not?*

Children may think three angles are required to work out a missing angle in a quadrilateral. Encourage them to consider the properties of the shapes they are dealing with. Ask:
• *Can you work out the two missing angles?*

STRENGTHENING UNDERSTANDING

If children find it a challenge to calculate missing angles in polygons, recap finding missing angles in triangles and quadrilaterals. Children will also need a sound understanding of properties of shapes. When calculating missing angles, encourage children to use a bar model to identify the calculations needed and to complete the calculations in steps, showing each stage of their working.

GOING DEEPER

Children could be encouraged to calculate the sum of the angles in polygons with many sides and to solve missing angle problems involving these. Give children some missing angle problems in word format where they also have to use their knowledge of properties of shapes to solve the problem.

KEY LANGUAGE

In lesson: quadrilateral, total, sum, angle, shape, measure, calculate, triangle, pentagon, hexagon, heptagon, kite, rhombus, regular, polygon

Other language to be used by the teacher: method, degrees, properties, interior, vertex

STRUCTURES AND REPRESENTATIONS

quadrilaterals and polygons

RESOURCES

Mandatory: ruler, coloured paper, scissors, protractors

 In the eTextbook of this lesson, you will find interactive links to a selection of teaching tools.

Before you teach

• Do children know the properties of polygons?
• Can children confidently add, subtract, multiply and divide numbers including decimal answers?
• Do children know the sum of the interior angles in a triangle is 180°?

Discover

WAYS OF WORKING Pair work

ASK

- Question ❶ a): *Which angles will stay the same? Which angles will be different?*
- Question ❶ b): *What is the angle total of Lexi's quadrilateral? How can you be sure the total will always be the same?*

IN FOCUS Question ❶ b) introduces children to the concept of the sum of the interior angles of any quadrilateral equalling 360°. It will be important to ensure that children are confident with the sum of the angles in a triangle.

PRACTICAL TIPS The context in this lesson is joining two triangles together to make a quadrilateral. This could be made into a practical activity where children make their own triangles from paper and form quadrilaterals while discussing the angles that are created and the sum of the angles.

ANSWERS

Question ❶ a): Lexi has created angles of 40°, 80°, 165° and 75° in her quadrilateral. These total 360°.

Question ❶ b): Any quadrilateral can be split into two triangles, so the total of all the angles must be 180 × 2 = 360°.

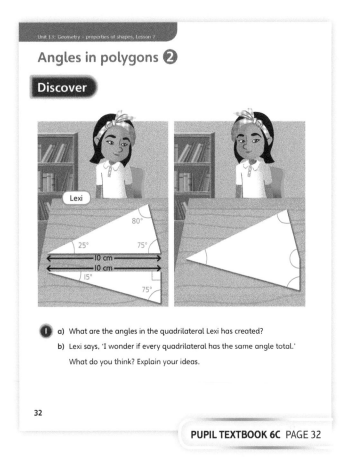

Unit 13: Geometry – properties of shapes, Lesson 7

Angles in polygons ❷

Discover

❶ a) What are the angles in the quadrilateral Lexi has created?

b) Lexi says, 'I wonder if every quadrilateral has the same angle total.'

What do you think? Explain your ideas.

32

PUPIL TEXTBOOK 6C PAGE 32

Share

WAYS OF WORKING Whole class teacher led

ASK

- Question ❶ a): *What does the diagram show you? How can you calculate the new angles that are created? What operation do you need to use? What is the total of these angles?*
- Question ❶ b): *What shapes can be made from quadrilaterals? Is this true for any quadrilateral? What can you say about the total of the angles in a quadrilateral?*

IN FOCUS Question ❶ a) aims to help children understand how quadrilaterals can be created by putting two triangles together. Explore with children which angles will stay the same and which angles are newly formed in the quadrilateral. Use the diagram to help children understand that to calculate the angles in the quadrilateral it is necessary to add. Emphasise how these angles total 360° and reinforce links with the previous lesson.

Question ❶ b) develops this concept by giving children an opportunity to explore a range of quadrilaterals that are split into two triangles. Ensure children are confident with the sum of the angles in triangles and use the diagram for pictorial support.

STRENGTHEN In question ❶ b) it may be beneficial for children to draw their own quadrilaterals and see how they can split them into two triangles to strengthen understanding of this concept.

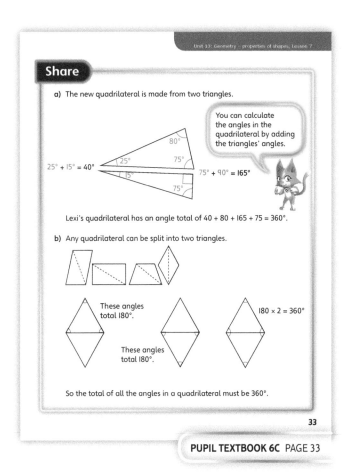

Unit 13: Geometry – properties of shapes, Lesson 7

Share

a) The new quadrilateral is made from two triangles.

You can calculate the angles in the quadrilateral by adding the triangles' angles.

25° + 15° = 40°

75° + 90° = 165°

Lexi's quadrilateral has an angle total of 40 + 80 + 165 + 75 = 360°.

b) Any quadrilateral can be split into two triangles.

These angles total 180°.

These angles total 180°.

180 × 2 = 360°

So the total of all the angles in a quadrilateral must be 360°.

33

PUPIL TEXTBOOK 6C PAGE 33

Think together

Whole class teacher led (I do, We do, You do)

ASK

- Question **1**: *What do the angles add up to? How can you work out the missing angles?*
- Question **2**: *What are the properties of a kite and a rhombus? Which angles would you need to know?*
- Question **3**: *How many triangles can you see in the polygons? What does this tell you about the interior angles of the polygons?*

IN FOCUS Question **1** requires children to calculate missing angles in a quadrilateral when given three of the angles. Watch out for children who mistake shape c) for a triangle. Encourage children to do their calculations in steps and show their working.

Question **2** develops children's thinking about the angles required to work out other missing angles. Encourage children to consider the properties of these shapes.

Question **3** introduces the sum of the interior angles in other shapes. It may be beneficial to revisit the definitions of polygon and regular.

STRENGTHEN To strengthen understanding encourage children to represent the numbers on a bar model to help them decide which operations they need to use.

DEEPEN Extend question **3** by asking: *Can you find the total of the interior angles in other polygons?* Give children some irregular polygons with some angles labelled and ask them to calculate one unknown angle.

ASSESSMENT CHECKPOINT Question **2** assesses children's ability to recall properties of shapes. If children think it is necessary to measure three angles in order to calculate the rest they are likely to need more support.

In question **3** children should be able to use the total of the interior angles to calculate one of the angles confidently using division.

ANSWERS

Question **1**: a) 85°; b) 103°; c) 210°

Question **2**: Only one pair of missing angles is equal in a kite; hence it is necessary to measure two different angles in order to calculate the rest. Opposite angles are equal in a rhombus, hence it is only necessary to measure one of the angles in order to calculate the rest.

Question **3**:

Shape	Number of sides	Number of triangles	180 × number of triangles	Sum of internal angles
Hexagon	6	4	180 × 4	720°
Heptagon	7	5	180 × 5	900°

a) The interior angle of a regular pentagon is 108°.
b) The interior angle of a regular hexagon is 120°.
c) The interior angle of a regular heptagon is 128·6° (1 d.p.).

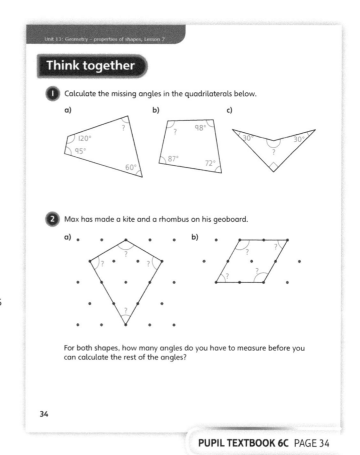

Think together

1 Calculate the missing angles in the quadrilaterals below.

a) 120° 95° 60° ?

b) 98° ? 87° 72°

c) 30° 30° ?

2 Max has made a kite and a rhombus on his geoboard.

a) b)

For both shapes, how many angles do you have to measure before you can calculate the rest of the angles?

34

PUPIL TEXTBOOK 6C PAGE 34

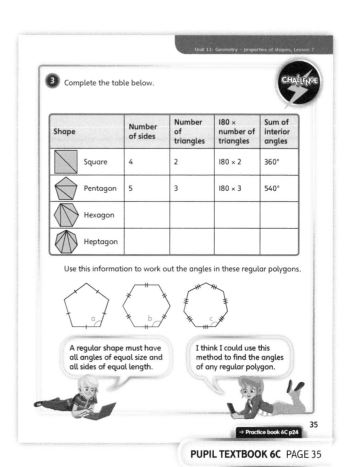

3 Complete the table below.

CHALLENGE

Shape		Number of sides	Number of triangles	180 × number of triangles	Sum of interior angles
	Square	4	2	180 × 2	360°
	Pentagon	5	3	180 × 3	540°
	Hexagon				
	Heptagon				

Use this information to work out the angles in these regular polygons.

a b c

A regular shape must have all angles of equal size and all sides of equal length.

I think I could use this method to find the angles of any regular polygon.

35

→ Practice book 6C p24

PUPIL TEXTBOOK 6C PAGE 35

Practice

Independent thinking

IN FOCUS Question ❶ develops children's understanding of using the sum of the interior angles of quadrilaterals to find unknown angles. Question ❷ allows children to find incorrect angles and consolidates using a protractor.

Question ❸ asks children to split polygons into triangles to work out the total of the interior angles. Watch out for children who overlap the triangles or do not have vertices touching the edges of the polygons.

Question ❺ is more abstract; encourage children to split the decagon into triangles to help.

In question ❻, children need to use other angle facts and explore all the possible angles that can be found on a diagram.

STRENGTHEN If children are finding it a challenge to calculate missing angles in polygons, remind them of the total of the interior angles and encourage them to use a bar model to show what they know and what they need to find.

DEEPEN Extend question ❺ by encouraging children to find the interior angles of other polygons with more than 10 sides. In question ❻, challenge children to find all the angles in the second diagram.

THINK DIFFERENTLY Question ❹ addresses the misconception of children drawing triangles incorrectly in shapes. Encourage children to explain why splitting the shape in this way does not work.

ASSESSMENT CHECKPOINT In questions ❸, ❹ and ❺, look for children fluently using multiplication and those who are able to draw triangles confidently where each vertex touches the edges of the polygons.

In question ❻, children should be able to fluently use the total of the interior angles in polygons to find one interior angle, while confidently using other angle facts and explaining their steps and reasoning.

ANSWERS Answers for the **Practice** part of the lesson appear in the separate **Practice and Reflect answer guide**.

Reflect

Pair work

IN FOCUS This reflection gives children an opportunity to work backwards and create a problem with a specific answer. Encourage them to draw a diagram to represent the problem and to use more than one operation if possible. Encourage children to describe the steps needed to answer the problem, writing their explanation in their own words. Ask them to give their problem to their partner to check.

ASSESSMENT CHECKPOINT Look for children fluently working backwards to create a problem, using their understanding of inverse operations while confidently checking their work and their partner's.

ANSWERS Answers for the **Reflect** part of the lesson appear in the separate **Practice and Reflect answer guide**.

After the lesson ⏸

- Can children accurately draw triangles inside polygons?
- Can children calculate missing angles and solve problems in polygons, using the properties of shapes?
- Can children write their own problems?

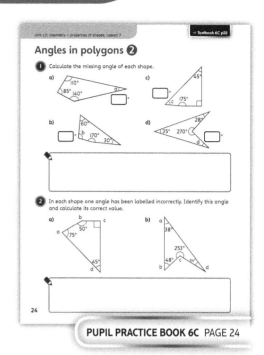

PUPIL PRACTICE BOOK 6C PAGE 24

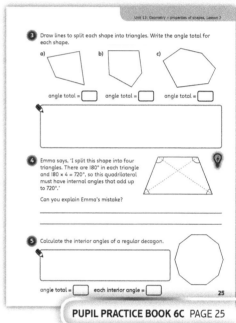

PUPIL PRACTICE BOOK 6C PAGE 25

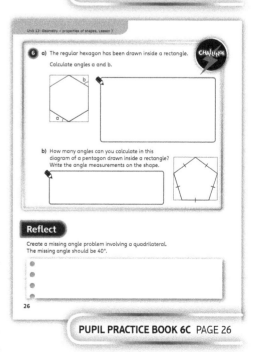

PUPIL PRACTICE BOOK 6C PAGE 26

Vertically opposite angles

Learning focus

In this lesson, children will extend their understanding of angles to discover vertically opposite angles are equal.

Small steps

→ Previous step: Angles in polygons (2)
→ **This step: Vertically opposite angles**
→ Next step: Equal distance

NATIONAL CURRICULUM LINKS

Year 6 Geometry – Properties of Shapes

Recognise angles where they meet at a point, are on a straight line, or are vertically opposite, and find missing angles.

ASSESSING MASTERY

Children understand that vertically opposite angles are equal using angles on a straight line which total to 180°. Children apply this understanding to solve missing angle problems, demonstrating fluency in associated angle facts.

COMMON MISCONCEPTIONS

Children may think that any opposite angles are equal (for example, they may think angle w is equal to angle y or that angle x is equal to angle z). Ensure children understand that vertically opposite angles are only formed by a pair of crossing straight lines. Ask:

• *How many lines are crossing?*

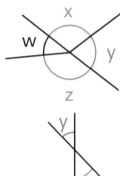

Another misconception occurs when the lines are different lengths or the angles are labelled with different curves (for example, children may think that angle x is not equal to angle y because of the way the angles have been marked or the fact that the lines are different lengths). Exposing children to examples like this and encouraging them to measure the angles using a protractor will help to strengthen understanding. Ask:

• *If the marking for these angles were removed and you concentrated on just the angles, do they look a similar size?*

STRENGTHENING UNDERSTANDING

Encourage children to identify straight lines where they can use the fact that angles on a straight line total 180°. Build confidence by encouraging children to measure one angle using a protractor and predict the other angles before measuring to confirm.

GOING DEEPER

Deepen learning by asking children to explore the different ways in which they can calculate a missing angle using a range of angle facts. Encourage children to discuss which methods are most efficient.

KEY LANGUAGE

In lesson: vertically opposite angle, measurement, equal, calculate, pattern, cross, predict

Other language to be used by the teacher: properties, less, twice, degrees, triangle, regular, polygon, fifth

STRUCTURES AND REPRESENTATIONS

angles in crossing lines, angles on straight lines, bar models

RESOURCES

Mandatory: paper, rulers, protractors, scissors, coloured paper, highlighter pens

Optional: tracing paper

 In the eTextbook of this lesson, you will find interactive links to a selection of teaching tools.

Before you teach

• Do children know angles on a straight line add to 180°?
• Can children measure and draw angles with a protractor?
• Can children find missing angles in regular polygons, including triangles?

Discover

Pair work

ASK

- Question **1** a): *What is the size of angle a? How can you work out the size of angle b?*
- Question **1** b): *What patterns can you see in the results? Why might this be?*

IN FOCUS In question **1** children are introduced to the concept of vertically opposite angles being equal, building on the known angle fact of angles on a straight line.

PRACTICAL TIPS A practical way to introduce vertically opposite angles is with a paper activity. Ask children to draw intersecting lines, label the angles and cut them out (or use tracing paper) to see that the angles are the same.

ANSWERS

Question **1** a): b = 40°, c = 140°, d = 40°

Question **1** b): Pairs of opposite angles where two straight lines cross must always be equal.

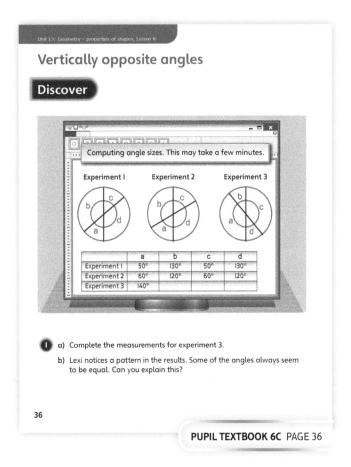

Vertically opposite angles

Discover

1 a) Complete the measurements for experiment 3.

b) Lexi notices a pattern in the results. Some of the angles always seem to be equal. Can you explain this?

36

PUPIL TEXTBOOK 6C PAGE 36

Share

WAYS OF WORKING Whole class teacher led

ASK

- Question **1** a): *How can you work out the missing angles? Do you need to use a protractor? What angle fact could you use? What does the diagram show you?*
- Question **1** b): *Which angles are equal? Why might this be? What do the bar models show you? What can you say about vertically opposite angles?*

IN FOCUS Question **1** a) introduces children to vertically opposite angles by using the known fact of angles on a straight line. Encourage children to reason that angle b must equal 40° since angle a is 140° and angles a and b form a straight line. Show children the diagram to strengthen their understanding and repeat this process for the other angles.

Question **1** b) requires children to find and explain patterns that occur within these results. It will be beneficial to refer children to the bar model that demonstrates how angle a must be equal to angle c, and angle b equal to angle d. Explore with children the straight lines that can be formed to show how these findings occur.

STRENGTHEN Watch out for children who think it is necessary to measure the angles with a protractor. Strengthen understanding by encouraging them to use the angle fact for angles on a straight line.

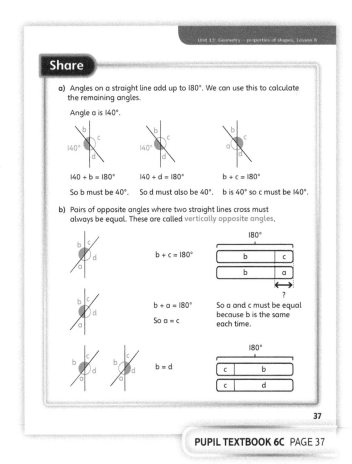

Share

a) Angles on a straight line add up to 180°. We can use this to calculate the remaining angles.

Angle a is 140°.

140 + b = 180°   140 + d = 180°   b + c = 180°

So b must be 40°.   So d must also be 40°.   b is 40° so c must be 140°.

b) Pairs of opposite angles where two straight lines cross must always be equal. These are called vertically opposite angles.

b + c = 180°

b + a = 180°
So a = c

b = d

So a and c must be equal because b is the same each time.

37

PUPIL TEXTBOOK 6C PAGE 37

Think together

WAYS OF WORKING Whole class teacher led (I do, We do, You do)

ASK

- Question **1**: *Which angles make a straight line? Which angles are vertically opposite? Which angles can you calculate? Are you able to calculate them all?*
- Question **2**: *How can you draw pairs of straight lines that cross at different angles? What equipment will you need?*
- Question **3**: *Which angle rules do you need to use? Can you find the answers straight away? What other angles could you find first to help?*

IN FOCUS Question **1** highlights a common misconception that all opposite angles are equal – watch out for children who assume that angle i in the last diagram is 62°.

Question **2** reinforces vertically opposite angles being equal. Ensure children use a ruler to draw the lines. Encourage children to measure one of the angles with a protractor then predict the other angles using angle facts before checking they are correct using the protractor.

Question **3** gives children an opportunity to explore angles and straight lines, while drawing on associated angle facts from previous lessons. Encourage children to discuss the order in which they found the angles.

STRENGTHEN Encourage children to identify which angles are vertically opposite. Ask: *Is this a pair of straight lines crossing? Can you check with a ruler? Which angles are vertically opposite?*

DEEPEN Question **3** can be explored further by asking children to find other angles in the diagrams. Encourage children to explore the order in which the angles can be found, depending on which rule is used.

ASSESSMENT CHECKPOINT Questions **1** and **2** give an opportunity to assess children's understanding of the different methods for calculating angles in crossing lines. Children who need to measure the angles with a protractor each time are likely to need more support with this concept.

Question **3** assesses children's ability to solve missing angle problems. Look for children who can draw on a range of angle facts, showing fluency in selecting the required operations to solve the problems. Children should also be able to describe the steps needed and the order in which they found the angles.

ANSWERS

Question **1**: Angles clockwise from given angle:
a) 100°, 80°, 100°, 80°; b) 43°, 137°, 43°, 137°;
c) 62°, 118°, unknown, unknown

Question **2**: Check that children have drawn a pair of crossing straight lines.

Question **3** a): a = 25°, b = 80°, c = 75°, d = 80°

Question **3** b): a = 38°, b = 142°, c = 52°

Question **3** c): y = 70°

Question **3** d): x = 108°

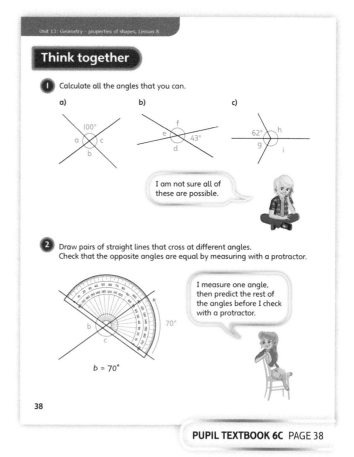

PUPIL TEXTBOOK 6C PAGE 38

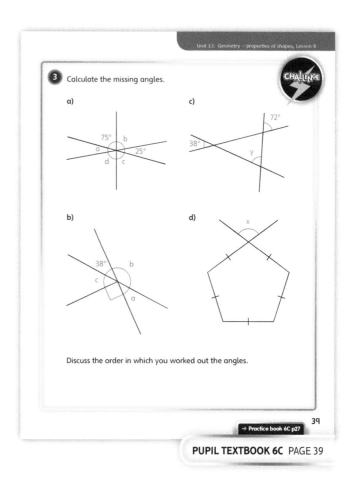

→ Practice book 6C p27

PUPIL TEXTBOOK 6C PAGE 39

Practice

WAYS OF WORKING Independent thinking

IN FOCUS Questions ❶ and ❸ aim to consolidate children's understanding of vertically opposite angles and angles on a straight line.

Question ❷ addresses a common misconception where children think that any opposite angles are equal. Ensure they understand that vertically opposite angles are only formed by a pair of crossing straight lines.

Question ❻ asks children to calculate missing angles. Encourage them to discuss the order in which they found the angles and the angle facts used.

STRENGTHEN Strengthen learning by encouraging children to use bar models. It may also be useful to colour vertically opposite angles with a highlighter pen, especially in question ❺.

DEEPEN Extend question ❻ by asking children to find the other unknown angles.

ASSESSMENT CHECKPOINT Questions ❶ to ❹ assess children's ability to calculate vertically opposite angles. Look for children confidently using this new angle rule, along with angles on a straight line.

In question ❺, look for children who can use angle facts to find the total of the given angles, showing fluency in identifying the required operations.

Question ❻ assesses children's ability to solve more complex missing angle problems. Children should be able to use associated angle facts, showing fluency in addition, subtraction and division.

ANSWERS Answers for the **Practice** part of the lesson appear in the separate **Practice and Reflect answer guide**.

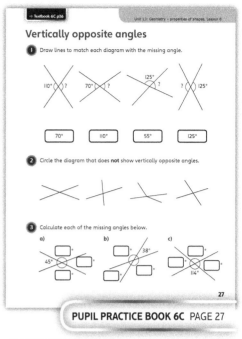

PUPIL PRACTICE BOOK 6C PAGE 27

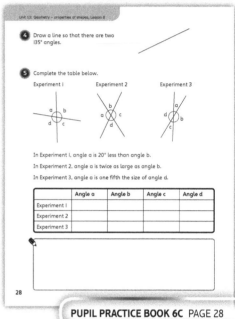

PUPIL PRACTICE BOOK 6C PAGE 28

Reflect

WAYS OF WORKING Pair work

IN FOCUS This reflection question involves children explaining the steps that show vertically opposite angles are equal. Encourage children to use angle facts to justify their reasoning.

ASSESSMENT CHECKPOINT This reflection assesses children's understanding of vertically opposite angles. Look for children confidently explaining in their own words why they must be equal.

ANSWERS Answers for the **Reflect** part of the lesson appear in the separate **Practice and Reflect answer guide**.

After the lesson

- Can children calculate missing angles on straight lines?
- Can children explain what makes vertically opposite angles and why they are equal?
- Can children calculate missing angles in shapes, drawing on a range of angle facts?

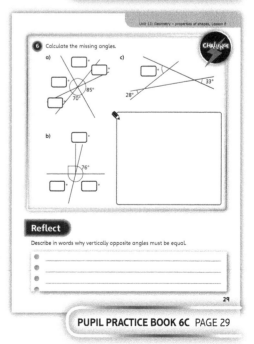

PUPIL PRACTICE BOOK 6C PAGE 29

Equal distance

Learning focus

In this lesson, children will understand that as the number of vertices increases an equal distance from the centre, a circle is formed. They learn the definition of radius and diameter and can solve problems involving radius and diameter.

Small steps

→ Previous step: Vertically opposite angles
→ **This step: Equal distance**
→ Next step: Parts of a circle

NATIONAL CURRICULUM LINKS

Year 6 Geometry – Properties of Shapes

Illustrate and name parts of circles, including radius, diameter and circumference and know that the diameter is twice the radius.

ASSESSING MASTERY

Children can recognise that a circle is formed by creating many points that are equal distances from the centre. They can identify the radius and diameter and calculate with them. They can use multiplication and division fluently, drawing circles accurately and solving problems, explaining the steps in their own words.

COMMON MISCONCEPTIONS

Children may think the radius goes from the centre of a circle in a horizontal or vertical direction only. Expose children to diagrams of circles that show the radius can be in any orientation from the centre. Ask:
• *Can you draw the radius at any angle?*

When asked to draw a circle given a diameter, children may forget to divide by 2 to find the radius. Encourage them to identify the radius and diameter before completing any questions and to check their answers. Ask:
• *Which is longer, the radius or the diameter? If the diameter is x, how can you work out the radius?*

STRENGTHENING UNDERSTANDING

Children who have difficulty identifying the radius from the diameter should draw this on the circle to help them see that they need to divide the diameter by 2. Children who find it a challenge to draw circles using a pair of compasses could be encouraged to rotate the paper instead as children often find this easier.

GOING DEEPER

Children can be encouraged to solve more complex problems involving circles. For example: *In a diagram of 5 concentric circles the smallest circle has a radius of 6 cm. Each circle increases by a 1 cm diameter. What is the diameter of the largest circle?* Ask children to explore the different methods they can use to solve the problems.

KEY LANGUAGE

In lesson: distance, vertices, triangle, quadrilateral, **radius**, circle, centre, pair of compasses, **concentric**, **diameter**

Other language to be used by the teacher: approximate, twice, equal, vertex, perimeter

STRUCTURES AND REPRESENTATIONS

polygons, circles

RESOURCES

Mandatory: pair of compasses, ruler, paper, string, pin (to hold string)

Optional: 2p and 5p coins, counters

 In the eTextbook of this lesson, you will find interactive links to a selection of teaching tools.

Before you teach

• Can children use a ruler to measure lines?
• Do children understand the word perimeter?
• Can children find the length of an equilateral triangle when given the perimeter?

Discover

WAYS OF WORKING Pair work

ASK
- Question ❶ a): *What shape will three people form? What shapes will be formed as more people join?*
- Question ❶ b): *What shape will the second class form?*

IN FOCUS This question introduces children to placing points an equal distance from a centre and exploring the shapes that are formed.

PRACTICAL TIPS It will be beneficial to use counters to represent the class in the **Discover** scenario, so children have an overhead view. This will help them to see the shapes formed.

ANSWERS

Question ❶ a): Three people form a triangle and four people form a quadrilateral. As more people join, the shape has more vertices and starts to form a circle.

Question ❶ b): The second class will form another circle, with a radius of 6 m.

PUPIL TEXTBOOK 6C PAGE 40

Share

WAYS OF WORKING Whole class teacher led

ASK
- Question ❶ a): *What do the diagrams show? What shape is formed when three people stand around Amelia? How about four people? Or five people? What happens as more people stand around Amelia? What shape is created? What is the distance from the centre called in a circle? How can you draw a circle? What equipment do you need?*
- Question ❶ b): *What shape will the second class form? Will the circle be smaller or bigger than the first one? How do you know? What is the special name for circles with the same centre?*

IN FOCUS Question ❶ a) asks children to explore the different shapes created by points placed around a central location. It would be beneficial to act this out with children, maybe using a smaller distance than 5 m.

Children should recognise that, as more people join, a circle is eventually formed. Define the term radius and discuss how to draw a circle using the correct equipment (a pair of compasses).

Part b) further develops the concept of equal distance from the centre and introduces the meaning of concentric circles. It will be useful to discuss how concentric circles can be drawn using a pair of compasses and a ruler.

STRENGTHEN In question ❶ a) encourage children to look at the diagram to strengthen understanding of the concept that as the number of vertices increases the shape will eventually become a circle.

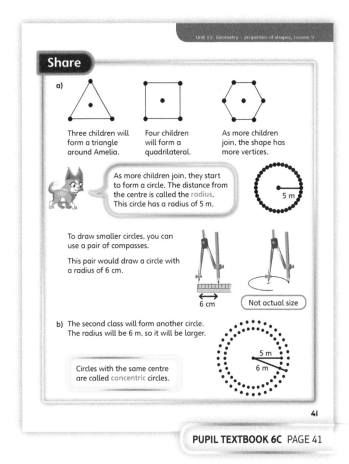

PUPIL TEXTBOOK 6C PAGE 41

Think together

WAYS OF WORKING Whole class teacher led (I do, We do, You do)

ASK

- Question **1**: *How can you identify the radius? Which direction does it go in? What equipment do you need? How can you ensure your answer is accurate?*
- Question **2**: *What do you need to draw first? Which circle should you start with? Does it matter?*
- Question **3**: *What is the diameter? How could this help? How can you find the diameter of a circle?*

IN FOCUS Question **1** develops children's understanding of identifying and measuring the radius. Ensure children are confident using the centre of the circle to measure the radius. Explore with them how the radius can go in any direction and will always be the same.

In question **2**, children are encouraged to use a pair of compasses, string or a ruler. Encourage them to explain which piece of equipment will give them the most accurate copy.

In question **3** ensure children measure the widest part of the circles by estimating where the diameter is and then adjusting as necessary.

STRENGTHEN When drawing circles with a pair of compasses it can be useful to encourage children to rotate the page rather than the compasses.

DEEPEN Extend question **2** by asking children to create other concentric circle patterns. Encourage them to calculate the distance between the circumference of the circles and ask if this will always be the same.

ASSESSMENT CHECKPOINT Question **1** assesses children's ability to identify and measure the radius of a circle. Look for children who are confident with the definition and can use a ruler accurately.

In question **2**, look for children who can measure accurately using the correct equipment and those who create an accurate copy of the design.

Question **3** assesses children's ability to identify and measure the diameter of a circle. Look for children who can confidently divide the diameters by 2 using an appropriate method. If children simply guess where the centre is, they may need more support.

ANSWERS

Question **1**: a) 4 cm; b) 5·5 cm

Question **2**: Make sure an accurate design is completed.

Question **3**: i) 2·5 cm; ii) 4 cm; iii) 2·3 cm

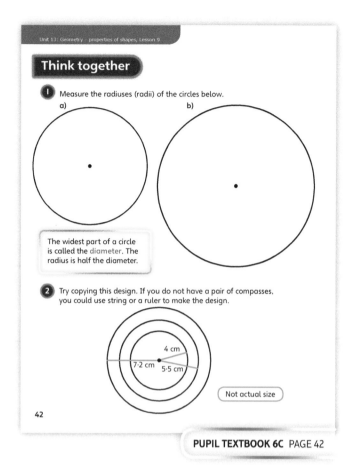

PUPIL TEXTBOOK 6C PAGE 42

PUPIL TEXTBOOK 6C PAGE 43

Practice

WAYS OF WORKING Independent thinking

IN FOCUS Question **1** requires children to make dots an equal distance from the centre. Encourage children to spread the dots to create a circle.

Questions **2**, **3** and **4** develop children's understanding of the radius and diameter. Watch for children who try to use a ruler in question **4**.

In question **6** explore with children the type of triangle shown and encourage them to reason about how they could calculate the length of one side. Children may need a reminder of the definition of perimeter. Encourage children to show their method clearly and use the correct units for their answers.

STRENGTHEN In question **3** encourage children to represent the sentences on diagrams to support their thinking. Get them to replace the x with a number to help them decide if the statement is correct.

DEEPEN Extend questions **5** and **6** by asking children to explain and explore the different ways in which the answers can be calculated.

Deepen learning in question **6** by asking children to draw other shapes on tessellated circles.

THINK DIFFERENTLY In question **5**, look out for children who divide by the wrong amount (for example, divide 13 cm by 5 since there are 5 coins). Encourage children to show their method clearly and to use the correct units.

ASSESSMENT CHECKPOINT Questions **2**, **3** and **4** assess children's ability to work with the radius and diameter of a circle.

In questions **5** and **6**, look for children fluently using division or multiplication in their calculations, while explaining the different steps in their own words.

ANSWERS Answers for the **Practice** part of the lesson appear in the separate **Practice and Reflect answer guide**.

Reflect

WAYS OF WORKING Pair work

IN FOCUS This reflection question checks children's understanding of drawing a circle when given a diameter. It addresses a common misconception where children may draw a circle with a radius of 4 cm rather than a diameter of 4 cm.

ASSESSMENT CHECKPOINT Children should be able to describe the steps needed to draw the circle. Look for children who recognise the need to divide by 2 to calculate the radius and identify the correct equipment to draw an accurate circle.

ANSWERS Answers for the **Reflect** part of the lesson appear in the separate **Practice and Reflect answer guide**.

After the lesson ⏸

- Can children differentiate between the radius and diameter of a circle and solve problems involving these lengths?
- Can children accurately draw a circle and describe the steps required?
- Can children draw concentric circles?

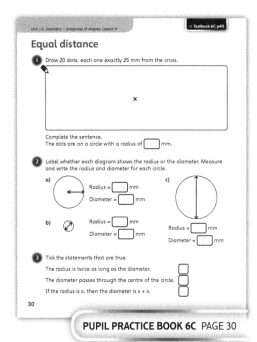

PUPIL PRACTICE BOOK 6C PAGE 30

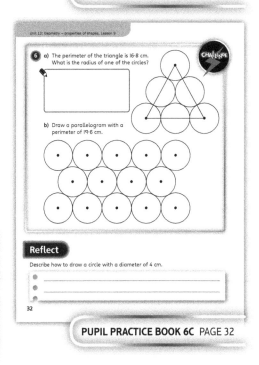

PUPIL PRACTICE BOOK 6C PAGE 31

PUPIL PRACTICE BOOK 6C PAGE 32

Parts of a circle

Learning focus

In this lesson, children will learn more about the parts of a circle and their properties.

Small steps

→ Previous step: Equal distance
→ **This step: Parts of a circle**
→ Next step: Nets (1)

NATIONAL CURRICULUM LINKS

Year 6 Geometry – Properties of Shapes

Illustrate and name parts of circles, including radius, diameter and circumference and know that the diameter is twice the radius.

ASSESSING MASTERY

Children can confidently identify the radius, diameter and circumference of a circle and can measure these accurately. They can draw shapes in circles and explore the properties of them showing fluency in measuring angles and calculating unknown angles, demonstrating an understanding of associated angle facts.

COMMON MISCONCEPTIONS

Children may not understand that the radius of a circle can come from the centre at any angle and thus, they may find it a challenge to identify isosceles triangles. To address this misconception, it is important to expose children to circles with the radius and diameter marked at different angles. Ask:
• *Can the radius be drawn at an angle that is not horizontal or vertical?*

STRENGTHENING UNDERSTANDING

To support children with drawing shapes within circles, provide circles with either the diameter or the radius pre-drawn. It may be beneficial for children to practise drawing a radius and diameter on a circle in different orientations before attempting to draw triangles.

GOING DEEPER

Children could be encouraged to investigate a range of shapes that can be drawn in circles, to develop their understanding of parts of a circle. For example, you could challenge children to draw a hexagon in a circle by accurately drawing six equilateral triangles from the centre.

KEY LANGUAGE

In lesson: circumference, diameter, radius, perimeter, polygon, centre, triangle, angle, isosceles

Other language to be used by the teacher: measure, shapes, properties, accurate, twice, equilateral, kite, parallelogram, trapezium, rhombus

STRUCTURES AND REPRESENTATIONS

circles, triangles, polygons

RESOURCES

Mandatory: string, ruler, pin (to hold string)

Optional: rope (for outdoor activities), squared paper, pair of compasses

 In the eTextbook of this lesson, you will find interactive links to a selection of teaching tools.

Before you teach

• Do children understand the terms radius, diameter and perimeter?
• Can children reliably measure using a ruler and a protractor?
• Can children calculate missing angles in triangles using angle facts?

Discover

WAYS OF WORKING Pair work

ASK

- Question ① a): *What equipment is needed to measure the edge of the bike wheel?*
- Question ① b): *What is the radius? What is the diameter?*

IN FOCUS Question ① a) introduces children to the circumference of a circle. Question ① b) develops this, requiring children to explore the longest length, using their knowledge of radius and diameter. This is a good opportunity to assess children's confidence with these definitions.

PRACTICAL TIPS Children could be introduced to the circumference of circles in a practical setting, such as measuring the circumference of a circular object outside. Encourage them to use string/rope to understand the circumference is the distance around the outside of a circle.

ANSWERS

Question ① a): Bella could wrap a piece of string or rope around the circumference, then measure it in a straight line using a ruler. Alternatively, Bella could choose a point on the wheel, and roll it until this point returns to the starting position. The distance it has rolled is the circumference.

Question ① b): The circumference is longest.

Share

WAYS OF WORKING Whole class teacher led

ASK

- Question ① a): *What is the name for the distance around the edge of a circle? What is this similar to? In method 1, how could you measure the piece of string or rope? In method 2, how would you measure the distance travelled?*
- Question ① b): *What does a radius look like? A diameter? Which is longer? Is the circumference bigger or smaller?*

IN FOCUS Question ① a) introduces the term 'circumference'. Watch out for children who think a valid way of measuring the circumference would be to put a ruler around the outside of the circle. Explain that a more accurate way of measuring the circumference is needed. Explore methods 1 and 2 with children; when discussing method 2, emphasise the need to mark a dot on the circle so the measurement is accurate. It would be beneficial to complete this activity in a physical way, so children can see how the wheel (i.e. circle) moves rather than just looking at the diagram.

In question ① b), encourage children to compare the radius and diameter first so they can eliminate one of these parts. Use the diagrams to support understanding that the circumference is longest.

STRENGTHEN It may be useful to link the concept of circumference with children's prior knowledge of the perimeter of polygons, using diagrams to strengthen understanding.

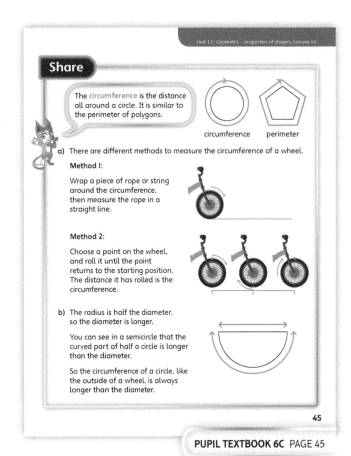

Parts of a circle

Discover

a) How could Bella find the distance around the edge of her bike's wheel?

b) Which is longest: the diameter, the radius or the distance around the edge of the wheel?

44

PUPIL TEXTBOOK 6C PAGE 44

Share

The circumference is the distance all around a circle. It is similar to the perimeter of polygons.

circumference   perimeter

a) There are different methods to measure the circumference of a wheel.

Method 1:

Wrap a piece of rope or string around the circumference, then measure the rope in a straight line.

Method 2:

Choose a point on the wheel, and roll it until the point returns to the starting position. The distance it has rolled is the circumference.

b) The radius is half the diameter, so the diameter is longer.

You can see in a semicircle that the curved part of half a circle is longer than the diameter.

So the circumference of a circle, like the outside of a wheel, is always longer than the diameter.

45

PUPIL TEXTBOOK 6C PAGE 45

Think together

Unit 13: Geometry – properties of shapes, Lesson 10

Think together

WAYS OF WORKING Whole class teacher led (I do, We do, You do)

ASK

- Question ①: *What can you use to measure accurately?*
- Question ②: *What is the word for the length from the centre of a circle to the circumference? What type of triangles are formed? Why? Is it possible to create any different types of triangle if the centre is always used?*
- Question ③ a): *What is the same and what is different about the triangles? What do you notice about the angles?*
- Question ③ b): *How has Isla split up the triangle? What type of triangles are the smaller ones? How do you know? What do the two angles a and two angles b add up to? What does this tell you about the total of one angle a and one angle b? Can you explain Isla's reasoning?*

IN FOCUS Question ① supports children in developing their understanding of the circumference of a circle and asks them to measure using a piece of string. Encourage children to work in pairs in order to measure more accurately.

Question ② gives children an opportunity to explore the types of triangle that can be formed within a circle. Encourage them to think about the two lines that come from the centre of the circle and consequently the types of triangles formed. Encourage children to use a protractor to check an equilateral triangle, if they try to create one.

Question ③ requires children to explore triangles in circles with the diameter as an edge. Children should notice that the angle between the lines that touch the circumference is always a right angle. A basic proof of this theorem is explained in part b).

STRENGTHEN To help children measure the circumference of the circle encourage them to make paper versions of circles and try method 2 from the **Share** section.

DEEPEN Questions ② and ③ extend children's understanding of parts of circles by drawing triangles within them. Encourage children to explore other shapes they could draw using parts of a circle to deepen this further.

ASSESSMENT CHECKPOINT In question ①, look for children who measure accurately and use the correct units.

Questions ② and ③ give an opportunity to assess children's ability to use parts of circles to draw triangles while understanding more complex reasoning, showing fluency in types of triangle and measuring angles.

ANSWERS

Question ① a): Circumference is 94 mm.

Question ① b): Circumference is 141 mm.

Question ②: Bella will form triangles which always have at least two equal lengths (the radii). She can form an isosceles triangle, an isosceles right-angle triangle or an equilateral triangle.

Question ③ a): The angle between the two lines at the circumference is always 90°

Question ③ b): Angles a + a + b + b = 180°. Therefore angles a + b = 90°.

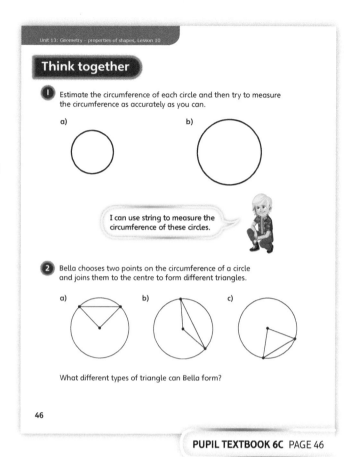

PUPIL TEXTBOOK 6C PAGE 46

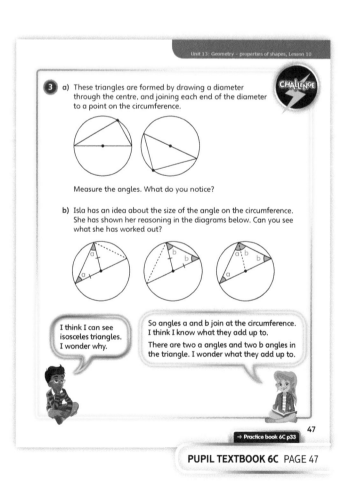

PUPIL TEXTBOOK 6C PAGE 47

Practice

WAYS OF WORKING Independent thinking

IN FOCUS Question ❶ consolidates children's understanding of identifying parts of a circle from a diagram.

Question ❷ allows children to explore forming isosceles triangles in circles and builds on prior knowledge of calculating two unknown angles. Watch out for children who try to measure all the angles using a protractor – encourage a more efficient method.

Question ❸ looks at creating other shapes in a circle. Ensure children are confident with the properties of each shape by discussing them beforehand.

Question ❹ develops children's understanding of the 90-degree angle at the circumference.

Question ❺ requires children to demonstrate an understanding of area and develops the concept of counting squares to find the area.

STRENGTHEN If children are finding it challenging to draw shapes inside circles, support them by drawing the first line for them and ask them to complete the shapes. Ensuring that children are confident with the properties of the shapes they are drawing will also be beneficial.

DEEPEN Question ❺ can be explored further by asking children to find areas of other circles drawn on squared paper.

ASSESSMENT CHECKPOINT Questions ❷, ❸ and ❹ assess children's ability to create shapes inside circles. Children should be able to identify and use parts of the circle to accurately form these shapes, showing fluency in measuring angles and calculating missing angles.

Question ❺ gives an opportunity to assess children's ability to approximate the area of a circle. Children should be able to count the full squares and half squares to find an estimate for the area.

ANSWERS Answers for the **Practice** part of the lesson appear in the separate **Practice and Reflect answer guide**.

Reflect

WAYS OF WORKING Independent thinking

IN FOCUS This reflection question will allow you to assess children's understanding of how to draw an isosceles triangle using a circle. Encourage children to describe the steps using key language, such as circumference, centre and radius. Look for children who can do this without any support and those who do need support.

ASSESSMENT CHECKPOINT Children should be able to describe the process confidently, clearly explaining the steps in their method and showing fluency with parts of a circle and the properties of shapes.

ANSWERS Answers for the **Reflect** part of the lesson appear in the separate **Practice and Reflect answer guide**.

After the lesson ⏸

- Can children confidently identify the radius, diameter and circumference of a circle, and measure the circumference of a circle using appropriate equipment?
- Can children draw shapes within circles and reason with shapes and angles inside circles?
- Can children find an approximate area of a circle by counting squares?

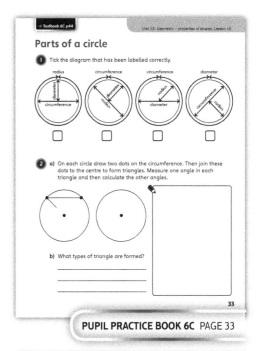

PUPIL PRACTICE BOOK 6C PAGE 33

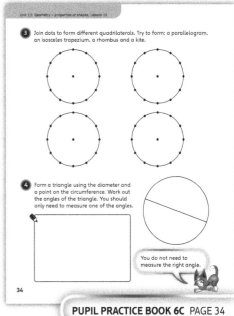

PUPIL PRACTICE BOOK 6C PAGE 34

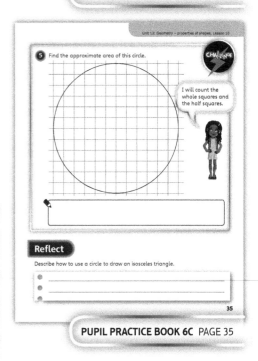

PUPIL PRACTICE BOOK 6C PAGE 35

Nets ①

Learning focus

In this lesson, children will use their understanding of properties of 3D shapes to develop their ability to identify shapes from nets and draw nets.

Small steps

→ Previous step: Parts of a circle
→ **This step: Nets (1)**
→ Next step: Nets (2)

NATIONAL CURRICULUM LINKS

Year 6 Geometry – Properties of Shapes
· Recognise, describe and build simple 3D shapes, including making nets.
· Identify 3D shapes, including cubes and other cuboids, from 2D representations.

ASSESSING MASTERY

Children can confidently identify 3D shapes from nets using the properties of shapes and can sketch nets demonstrating understanding of the different ways in which nets can be represented.

COMMON MISCONCEPTIONS

Children may focus on just some of the shapes of the faces in the net and become mixed up between 3D shapes. For example, children may see a triangular face and assume it must be a net for a pyramid. Also, children may forget to include one of the faces (usually the face that would be seen as the 'top' of the 3D shape). Ensure children are confident with identifying 3D shapes and their properties before completing this lesson. Ask:
· *Have you looked at all of the faces?*

Children may draw the correct faces for the net but join them in such a way that it would be impossible to fold up the net to make a 3D shape where all the edges touch. Ask:
· *Which edges will meet when the net is folded to make a 3D shape?*

STRENGTHENING UNDERSTANDING

Encourage children to consolidate learning by focusing on paper versions of nets, so they can manipulate them to make 3D shapes.

GOING DEEPER

Children could be challenged to explore all the possible nets for a particular 3D shape.

Give children a 3D shape with measurements on it and ask them to create a net that is to scale and can be folded to make an accurate copy of the 3D shape.

KEY LANGUAGE

In lesson: nets, 3D, 2D, shape, face, sketch, overlap, pentagonal-based pyramid, **tetrahedron**, square-based pyramid, triangular prism, cuboid

Other language to be used by the teacher: accurate, form, edge, vertex, draw, cylinder, hexagonal-based pyramid, pentagonal prism, hexagonal prism

STRUCTURES AND REPRESENTATIONS

nets, 3D shapes

RESOURCES

Mandatory: paper, scissors, ruler, protractor

Optional: paper nets

 In the eTextbook of this lesson, you will find interactive links to a selection of teaching tools.

Before you teach

· Can children recognise and name 3D shapes?
· Can children identify the properties of 3D shapes?

Discover

WAYS OF WORKING Pair work

ASK

- Question ❶ a): *What is a net? What shapes do you recognise in the nets? Can you link these to 3D shapes?*
- Question ❶ b): *What are the properties of a pentagonal-based pyramid? What is a pyramid?*

IN FOCUS Question ❶ a) will introduce children to identifying 3D shapes from 2D nets. Question ❶ b) gives children an opportunity to explore the concept of nets by sketching a net for a 3D shape.

PRACTICAL TIPS You could give children copies of the nets or ask them to draw their own versions. They can then physically fold the nets to discover the 3D shapes that will be created. It may be best to do this activity after children have tried the problem themselves, to reinforce the concepts discussed.

ANSWERS

Question ❶ a): From top to bottom: a triangular prism, a square-based pyramid, a tetrahedron.

Question ❶ b): Various nets can be drawn for a pentagonal-based pyramid. One way is to have the base in the centre, and one triangular face for each side of the base.

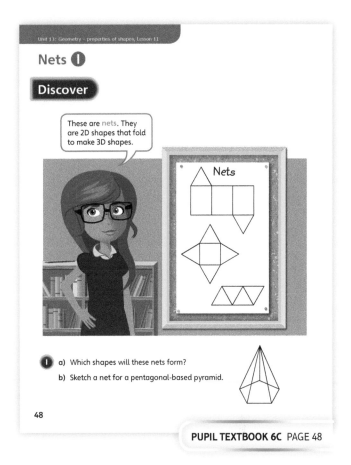

PUPIL TEXTBOOK 6C PAGE 48

Share

WAYS OF WORKING Whole class teacher led

ASK

- Question ❶ a): *What faces do the nets show? What 3D shapes have these faces? What are the properties of a prism? What are the properties of a pyramid?*
- Question ❶ b): *What faces must the net contain? What does the diagram show? Are there any other ways to make a net? How can you check your answer?*

IN FOCUS In question ❶ a), encourage children to use the descriptions of the 3D shapes and compare them with the nets, but ensure they do not rely on the diagrams of the 3D shapes to name them. Children should realise that they need to analyse the properties of the nets to identify the 3D shapes formed.

In question ❶ b) discuss the key properties of a pentagonal-based pyramid and explore with children the different ways that the net can be sketched. Discuss the difference between a *sketch* and an accurate *drawing* – the net needs to be easily identifiable but does not need to be completely accurate or to scale. Emphasise the need to check that the net would fold to make a pentagonal-based pyramid.

STRENGTHEN Strengthen learning by using paper versions of the nets, so children can manipulate them in a concrete way.

DEEPEN Extend question ❶ b) by challenging children to find all the possible nets for a pentagonal-based pyramid.

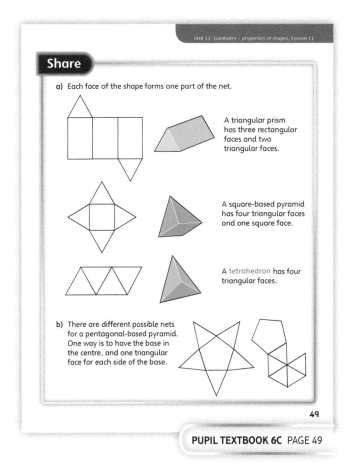

PUPIL TEXTBOOK 6C PAGE 49

Think together

WAYS OF WORKING Whole class teacher led (I do, We do, You do)

ASK

- Question ❶: *What are the properties of a cuboid? Can you tell if any of the nets would **not** form a cuboid based on their properties? Which faces need to be next to each other? Would any of the faces overlap when folded to make a 3D shape?*
- Question ❷: *What are the properties of each shape? Where would the faces need to be on the nets? How can you check your answers?*
- Question ❸: *What shape is shown? What are its properties? How can you draw an accurate net?*

IN FOCUS In question ❶, children should be encouraged to consider the properties of a cuboid and then visualise the nets forming to make a 3D shape, thinking about any overlapping that would occur.

Question ❷ builds on the **Discover** section asking children to sketch a range of nets. Encourage children to discuss the properties of the shapes first, highlighting the number of faces and the faces that will need to be next to each other in the net. Remind children to check that their nets will form the 3D shapes after sketching them. Watch out for children who are unsure where to place the circles for the cylinder. Since the rectangular part wraps round the circles, the circles can be placed anywhere along the edge of the rectangle.

Question ❸ is more challenging: children are required to identify the shape and its properties and create an accurate drawing of its net. Children will need to ensure all the lengths in the net correspond to the lengths that are labelled on the 3D shape. Explore different techniques for drawing the net accurately and discuss Ash's suggestion.

STRENGTHEN To support understanding, children can explore the shapes using paper versions of the nets.

DEEPEN Question ❶ can be deepened by asking children to explore all the possible ways of correctly representing a net for a cuboid. Questions ❷ and ❸ can be extended by challenging children to sketch and draw the nets in different ways.

ASSESSMENT CHECKPOINT Question ❶ assesses children's ability to identify nets that form a cuboid. Questions ❷ and ❸ develop this, giving an opportunity to assess children's ability to sketch and draw accurately nets of 3D shapes.

ANSWERS

Question ❶: Net D will form a cuboid.

Question ❷:

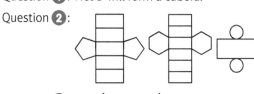

Question ❸:

Think together

❶ Which of these nets will form a cuboid?

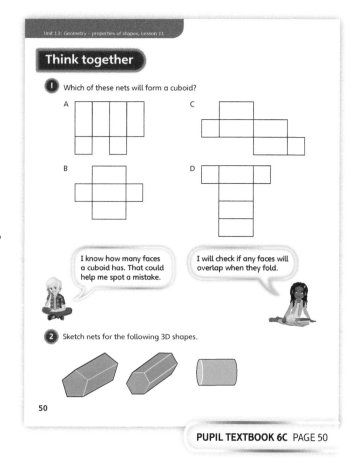

A

C

B

D

> I know how many faces a cuboid has. That could help me spot a mistake.

> I will check if any faces will overlap when they fold.

❷ Sketch nets for the following 3D shapes.

50

PUPIL TEXTBOOK 6C PAGE 50

---

❸ Draw a net for the following shape as accurately as you can. The base is a regular shape.

CHALLENGE

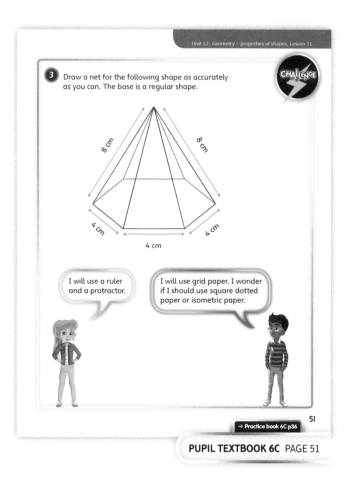

8 cm   8 cm

4 cm   4 cm

4 cm

> I will use a ruler and a protractor.

> I will use grid paper. I wonder if I should use square dotted paper or isometric paper.

→ Practice book 6C p36

51

PUPIL TEXTBOOK 6C PAGE 51

Practice

WAYS OF WORKING Independent thinking

IN FOCUS Question **1** aims to consolidate children's understanding of nets by asking them to complete a matching activity. Encourage children to compare the properties of the shapes.

Question **2** develops children's understanding of nets being represented in different ways.

Questions **3** and **4** require children to apply their knowledge of nets. Encourage them to think about which edges will meet.

STRENGTHEN Strengthen learning by encouraging children to represent the nets on paper and to cut them out, so they can make the 3D shapes.

DEEPEN Extend question **5** by challenging children to draw the net in a different way.

Deepen learning on question **6** by exploring with children if they can come up with more than one solution.

ASSESSMENT CHECKPOINT Questions **3** and **4** provide an opportunity to assess children's ability to reason with nets and visualise which faces will be where when the 3D shape is formed.

In questions **5** and **6**, look for children who can demonstrate understanding of where the faces need to be so the net forms a cuboid.

ANSWERS Answers for the **Practice** part of the lesson appear in the separate **Practice and Reflect answer guide**.

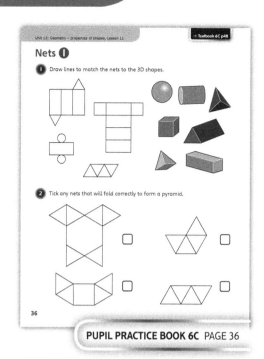

PUPIL PRACTICE BOOK 6C PAGE 36

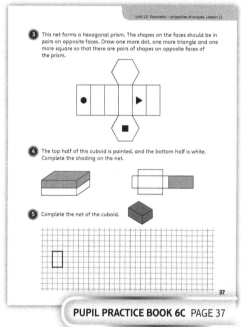

PUPIL PRACTICE BOOK 6C PAGE 37

Reflect

WAYS OF WORKING Independent thinking

IN FOCUS This reflection asks children to draw a net of a pyramid. Discuss the different pyramids they could draw, encouraging them to reflect on the pyramids they have met in the lesson. Children should be able to describe the properties of pyramids compared with other 3D shapes, for example, prisms.

ASSESSMENT CHECKPOINT Look for children confidently choosing an appropriate pyramid and drawing an accurate net.

ANSWERS Answers for the **Reflect** part of the lesson appear in the separate **Practice and Reflect answer guide**.

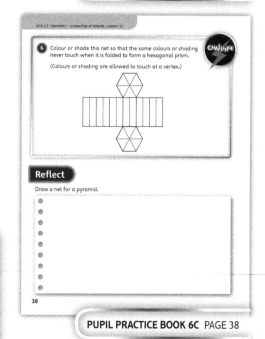

PUPIL PRACTICE BOOK 6C PAGE 38

After the lesson ⏸

- Can children match a net to its 3D representation?
- Can children name a 3D shape when given its net?
- Can children identify which nets will fold correctly to form a 3D shape and draw a net accurately?

Nets ②

Learning focus

In this lesson, children will build on their knowledge of nets of 3D shapes by exploring the multiple nets of a cube in the context of dice.

Small steps

→ Previous step: Nets (1)
→ **This step: Nets (2)**
→ Next step: Problem solving – place value

NATIONAL CURRICULUM LINKS

Year 6 Geometry – Properties of Shapes
- Recognise, describe and build simple 3D shapes, including making nets.
- Identify 3D shapes, including cubes and other cuboids, from 2D representations.

ASSESSING MASTERY

Children can confidently identify nets that will form cubes and can sketch nets, demonstrating understanding of faces that are opposite in cubes and the different ways in which the nets of a cube can be represented.

COMMON MISCONCEPTIONS

Children may not include all six faces of a cube in its net. Ensure they are confident with the properties of a cube. Ask:
- *How many faces make a cube?*

Children may draw the correct number of faces for the net of a cube, but have faces that overlap or edges that do not meet when the net is folded. When working with patterns on nets of cubes children often get the patterns in the wrong place. Ask:
- *Which edges will meet when the net is folded? Which faces will be opposite each other when the net is folded?*

STRENGTHENING UNDERSTANDING

Children should be encouraged to strengthen learning by using construction materials to make cubes. They can also focus on paper versions of nets.

GOING DEEPER

Encourage children to deepen learning by exploring different patterns on the nets of a cube. Give them a picture of a cube that has a pattern on the faces and ask them to create the net. Ask: *Can you find more than one solution using different nets?*

KEY LANGUAGE

In lesson: nets, cube, form, face, opposite, dice, sketch, solution, view, construction, fold

Other language to be used by the teacher: total, edge, sides

STRUCTURES AND REPRESENTATIONS

nets of cubes, cubes

RESOURCES

Mandatory: paper, scissors, ruler

Optional: dice, cubes, geometric construction set

 In the eTextbook of this lesson, you will find interactive links to a selection of teaching tools.

Before you teach

- Can children identify the properties of a cube?
- Can children sketch nets?

Discover

WAYS OF WORKING Pair work

ASK

- Question ❶ a): *What 3D shape is a dice? Which faces are opposite one another? How can you work out which net is correct?*
- Question ❶ b): *Which faces would be opposite each other?*

IN FOCUS Question ❶ a) introduces children to the properties of a dice and asks them to identify the net that forms a correct dice. Question ❶ b) gives children an opportunity to explore the various ways in which the dots on a net of a dice can be displayed.

PRACTICAL TIPS You could give children paper versions of the nets, which they can fold. However, children will need to be able to reason in an abstract way, so it may be beneficial to complete the practical activity after children have thought about the problem. This concept could also be introduced during an art session with children decorating the different sides of a cube and examining how the faces of the net fit together.

ANSWERS

Question ❶ a): The correct net is D.

Question ❶ b): There are multiple solutions. Pairs totalling 7 must be on opposite faces, for example:

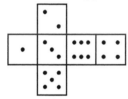

Share

WAYS OF WORKING Whole class teacher led

ASK

- Question ❶ a): *Which numbers must be opposite each other? How do you know? Which faces are opposite each other in the nets shown? How do you know? Do all the nets form cubes correctly? Which net is correct?*
- Question ❶ b): *Which faces must be opposite each other? What total must the numbers make? What does the diagram show? Are there any other ways to make a net of a cube?*

IN FOCUS Question ❶ a) introduces children to the properties of a net for a dice. First discuss with children what 3D shape a dice is and then discuss the properties before asking children which pairs of numbers total 7. Encourage children to analyse the given nets based on which faces are opposite one another. Children should realise that numbers which are next to each other in the net cannot be opposite each other in the 3D shape. With net B highlight that this would not form a cube correctly; this is an important concept that children need to be able to identify.

In question ❶ b) encourage children to discuss which faces are opposite on the net of the cube and challenge them to explore all possible solutions.

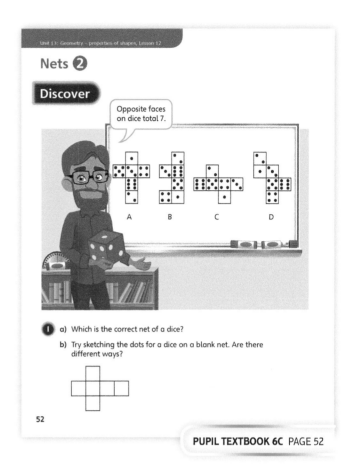

PUPIL TEXTBOOK 6C PAGE 52

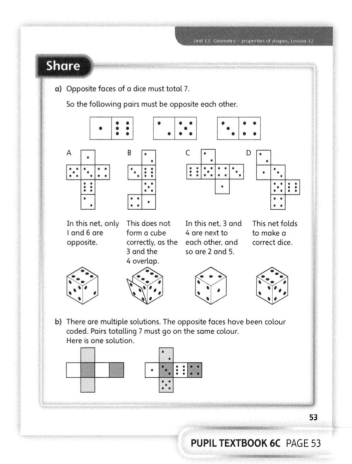

PUPIL TEXTBOOK 6C PAGE 53

Think together

WAYS OF WORKING Whole class teacher led (I do, We do, You do)

ASK

- Question ❶: *Can you tell if any of the nets would **not** form a cube? Would any of the faces overlap when folded to make a 3D shape?*
- Question ❷: *Are there any that you can rule out easily?*
- Question ❸: *How many faces need to be drawn?*

IN FOCUS Question ❶ aims to develop understanding of forming cubes from nets and addresses common misconceptions. Encourage children to consider the properties of a cube and to visualise each net folding to make a cube, thinking about any overlapping that would occur.

Question ❷ asks children to identify the cubes that could have been formed from a net. Watch out for children making common mistakes, such as choosing A because it shows three triangles even though it would be impossible for the faces to meet in this way. Encourage children to attempt the problem abstractly before making a paper version to fold and check.

Question ❸ allows children to explore the different possible nets of a cube. Discuss nets that are drawn in different orientations, as per Dexter's comment.

STRENGTHEN Encourage children to explore the shapes using paper versions of the nets or concrete materials.

DEEPEN Question ❷ can be deepened by asking children to explore all the possible views of the cube from this net. Challenge children by giving them another patterned cube and asking them to draw the net or vice versa.

ASSESSMENT CHECKPOINT Question ❶ assesses children's ability to identify nets that form a cube. Question ❷ develops this, giving an opportunity to assess children's ability to work out how the cube could look once it is formed. Look for children who can confidently identify which views are possible using a paper version or otherwise.

Question ❸ assesses children's ability to find nets of cubes. Look for children who can systematically work through the problem to find all possible solutions.

ANSWERS

Question ❶: Nets A and D will form a cube.

Question ❷: B and C could be views of the cube.

Question ❸: There are 11 different nets of a cube, for example:

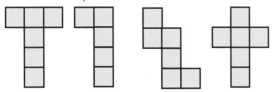

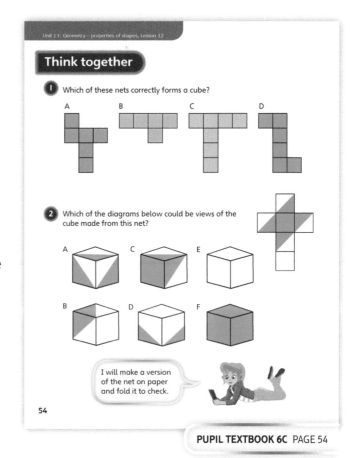

PUPIL TEXTBOOK 6C PAGE 54

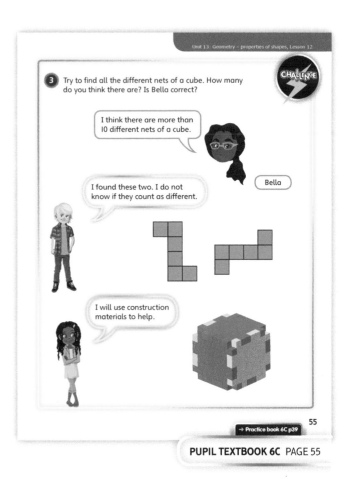

PUPIL TEXTBOOK 6C PAGE 55

86

Practice

WAYS OF WORKING Independent thinking

IN FOCUS Questions **1**, **2** and **3** aim to consolidate children's understanding of representing the net of a cube in different ways. The questions gradually reduce scaffolding by progressing from nets given, to completing a net, to drawing nets independently where children will need to identify opposite faces.

Question **4** allows children to apply their knowledge of nets in a different context and develops children's understanding of which vertices will meet when a cube is formed.

Question **5** asks children to use their knowledge of nets and volume to answer the question.

STRENGTHEN When identifying and sketching nets, encourage children to represent the nets on paper and cut them out, so they can make the 3D shapes. Ask: *How do the 3D shapes help you check the nets are correct? What faces are opposite each other? Do any of the sides overlap?*

DEEPEN Question **4** can be explored further by challenging children to draw the net in a different way.

ASSESSMENT CHECKPOINT Questions **1** and **2** assess children's ability to identify nets of a cube and complete nets when given four of the faces.

Question **3** gives an opportunity to assess children's ability to draw nets of cubes independently. Look for children who can confidently draw the net in three different ways, demonstrating understanding of opposite faces.

Question **4** assesses children's ability to complete a pattern on a net. Look for children who can complete this abstractly or those who make a paper version correctly, demonstrating an understanding of where the vertices and edges will meet so the pattern is formed correctly.

ANSWERS Answers for the **Practice** part of the lesson appear in the separate **Practice and Reflect answer guide**.

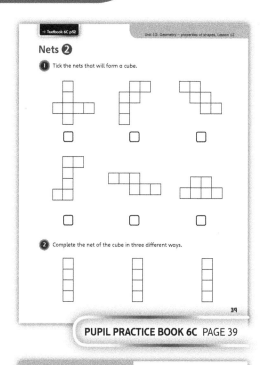

PUPIL PRACTICE BOOK 6C PAGE 39

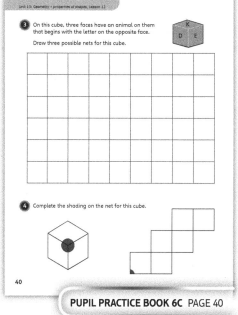

PUPIL PRACTICE BOOK 6C PAGE 40

Reflect

WAYS OF WORKING Independent thinking or pair work

IN FOCUS This reflection gives an opportunity to check children's understanding of identifying nets that form a cube. Encourage children to explain in their own words and to draw on key language, such as faces and edges.

ASSESSMENT CHECKPOINT Look for children who can confidently describe the way in which they can identify if a net will form a cube, demonstrating understanding of the properties of a cube and edges of faces that will meet.

ANSWERS Answers for the **Reflect** part of the lesson appear in the separate **Practice and Reflect answer guide**.

After the lesson

- Can children identify opposite faces on the net of a cube?
- Can children identify which nets will form a cube?
- Can children complete nets of cubes, including nets of cubes that contain patterns?

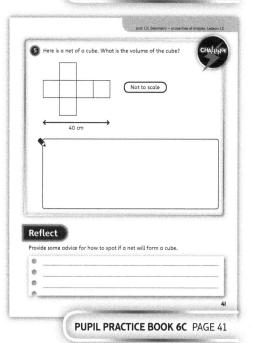

PUPIL PRACTICE BOOK 6C PAGE 41

End of unit check

> **Don't forget the *Power Maths* unit assessment grid on p26.**

WAYS OF WORKING Group work adult led

IN FOCUS

- Questions **2**, **3** and **5** assess children's ability to use angle facts to calculate missing angles in shapes and on lines.
- Question **4** assesses children's knowledge of properties of shapes.
- Question **6** is a SATs-style question which allows children to apply their skills to draw a 2D representation of a 3D shape. Encourage children to draw the net accurately.

ANSWERS AND COMMENTARY Children who have mastered the concepts in this unit are able to confidently measure angles, understand and recall facts for angles in shapes and lines, fluently use shape properties to reason and accurately draw and recognise nets of 3D shapes.

In questions **3** and **5**, encourage children to label any angles they know or can work out. Remind them that a right angle is 90° if necessary. Strengthen understanding by encouraging children to use a written method, such as the column method, for their calculations.

In question **6**, encourage children to identify the properties of the cuboid and to discuss the length and width of the faces. Common misconceptions include not drawing the correct number of faces, not drawing equivalent faces opposite one another, or drawing faces so that they will overlap when the net is folded to make the 3D shape.

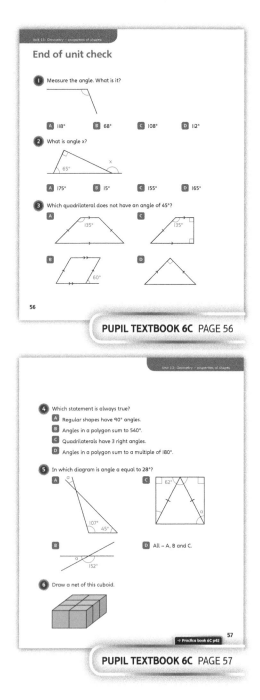

PUPIL TEXTBOOK 6C PAGE 56

PUPIL TEXTBOOK 6C PAGE 57

Q	A	WRONG ANSWERS AND MISCONCEPTIONS	STRENGTHENING UNDERSTANDING
1	D	A and C suggest that children have misread the numbers or not aligned the protractor correctly. B suggests children have looked at the wrong scale.	Encourage children to rotate the paper, so the baseline is at the bottom.
2	C	A and D suggest that children have miscalculated when adding the numbers. B suggests children have worked out the unknown in the triangle.	Encourage children to write on any angles they know or can work out. Recap the relevant angle rules.
3	B	Other answers suggest that children do not have a sound understanding of the properties of shapes or have miscalculated.	Encourage children to discuss the properties of each shape.
4	D	Other answers suggest that children do not have a sound understanding of the properties of shapes or have miscalculated.	Encourage children to discuss the properties of each shape.
5	D	Other answers suggest that children do not have a sound understanding of the properties of shapes or have miscalculated.	Encourage children to discuss the properties of each shape.
6	Correct net	Look out for and correct any common misconceptions.	Children could draw their net on paper and cut it out to check their answer.

My journal

WAYS OF WORKING Independent thinking

ANSWERS AND COMMENTARY

Question **1** aims to consolidate angle facts and assesses understanding of the steps needed to find unknown angles. Look for children who can identify where to start, explaining the steps needed confidently using angle facts, demonstrating understanding of the properties of a square and showing fluency in addition and subtraction.

a = b = h = 63°, c = 99°, d = 72°, e = g = 81°, f = 117°

Question **2** requires children to work 'backwards' to identify the 3D shapes that nets will make. Look for children who can confidently describe how they can identify if a net will form a 3D shape, demonstrating understanding of the properties of shapes and edges of faces that will meet.

Cube: A, D
Prism: E, G, H
Pyramid: B, C
Will not make a 3D shape: F

Power check

WAYS OF WORKING Independent thinking

ASK

• *How confident do you feel about the properties of shapes?*

Power puzzle

WAYS OF WORKING Pair work or small groups

IN FOCUS Use this activity to assess children's understanding of shape properties. Look for children who make the same polygons, but in different orientations – encourage them to make unique polygons each time.

ANSWERS AND COMMENTARY There are various answers to this puzzle.

Encourage experimentation with each polygon made and ask children to name the shapes and discuss their properties using key words, such as regular. Watch out for children who join the triangles like this: this is not a polygon as its sides do not intersect in exactly two places each.

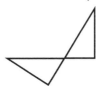

This question can be explored further by encouraging children to investigate the lines of symmetry and the interior angles of the polygons.

After the unit ⏸

• Can children measure angles and draw shapes accurately?
• Can they calculate unknown angles in shapes and on lines using known angle facts and properties of shapes?
• Can children draw and identify nets of 3D shapes?

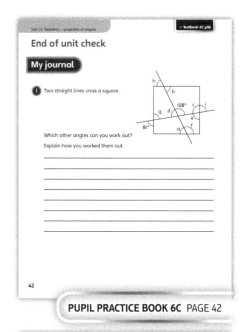

PUPIL PRACTICE BOOK 6C PAGE 42

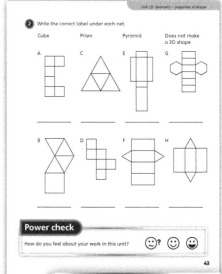

PUPIL PRACTICE BOOK 6C PAGE 43

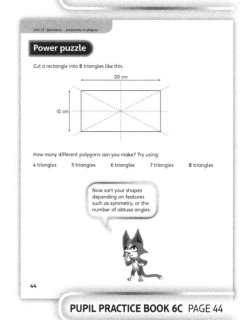

PUPIL PRACTICE BOOK 6C PAGE 44

Strengthen and **Deepen** activities for this unit can be found in the *Power Maths* online subscription.

Unit 14
Problem solving

Mastery Expert tip! "I found that representing problems using bar models and number lines helped children to develop an understanding of how to approach problems. Annotating their diagrams with information that they were given or found out helped them to work their way through the steps and ensured that they answered the question."

Don't forget to watch the Unit 14 video!

WHY THIS UNIT IS IMPORTANT

This unit draws on the extensive range of skills and knowledge acquired by children during Year 6, as well as building on learning from previous years, to solve problems about number, measurement and geometry. The emphasis is on reasoning and selecting appropriate methods, providing appropriate revision for end of key stage assessments. The unit will allow teachers to assess children's confidence and their ability to fluently apply their understanding in different ways, using both mental and written methods, and to use the relationships between numbers to consider more flexible or creative approaches.

WHERE THIS UNIT FITS

→ Unit 13: Geometry – properties of shapes
→ **Unit 14: Problem solving**
→ Unit 15: Statistics

The unit builds on children's work in previous units. Children apply their knowledge and skills in problems with and without context, some of which may appear less familiar because the problem is non-routine. They represent problems using bar models to help make sense of a problem and the relationships within it, exposing the operations needed.

Before they start this unit, it is expected that children:
- can identify the value of each digit in numbers up to 10,000,000
- can apply mental and written strategies for the four operations
- can represent a problem or steps in a problem using bar models
- can draw on knowledge including unit conversion, equivalence, coordinates and properties of shapes.

ASSESSING MASTERY

Children can reason about and solve a range of mathematical problems with and without a context. They can recognise which operations are required and in which order, explaining when calculations can be done in a different order because the relationships between the numbers make it easier. Children can apply learning in different areas of mathematics and can represent problems using bar models to support their thinking.

COMMON MISCONCEPTIONS	STRENGTHENING UNDERSTANDING	GOING DEEPER
Children may think that problems can only be solved in the order in which the information is presented.	Explore different types of question where the starting place is not always the first piece of information given, to encourage children to look at the problem as a whole.	Explore more flexible calculating as children use the relationships between the numbers to decide which operation to carry out first.
Children may make assumptions about what the question is asking them to find out, possibly relating it to other questions they have answered recently.	Encourage children to use bar models to represent problems, showing clearly what is known and what needs to be found out – and to check at the end that they have answered the actual question.	Ask children to compile a set of 'Helpful tips' that can be used to solve problems. Discuss the role of estimating and using the inverse to check answers.

WAYS OF WORKING

Use these pages to introduce the unit focus to children. You can use the characters to explore different ways of working.

STRUCTURES AND REPRESENTATIONS

Number line: This model helps children to work with positive and negative numbers, order numbers (including fractions) and calculate time intervals. It will also support their understanding of scales for measurement and statistics.

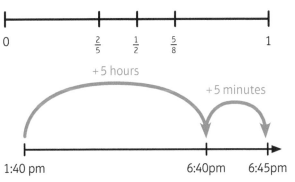

Bar model: Bar models help children to represent problems in a range of contexts, including fractions, percentages and ratio, to show what each part represents and what needs to be found.

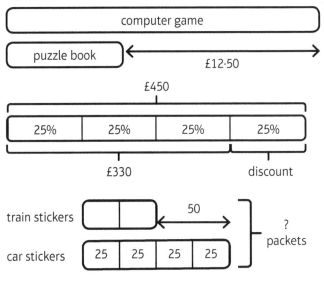

KEY LANGUAGE

There is some key language that children will need to know as part of the learning in this unit.

→ partition

→ estimate, round, compare

→ equivalent, common denominator

→ percentage, ratio, proportion, convert

→ coordinates, vertex (vertices), reflection, translation

→ sum of interior angles

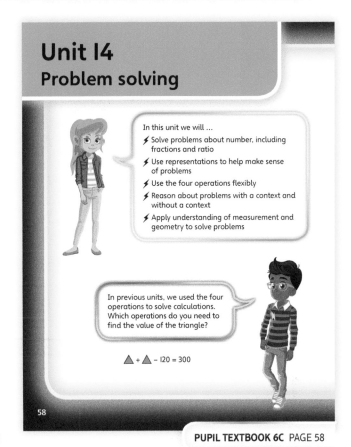

PUPIL TEXTBOOK 6C PAGE 58

PUPIL TEXTBOOK 6C PAGE 59

Problem solving – place value

Learning focus

In this lesson, children will use understanding of place value to solve problems involving rounding, estimating and positional values of digits.

Small steps

→ Previous step: Nets (2)
→ **This step: Problem solving – place value**
→ Next step: Problem solving – negative numbers

NATIONAL CURRICULUM LINKS

Year 6 Number – Number and Place Value

Solve number and practical problems that involve [place value].

ASSESSING MASTERY

Children can apply understanding of place value to a range of problems, including those in the context of measurement and statistics.

COMMON MISCONCEPTIONS

When identifying the intervals on a number line (or scale), children may divide the amount by the number of marks on the scale rather than the number of intervals (for example, dividing by 3 rather than 4, when there are three marks showing four intervals). Ask:

• *How many equal parts are there between 5,000 and 6,000? How can you work out what each interval represents?*

STRENGTHENING UNDERSTANDING

To develop children's confidence when working with number lines for large numbers, explore a range of number lines and scales with different intervals. Look at how the position of a number may change as it appears on different scales, for example the number 2,500 on number lines with intervals of 1,000 and 500. Practise rounding and ordering sets of numbers, placing them on number lines with different scales.

GOING DEEPER

Ask children to select five digit cards and to make a number using their cards. They can then give clues for a partner to find the number using the cards. Remind them that they need to be sure that combining all the clues only gives one possible answer.

KEY LANGUAGE

In lesson: digit, round, estimate, approximate, interval, scale, less than (<)

Other language to be used by the teacher: place value, greater than (>)

STRUCTURES AND REPRESENTATIONS

number line, sorting circles

RESOURCES

Optional: place value counters

 In the eTextbook of this lesson, you will find interactive links to a selection of teaching tools.

Before you teach

• Can children identify the value of each digit in numbers up to 10,000,000?
• Can they explain the rules for rounding?
• Can children identify the values represented by intervals on a number line or scale?

Discover

Unit 14: Problem solving, Lesson 1

Problem solving – place value

WAYS OF WORKING Pair work

ASK

- Question ❶ a): *What does the digit 6 represent each time in the number 6,068?*
- Question ❶ a): *How can you work out the missing values on the number line?*
- Question ❶ a): *What number is half-way between 5,000 and 6,000? Where will it appear on this number line?*
- Question ❶ b): *What digit do you need to look at when rounding to the nearest 1,000?*

IN FOCUS Question ❶ a) requires children to position a set of numbers on a given number line. The number line is only labelled every 1,000, so children need to work out the value each interval represents. In question ❶ b), children need to apply the rules for rounding to reason about distances that round to the same multiple of 1,000 km.

PRACTICAL TIPS Recreate the number line using place value counters. Then make each distance using place value counters. Children can then compare the value of each distance with the number line.

ANSWERS

Question ❶ a): Check for the sensible placement of numbers like the following:

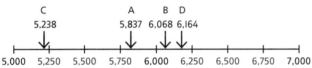

Question ❶ b): The distance from Paris to cities A, B and D rounds to 6,000 km.

Share

WAYS OF WORKING Whole class teacher led

ASK

- Question ❶ a): *Why is Dexter looking at the four intervals to work out the scale on the number line, rather than looking at the three marks?*
- Question ❶ a): *Is 6,164 closer to 6,000 or 7,000 on the number line? How do you know? How do you know that 6,068 is closer to 6,000 than 6,164 is to 6,000?*
- Question ❶ b): *Why do you check the hundreds digit when rounding to the nearest 1,000? Why not the thousands digit?*
- Question ❶ b): *What other numbers do you know that round to the same multiple of 1,000?*

IN FOCUS In question ❶ a), suggest that children could imagine each interval of 250 split into five equal intervals of 50; this may help them to position the numbers on the line. In question ❶ b), Flo and Dexter use different methods to round the numbers. The numbers have been chosen so that one rounds up and the others round down to the same 1,000.

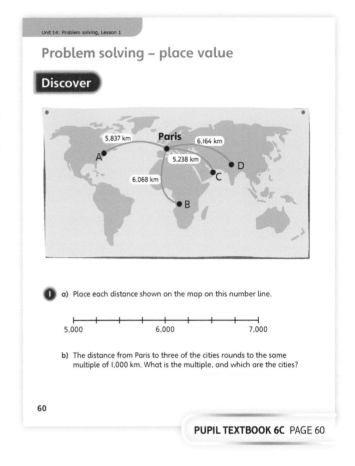

a) Place each distance shown on the map on this number line.

b) The distance from Paris to three of the cities rounds to the same multiple of 1,000 km. What is the multiple, and which are the cities?

60

PUPIL TEXTBOOK 6C PAGE 60

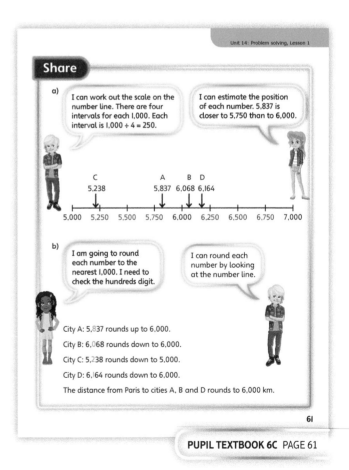

PUPIL TEXTBOOK 6C PAGE 61

Think together

WAYS OF WORKING Whole class teacher led (I do, We do, You do)

ASK

- Question ❶: *Can you explain Astrid's mistake? How can you work out the value of each interval?*
- Question ❷ b): *What do you know about the missing value?*
- Question ❸: *What are the properties of numbers in the overlapping section of the sorting circles? Why does 10,001 sit outside both sorting circles?*
- Question ❹: *How do you know that a number is odd? Which digit position is important?*

IN FOCUS Question ❷ requires children to reason about distances using the < and > symbols to show comparisons and order. An example with three values has been included to encourage children to think about the property of the middle value in relation to those on either side. Question ❸ uses a statistical representation; children need to apply knowledge of numbers and their properties, recognising when a number possesses one, both or neither of these properties. In question ❹, children are required to think about the digit in a number that determines a property, for example the ones digit to assess whether a number is odd or even.

STRENGTHEN In question ❶, once the interval value has been determined, ask children to label the number line and talk about other numbers that could or could not appear in each interval.

DEEPEN For question ❹, ask children to think about another set of criteria Luis can use to make a different set of numbers for his number line.

ASSESSMENT CHECKPOINT Use question ❶ to assess whether children can determine the intervals on a scale and estimate the positions of numbers on a number line. Use question ❷ to assess whether they can order numbers. Use question ❸ to assess whether they can sort numbers by their properties.

ANSWERS

Question ❶:

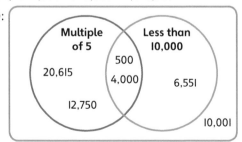

Question ❷ a): 942,000 > 924,500

Question ❷ b): 924,500 < 942,000 < 1,025,000

Question ❸:

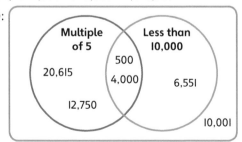

Question ❹: Section B: 4,605; Section D: 6,540 or 5,640, 5,460, 4,560; last number: 5,046 or 5,064, 5,406, 5,460, 5,604, 5,640

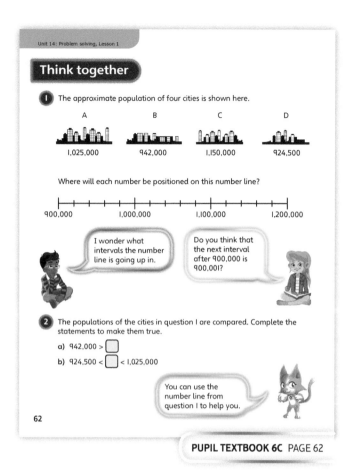

PUPIL TEXTBOOK 6C PAGE 62

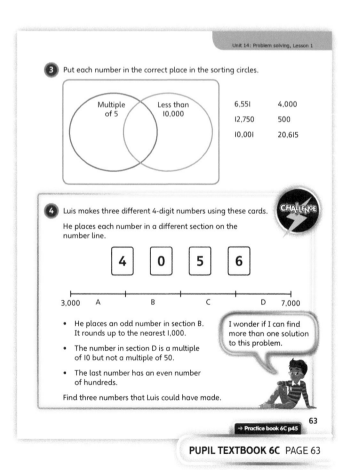

PUPIL TEXTBOOK 6C PAGE 63

Practice

WAYS OF WORKING Independent thinking

IN FOCUS In question ②, children need to reason about rules for rounding to complete the labels. Question ③ requires children to reason about a possible number that meets all the criteria. There is more than one solution to this problem so children need to think about making one number and altering single digits, rather than starting from scratch each time. Question ⑤ provides an opportunity for children to explain their reasoning. These questions are often less well answered as children have to think carefully about the language they use to explain clearly and consider any drawings that support their explanation.

STRENGTHEN For question ④, discuss different interval values for the scale first and reason about which ones could or could not be possible. This will give children a sense of the size of the scale before they find the actual interval values.

DEEPEN Tell children that the line graph used in question ④ now represents a different set of data. Give the value for Monday as 3,600 and ask children to explain what the other values are. Then ask them to suggest alternative values for Monday that would give a sensible scale, explaining their choices.

THINK DIFFERENTLY In question ④, children apply their knowledge of place value to a new context. They need to realise that the vertical scale is like a number line and use the number line skills they practised in question ① to identify the value of the intervals on the scale, using Monday as a starting point.

ASSESSMENT CHECKPOINT Use question ① to assess whether children can compare and order a set of numbers in context. Look to see whether they use a number line or can compare the numbers directly using place value. Use question ④ to assess whether children can transfer their knowledge of working out intervals on a number line to a scale on a graph. Use question ⑤ to check that children understand the effect of rounding to different degrees of accuracy and the possible ranges each time.

ANSWERS Answers for the **Practice** part of the lesson appear in the separate **Practice and Reflect answer guide**.

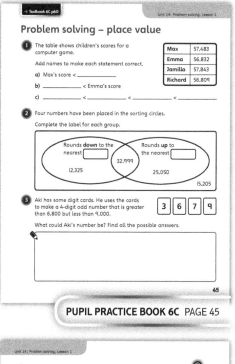

PUPIL PRACTICE BOOK 6C PAGE 45

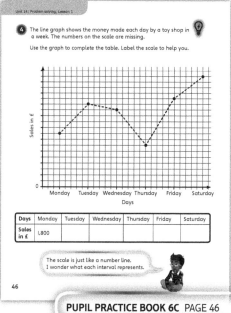

PUPIL PRACTICE BOOK 6C PAGE 46

Reflect

WAYS OF WORKING Pair work

IN FOCUS Children use their knowledge of number properties to find numbers that would be placed in each section of the sorting circles. They need to know both how to round numbers and how to compare numbers.

ASSESSMENT CHECKPOINT Check that children can explain why some numbers belong in both circles and why other numbers belong in none of the circles.

ANSWERS Answers for the **Reflect** part of the lesson appear in the separate **Practice and Reflect answer guide**.

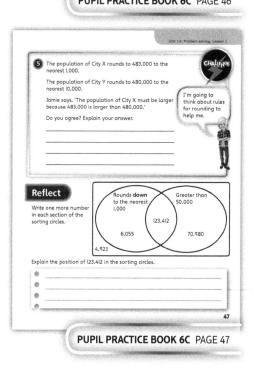

PUPIL PRACTICE BOOK 6C PAGE 47

After the lesson ⏸

- Can children apply understanding of place value and number to a range of different contexts?
- Can they interpret scales and use known points to identify the value of each interval?

Problem solving – negative numbers

Learning focus

In this lesson, children will use what they have learnt about positive and negative numbers to help solve problems with and without a context. They will build on the previous lesson as they identify the intervals on different scales.

Small steps

→ Previous step: Problem solving – place value
→ **This step: Problem solving – negative numbers**
→ Next step: Problem solving – addition and subtraction

NATIONAL CURRICULUM LINKS

Year 6 Number – Number and Place Value

Solve number and practical problems that involve [negative numbers].

ASSESSING MASTERY

Children can use knowledge of scales and the number system to solve problems that involve counting on and counting back across 0 and calculating a difference. They can apply their understanding in the context of temperature.

COMMON MISCONCEPTIONS

When ordering negative numbers, children may reason that a number such as ⁻20 must be larger than ⁻5 because 20 is larger than 5. Practise counting on and back over 0 looking at the symmetry of positive and negative numbers as they move away from 0. Ask:

• *When you move to the right on the number line, do the numbers get larger or smaller? In which direction do you move to go from ⁻20 to ⁻5?*

STRENGTHENING UNDERSTANDING

Explore differences between pairs of positive and negative numbers, drawing on number bonds to partition differences across 0. For example, ask: *What number is 5 more than 0? What number is 5 less than 0?* Ask children to explain why the difference between these two numbers must be 10.

GOING DEEPER

Give children a difference, for example 13. Ask them to find pairs of positive and negative numbers, or two negative numbers, separated by this difference. Challenge children to make up problems, possibly in the context of temperature, related to a difference of 13.

KEY LANGUAGE

In lesson: negative, positive, sequence, difference, half-way

Other language to be used by the teacher: scale

STRUCTURES AND REPRESENTATIONS

number line, bar model, line graph

 In the eTextbook of this lesson, you will find interactive links to a selection of teaching tools.

Before you teach

• Can children count on and back across 0?
• Can they explain why ⁻1 is larger than ⁻10?
• Can they identify the value of the intervals on a number line or scale?

Discover

WAYS OF WORKING Pair work

ASK

- Question ① a): *Zero is given as a value on the number line. What does this tell you about A and B?*
- Question ① a): *How can you work out the value of A and B? What should you do first?*
- Question ① a): *How is this problem similar to the number line problems you solved in the previous lesson?*
- Question ① b): *Where will the half-way point be? Is it before or after 0?*

IN FOCUS Question ① a) requires children to interpret a scale involving positive and negative numbers and find the value of two points with a given difference. It builds on the number line work in the previous lesson, but this time children are given the difference between two points, rather than working it out.

Question ① b) has been chosen so that children revisit finding the half-way point between two values. This skill is vital when reading scales for measurement and statistics.

PRACTICAL TIPS Practise counting in different intervals across 0. Ask questions such as: *I'm counting on in intervals of 5 from ⁻21. How do you know that I won't say 0 in my count?*

ANSWERS

Question ① a): The value of point A is ⁻100. The value of point B is 60.

Question ① b): The value of the half-way point between A and B is ⁻20.

Share

WAYS OF WORKING Whole class teacher led

ASK

- Question ① a): *Why can't Astrid's interval value of 10 be correct? What does this tell you about the interval value?*
- Question ① a): *What is the relationship between a difference of 80 and a difference of 160? Can you use this relationship to explain why the interval must be 20?*
- Question ① b): *What is the same and what is different about Flo's two strategies?*

IN FOCUS In question ① a) ensure that children recognise why 160 is divided by 8 to find the value of each interval on the number line. In question ① b) children often halve the difference when finding the half-way point, but forget to add this value to the lowest number; for example, they might say that the half-way point is 80 because this is half of the difference (160). Ensure they remember to add 80 to ⁻100, to find the answer of ⁻20.

STRENGTHEN Once the the value of the intervals has been identified, count on and back in intervals of 20 from 0. Use this count to agree the values of A and B, relating A to 5 intervals of 20 less than 0 and B to 3 intervals of 20 greater than 0.

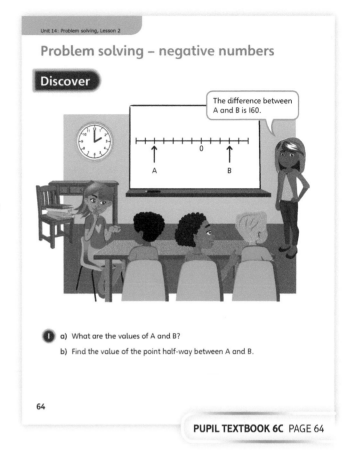

Problem solving – negative numbers

Discover

The difference between A and B is 160.

① a) What are the values of A and B?

b) Find the value of the point half-way between A and B.

64

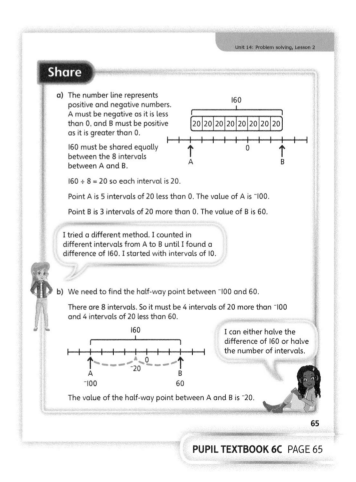

Share

a) The number line represents positive and negative numbers. A must be negative as it is less than 0, and B must be positive as it is greater than 0.

160 must be shared equally between the 8 intervals between A and B.

160 ÷ 8 = 20 so each interval is 20.

Point A is 5 intervals of 20 less than 0. The value of A is ⁻100.

Point B is 3 intervals of 20 more than 0. The value of B is 60.

I tried a different method. I counted in different intervals from A to B until I found a difference of 160. I started with intervals of 10.

b) We need to find the half-way point between ⁻100 and 60.

There are 8 intervals. So it must be 4 intervals of 20 more than ⁻100 and 4 intervals of 20 less than 60.

I can either halve the difference of 160 or halve the number of intervals.

The value of the half-way point between A and B is ⁻20.

65

Think together

WAYS OF WORKING Whole class teacher led (I do, We do, You do)

ASK

Question **1**: *How do you know that one of the temperatures must be negative and the other positive?*

Question **2**: *What is the same and what is different about finding missing numbers in a sequence and finding missing numbers on a scale?*

Question **2**: *What will the next number in the sequence be? What is the difference between this number and ⁻22?*

Question **3**: *How do you know that the temperature at 7 pm must be below 0?*

Question **4**: *There are no intervals on this number line. How can you find the half-way point?*

IN FOCUS Questions **1** and **2** provide opportunities for children to apply the same skills but now in the context of temperature or as part of a linear sequence. In question **1**, they need to make a connection between intervals on number lines and scales. In both questions, children have to calculate across 0.

In question **4**, no intervals are shown on the number line but children should recognise that the half-way point can be found by applying the same strategies used in **Share**.

STRENGTHEN For question **4**, model using 0 as a stopping point to calculate the difference between two points, for example ⁻24 and 6. Children can then attempt to answer question **4** using the same strategy.

DEEPEN Ask children to explain how they can quickly work out the values of the 8th and 10th terms in the sequence in question **2**. Ask them to investigate whether ⁻181 is in the sequence. Encourage them to reason rather than working out the values up to ⁻190.

ASSESSMENT CHECKPOINT Use questions **1** and **2** to assess whether children can apply strategies to interpret scales and intervals in other contexts. Check that they can use the number of intervals and the difference to find the interval value. Use question **3** to assess whether children can find the difference between positive and negative values and find a drop or rise in temperature. Check that children can interpret data presented on a graph.

ANSWERS

Question **1** a): The inside temperature is 30 °C.

Question **1** b): The outside temperature is ⁻15 °C.

Question **2**: 2, ⁻10, ⁻34

Question **3** a): It was 12 °C warmer.

Question **3** b): The temperature at 7 pm was ⁻1 °C.

Question **4**: The half-way point is ⁻6.

PUPIL TEXTBOOK 6C PAGE 66

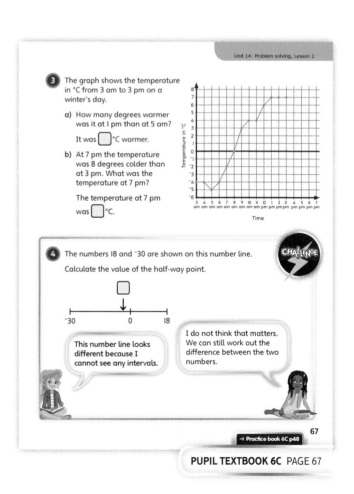

PUPIL TEXTBOOK 6C PAGE 67

Practice

WAYS OF WORKING Independent thinking

IN FOCUS Question ❶ requires children to identify the biggest difference between pairs of positive and negative numbers. They should reason about each pair first before calculating the difference. The numbers have been chosen so that two of the differences involve counting across 0 and the third pair involves the difference between two negative numbers.

In question ❷, children work with increasing and decreasing sequences. In part b), the interval value is not given, so they need to calculate this first by adapting the strategies developed in the lesson.

In question ❻, children solve a puzzle as they reason about differences between positive and negative numbers. They may find it useful to write each value on a small piece of paper so they can be easily rearranged on the diagram.

STRENGTHEN For question ❸, encourage children to label intermediate points on the vertical scale to help make sense of values that lie within intervals on the bar chart.

DEEPEN Ask children to make up linear sequence problems for a partner to solve. Ensure their sequences cross 0. Encourage children to use both increasing and decreasing sequences.

ASSESSMENT CHECKPOINT Use questions ❶ and ❻ to assess whether children can reason and fluently calculate the difference between positive and negative numbers. Check whether they use a number line to work out the differences or can apply reasoning.

Use questions ❸ and ❹ to assess whether children can apply understanding of positive and negative numbers in the context of measurement and statistical representation. In question ❹, check that children can work out the interval size from the given difference.

ANSWERS Answers for the **Practice** part of the lesson appear in the separate **Practice and Reflect answer guide**.

Reflect

WAYS OF WORKING Independent thinking

IN FOCUS This question requires children to explain the steps in their strategy to find a point half-way between given positive and negative numbers. They should recognise that the same strategy can be used to find the point half-way between any two numbers.

ASSESSMENT CHECKPOINT Check that children remember to add half the difference to ⁻40 (or subtract half the difference from 24) rather than incorrectly giving the half-way point as 32.

ANSWERS Answers for the **Reflect** part of the lesson appear in the separate **Practice and Reflect answer guide**.

After the lesson ⏸

- Can children calculate the difference between pairs of positive and negative numbers, applying this to problems with or without a context?
- Can they interpret scales that include both positive and negative numbers, including finding a half-way point?

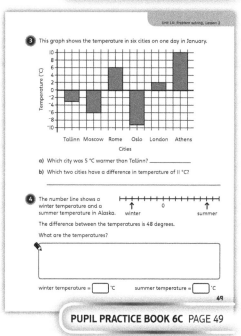

PUPIL PRACTICE BOOK 6C PAGE 48

PUPIL PRACTICE BOOK 6C PAGE 49

PUPIL PRACTICE BOOK 6C PAGE 50

Problem solving – addition and subtraction

Learning focus

In this lesson, children will flexibly apply their understanding of addition and subtraction to a range of problems. They will have the opportunity to consider different strategies dependent on the numbers and operations. They will use estimation to check answers.

Small steps

→ Previous step: Problem solving – negative numbers
→ **This step: Problem solving – addition and subtraction**
→ Next step: Problem solving – four operations (1)

NATIONAL CURRICULUM LINKS

Year 6 Number – Addition, Subtraction, Multiplication and Division
• Use estimation to check answers to calculations and determine, in the context of a problem, an appropriate degree of accuracy.
• Solve addition and subtraction multi-step problems in contexts, deciding which operations and methods to use and why.
• Solve problems involving addition, subtraction, multiplication and division.

ASSESSING MASTERY

Children can work flexibly with addition and subtraction to solve a range of problems, with or without a context. They recognise and can explain why it may be easier to calculate in a different order than the steps given in a problem, drawing on their understanding of the order of operations.

COMMON MISCONCEPTIONS

Most children recognise that addition can be carried out in any order but subtraction cannot. Although 3,250 – 1,925 – 250 cannot be carried out in any order (for example, 1,925 – 250 – 3,250), children may not recognise that they can reorder the numbers to be subtracted (for example, 3,250 – 250 – 1,925). Similarly, 3,250 + 895 – 250 gives the same result as 3,250 – 250 + 895, but the latter is easier to work out. Ask:
• *For 3,250 + 895 – 250, why might it be easier to subtract 250 from 3,250 first and then add 895?*

STRENGTHENING UNDERSTANDING

Explore test questions involving both addition and subtraction. Sort them into examples where the calculation is best carried out in the order given and those where the calculation is made easier by reordering the values.

GOING DEEPER

Ask children to make up calculations or problems where reordering the numbers to be added and subtracted makes the calculation simpler. They should be able to explain their reasoning for the choice of numbers.

KEY LANGUAGE

In lesson: add, subtract, estimate, total, difference
Other language to be used by the teacher: order

STRUCTURES AND REPRESENTATIONS

column method, bar chart, number line

RESOURCES

Optional: sticky notes

 In the eTextbook of this lesson, you will find interactive links to a selection of teaching tools.

Before you teach

• Can children explain why a problem requires them to add and/or subtract?
• Can they use rounding appropriately to make estimations?
• Do they recognise different contexts where addition and subtraction are used, for example statistics?

Discover

WAYS OF WORKING Pair work

ASK

- Question ❶ a): *How do Max and Kate's methods differ?*
- Question ❶ a): *Will you use a mental or a written method? Why?*
- Question ❶ b): *What has Max noticed about the numbers involved?*
- Question ❶ b): *Does it matter whether you add or subtract first? Why?*

IN FOCUS The numbers in this two-step problem have been chosen to encourage children to consider the order in which they carry out a calculation. In this example it is easier to find the answer by working through the steps in a different order from that given in the problem. In question ❶ a), Kate works through the steps in the order in which the numbers are given; in question ❶ b), Max recognises that the numbers 875 and 1,975 make the calculation easier if he does the subtraction first.

PRACTICAL TIPS Write the numbers to be added and subtracted on separate sticky notes so they can be reordered easily to match the different methods.

ANSWERS

Question ❶ a): 2,692 − 875 = 1,817; 1,817 + 1,975 = 3,792

Question ❶ b): 1,975 − 875 = 1,100; 2,692 + 1,100 = 3,792

Max chose this method because 875 can easily be subtracted from 1,975 to leave a multiple of 100.

1,975 can be partitioned as 1,100 + 875 so 875 can be subtracted easily.

PUPIL TEXTBOOK 6C PAGE 68

Share

WAYS OF WORKING Whole class teacher led

ASK

- Question ❶ a): *How has Dexter rounded the numbers 2,692 and 875 to get the estimated answer of 1,800?*
- Question ❶ a): *How would you round the numbers 1,817 and 1,975 to estimate the addition?*
- Question ❶ b): *Why has Astrid chosen a mental method this time?*
- Question ❶ b): *Why will Flo's method give the same answer even though she is adding first?*

IN FOCUS Question ❶ a) revisits the use of a written method for subtraction and addition. It also demonstrates the use of estimation to check an answer. Children should be able to explain why a mental method is more appropriate in question ❶ b). Question ❶ b) requires children to think about why Max has chosen to subtract 875 from 1,975, rather than from 2,692. Discuss other examples where the operations of addition and subtraction can be reordered within a calculation, explaining why this may be useful.

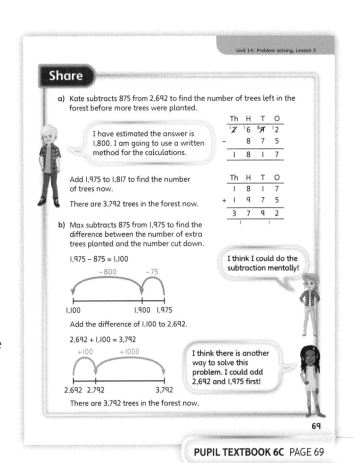

PUPIL TEXTBOOK 6C PAGE 69

Think together

Unit 14: Problem solving, Lesson 3

WAYS OF WORKING Whole class teacher led (I do, We do, You do)

ASK

- Question **1**: *What can you tell me about the scale? What is the value of each interval? How do you know?*
- Question **2**: *Why might Ash choose to complete the calculations in a different order? What has he noticed?*
- Question **3** b): *How do you know that the hundredths digit must be less than 6?*
- Question **4**: *What bar model should Flo draw? How will this help her to solve the problem?*
- Question **4**: *Will you add or subtract first? Why?*

IN FOCUS Question **1** has been chosen to help children recognise the application of addition and subtraction to statistics. The questions can be solved in more than one way so children can demonstrate their flexibility with calculation. Question **2** provides a de-contextualised example, so children recognise that similar strategies can be applied and that the numbers involved may determine what part of the calculation they carry out first. In question **3**, children reason about missing values in an addition and a subtraction using the column method. They are required to think about the effect of any regrouping.

STRENGTHEN For question **4**, look together at the difference between the items that Aki and Jamie bought. Encourage children to draw a bar model to illustrate their purchases: they both bought 1 rubber and 1 pen but Jamie bought 1 pen more. Therefore, a pen must cost 65p, so the cost of the rubber can be calculated using £1·10 – 65p = 45p.

DEEPEN For question **1**, ask children to describe different strategies to complete the calculations. For example, in part a) they could find the total for each year and then compare, or they could see that £700 more was raised by fun runs in 2017 and £500 more was raised by singing competitions in 2017, giving a total of £1,200 more. In part b), they may identify that in 2015, £500 more was raised by fun runs, but in 2017, £500 more was raised by singing competitions; therefore, the total difference is only the difference in 2017. Challenge them to make up a similar question for a partner to solve.

ASSESSMENT CHECKPOINT Use questions **1** and **2** to assess whether children can choose a strategy and an appropriate order for operations depending on the numbers. Check that they can explain their strategy. Use question **3** to assess whether children can use the structure of a column method to help them reason about missing digits.

ANSWERS

Question **1** a): £1,200 more was raised in 2017 than in 2015.

Question **1** b): The difference is £700.

Question **2**: The value of the triangle is 2,000.
The value of the square is 299.

Question **3** a): 5,364 + 6,539 = 11,903

Question **3** b): 69·85 – 23·56 = 46·29

Question **4**: A rubber costs 45p.

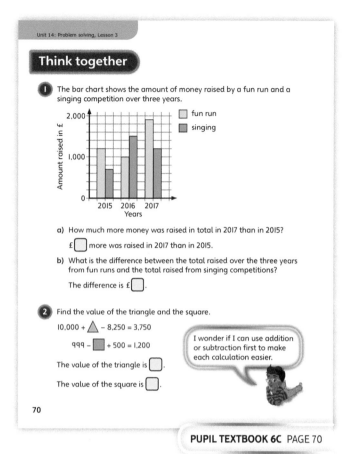

1 The bar chart shows the amount of money raised by a fun run and a singing competition over three years.

a) How much more money was raised in total in 2017 than in 2015?
£ ☐ more was raised in 2017 than in 2015.

b) What is the difference between the total raised over the three years from fun runs and the total raised from singing competitions?
The difference is £ ☐.

2 Find the value of the triangle and the square.

$10{,}000 + \triangle - 8{,}250 = 3{,}750$

$999 - \blacksquare + 500 = 1{,}200$

The value of the triangle is ☐.

The value of the square is ☐.

I wonder if I can use addition or subtraction first to make each calculation easier.

70

PUPIL TEXTBOOK 6C PAGE 70

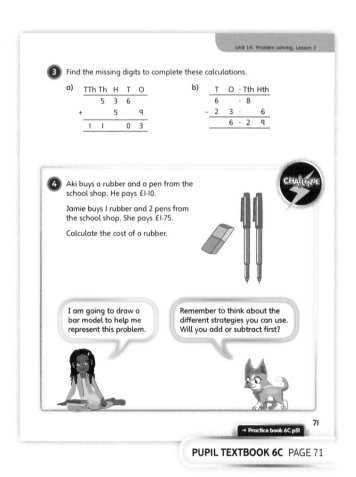

Unit 14: Problem solving, Lesson 3

3 Find the missing digits to complete these calculations.

a)
```
  TTh Th  H  T  O
        5  3  6
   +       5  ⬚  9
  ─────────────────
     1  1     0  3
```

b)
```
   T  O . Tth Hth
   6  ⬚ .  8
 - 2  3 . ⬚   6
 ────────────────
   6  ⬚ . 2   9
```

4 Aki buys a rubber and a pen from the school shop. He pays £1·10.

Jamie buys 1 rubber and 2 pens from the school shop. She pays £1·75.

Calculate the cost of a rubber.

I am going to draw a bar model to help me represent this problem.

Remember to think about the different strategies you can use. Will you add or subtract first?

71

→ Practice book 6C p51

PUPIL TEXTBOOK 6C PAGE 71

Practice

WAYS OF WORKING Independent thinking

IN FOCUS Question ❶ requires children to think about the order in which they will carry out an addition and a subtraction, making decisions based on the numbers involved. Question ❸ has been designed to be slightly more complex than the question in **Think together**, with the bar chart shown in a horizontal orientation and each set of data comprising three bars. Question ❹ is a multi-step problem, so children must be careful to complete all steps. In question ❻, children need to reason about which statement provides the best starting place to help find the unknown values.

STRENGTHEN Encourage children to make estimates first and then check their answers against those estimates.

DEEPEN Give children algebraic problems similar to question ❻, where unknown values have to be determined. For example:

$$4,599 - \triangle + 401 = 3,500 + \square$$
$$\square + \triangle - 975 = 525$$
$$\triangle + \triangle - 545 = 655$$

ASSESSMENT CHECKPOINT Use questions ❶ to ❸ to assess whether children can fluently apply strategies of addition and subtraction in different contexts, including statistics. Look to see what strategy they choose each time. Use question ❹ to assess whether children can complete a multi-step problem. Check whether they make estimates and check their answer against these.

ANSWERS Answers for the **Practice** part of the lesson appear in the separate **Practice and Reflect answer guide**.

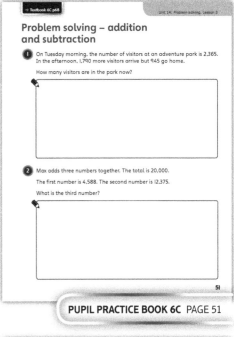

PUPIL PRACTICE BOOK 6C PAGE 51

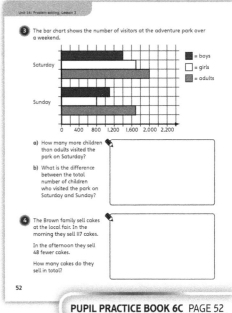

PUPIL PRACTICE BOOK 6C PAGE 52

Reflect

WAYS OF WORKING Independent thinking

IN FOCUS Drawing a bar model to represent the problem in question ❹ requires children to recognise that they are showing the difference between the cakes sold in the morning and the afternoon.

ASSESSMENT CHECKPOINT Check that children can explain how their bar model matches the problem.

ANSWERS Answers for the **Reflect** part of the lesson appear in the separate **Practice and Reflect answer guide**.

After the lesson ⏸

- Can children flexibly work with addition and subtraction, explaining the order in which they should calculate?
- Can they solve a range of problems, recognising when they need to add or subtract?

PUPIL PRACTICE BOOK 6C PAGE 53

Problem solving – four operations

Learning focus

In this lesson, children will use the four operations to solve a range of problems. They will make decisions about which operation to use first, and recognise when and why a calculation can be carried out in a different order.

Small steps

→ Previous step: Problem solving – addition and subtraction
→ **This step: Problem solving – four operations (1)**
→ Next step: Problem solving – four operations (2)

NATIONAL CURRICULUM LINKS

Year 6 Number – Addition, Subtraction, Multiplication and Division
- Solve problems involving addition, subtraction, multiplication and division.
- Use their knowledge of the order of operations to carry out calculations involving the four operations.
- Use estimation to check answers to calculations and determine, in the context of a problem, an appropriate degree of accuracy.

ASSESSING MASTERY

Children can use representations to help make sense of problems and use them to determine the operations required. They can apply mental and written strategies to work with two- and multi-step problems.

COMMON MISCONCEPTIONS

Children may choose the wrong operations to answer problem-solving questions. This is principally due either to failure to comprehend the text or to insecurity in their understanding of the effect of the operations. Encourage children always to draw a diagram to represent the problem. Ask:
- *What information are you given? How can you represent this in a diagram?*
- *What operation does the diagram suggest you should use?*

STRENGTHENING UNDERSTANDING

Revisit the effect of the four operations, discussing examples of contexts and language related to them. Give a range of contextualised problems to groups of four children to reinforce the steps required for problem solving. Each child within the group has a role: making sense of the problem and explaining; making an estimate, explaining any rounding; calculating, explaining and justifying the strategies used; checking the calculated answer, comparing with the estimate and ensuring the actual question has been answered.

GOING DEEPER

Look at problems involving two operations with the same order of priority, for example multiplication and division. Discuss why we may choose to complete a division before a multiplication (or vice versa) even when this is not the order suggested by the problem; children should recognise that this will depend on the numbers involved. For example, when solving a problem using $45 \times 12 \div 15$, work out $45 \div 15$ first and then multiply 3 by 12. Some children may also see this as $45 \times \frac{4}{5}$ by expressing $12 \div 15$ as a fraction first.

KEY LANGUAGE

In lesson: divide, subtract

Other language to be used by the teacher: add, multiply, estimate, order

STRUCTURES AND REPRESENTATIONS

bar model

RESOURCES

Optional: pictures of puzzle books, computer games and boxes of colouring pencils

 In the eTextbook of this lesson, you will find interactive links to a selection of teaching tools.

Before you teach
- Can children explain what a problem is asking them to do?
- Can they explain what steps are required and the operations needed?
- Can they represent the problem with a diagram?

Discover

WAYS OF WORKING Pair work

ASK

- Question ❶ a): *If the computer game is £15, how much is the puzzle book? If the puzzle book is £15, how much is the computer game?*
- Question ❶ a): *How can the problem be represented? You don't know the price of either item – what could you do?*
- Question ❶ b): *Using the information given in part a), how do you know that at least two boxes of pencils can be purchased for £35 before doing any calculations?*
- Question ❶ b): *How can this problem be represented? What operation will you need to use?*

IN FOCUS Questions ❶ a) and ❶ b) both require children to draw on a range of information and use relationships between prices to solve the problems. They need to be able to think through each problem systematically.

PRACTICAL TIPS Use pictures of puzzle books, computer games and boxes of colouring pencils so children can role play the scenario with different prices for the items. Look at other possible prices for the puzzle book and the computer game with a difference of £12·50, agreeing that although this could be used to help solve the problem, it is a less efficient method.

ANSWERS

Question ❶ a): A puzzle book costs £7·50. A computer game costs £20.

Question ❶ b): Isla can buy 3 boxes of pencils for £35.

Share

WAYS OF WORKING Whole class teacher led

ASK

- Question ❶ a): *What does the first bar model represent?*
- Question ❶ a): *You are told that two puzzle books and a computer game cost £35. Why does the bar model show three puzzle books and an additional £12·50?*
- Question ❶ b): *Why will both of Flo's strategies work?*
- Question ❶ b): *35 divided by 10 is 3·5, so why is the answer to the problem 3, not 3·5?*

IN FOCUS Question ❶ a) requires children to think flexibly as they use more than one bar model to represent different aspects of the problem. In question ❶ b) they need to round after division, using the context of the question to decide whether to round up or down. They can also be asked how much more money Isla would need to buy a fourth box of pencils.

STRENGTHEN Work through the problems in question ❶ a), step-by-step, so children understand the order in which calculations must be done. Check that the solution is correct by working out £7·50 × 2 and then adding £20.

DEEPEN Ask children to think of a different question for question ❶ b) that would require 3·5 to be rounded up to 4 rather than keeping 3 with a remainder.

Problem solving – four operations ❶

Discover

❶ a) A computer game costs £12·50 more than a puzzle book.
Zac buys 1 computer game and 2 puzzle books for £35.
How much does each item cost?

b) A box of pencils is half the price of a computer game.
How many boxes of pencils can Isla buy for £35?

72

PUPIL TEXTBOOK 6C PAGE 72

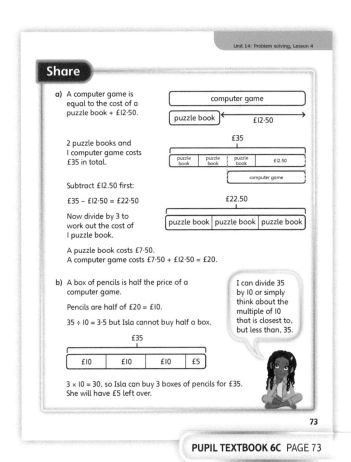

Share

a) A computer game is equal to the cost of a puzzle book + £12·50.

2 puzzle books and 1 computer game costs £35 in total.

Subtract £12·50 first:

£35 – £12·50 = £22·50

Now divide by 3 to work out the cost of 1 puzzle book.

A puzzle book costs £7·50.
A computer game costs £7·50 + £12·50 = £20.

b) A box of pencils is half the price of a computer game.

Pencils are half of £20 = £10.

35 ÷ 10 = 3·5 but Isla cannot buy half a box.

I can divide 35 by 10 or simply think about the multiple of 10 that is closest to, but less than, 35.

3 × 10 = 30, so Isla can buy 3 boxes of pencils for £35. She will have £5 left over.

73

PUPIL TEXTBOOK 6C PAGE 73

Think together

WAYS OF WORKING Whole class teacher led (I do, We do, You do)

ASK

- Question ❶: *How is this problem similar to part a) in* **Share**? *How is it different?*
- Question ❶: *How can you show the value of the toy car using what you know about the cost of a whistle?*
- Question ❷: *How can you estimate the mass of a small bag? Is your calculated answer similar to your estimate?*
- Question ❷: *What method can you use for each division? What can you do to help divide by a multiple of 10?*
- Question ❸: *What information do you already know? How can you represent this using bar models?*
- Question ❹: *How can you work out the perimeter of the square?*
- Question ❹: *Why could Ash's method be used to solve this problem? What is the same and what is different about Ash and Astrid's methods?*

IN FOCUS Question ❶ requires children to recognise that although the language is slightly different ('less than' instead of 'more than'), the same strategy can be used. Question ❸ requires children to round to the nearest pound and to reason about the result. Question ❹ is written in the context of shape and measurement, encouraging children to recognise why similar strategies can be used. This is a multi-step problem, so children are required to check carefully that they have answered the question and have not missed any steps.

STRENGTHEN Encourage children to use bar models to represent the problems, looking carefully at the language of the question to help them. They should remember to estimate before calculating and to check their answer against the estimate.

DEEPEN Look at different strategies to solve question ❷. Similarly, encourage children to explain the alternative strategies for question ❹.

ASSESSMENT CHECKPOINT Use questions ❷ and ❸ to assess whether children can solve multi-step problems, checking that they recognise what operations need to be carried out. Use question ❹ to assess whether children can apply the four operations to problems relating to shape and measurement.

ANSWERS

Question ❶: A whistle costs £1·10. A toy car costs £1·95.

Question ❷: A large bag is 6 kg heavier than a small bag.

Question ❸ a): Each child pays £27·75.

Question ❸ b): No, because each share of the coach cost was rounded down from £13·45 to £13 so there is 40 × 45p less than £538.

Question ❹: The length of side *x* of the rectangle is 50 cm.

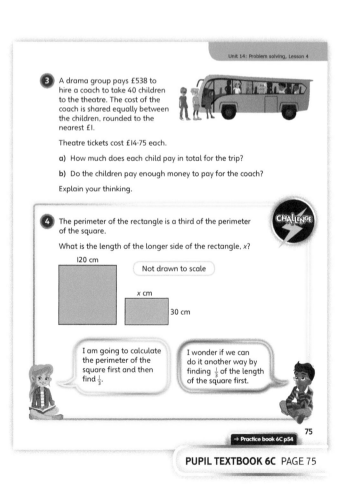

Practice

WAYS OF WORKING Independent thinking

IN FOCUS In question **2**, children must round up after the division to solve the problem. They can use what they know about the number of 25s in 100 to solve the calculation mentally. Question **3** requires children to recognise that they need to do two separate divisions, rather than simply dividing the total number of fruits by 10. In contrast to question **2**, they need to round both numbers down. Question **4** has been chosen so that children can think about possible strategies, as used in previous lessons. They can find the difference between 250 × 5 and 375 × 5, or they can simply calculate 125 × 5 as both calculations involve multiplying by 5.

STRENGTHEN For question **6**, encourage children to draw bar models to represent the problem first. Focus on the relationship between the number of litres in a tin of red paint compared to a tin of blue, and the total number of litres of red paint compared to the number of litres of blue paint (half).

DEEPEN Ask children to look together at question **5**. Ask them to explain whether Reena's statement is still true if a number is divided by 3 and then multiplied by 6; or multiplied by 3 and then divided by 6.

THINK DIFFERENTLY Question **5** considers the replacement of two calculations by a single calculation, rather than only looking at the order in which calculations are carried out. Children need to reason about the effect of multiplying by 6 and dividing by 3.

ASSESSMENT CHECKPOINT Use question **1** to assess whether children can represent problems using bar models. Check that they recognise when one value can be replaced and represented using its relationship with another. Use questions **2** and **3** to assess whether they understand when to round up or down in the context of the problem.

ANSWERS Answers for the **Practice** part of the lesson appear in the separate **Practice and Reflect answer guide**.

Reflect

WAYS OF WORKING Pair work

IN FOCUS Children discuss strategies for problem solving, thinking about the steps they should take to make sense of the problem and to check that they have answered the question posed.

ASSESSMENT CHECKPOINT Check that children consider estimates when solving problems.

ANSWERS Answers for the **Reflect** part of the lesson appear in the separate **Practice and Reflect answer guide**.

After the lesson ⏸

- Can children make sense of a problem and represent it using bar models?
- Can they use a range of strategies for calculations, both written and mental?
- Can children explain which operations they should use and what language tells them this?

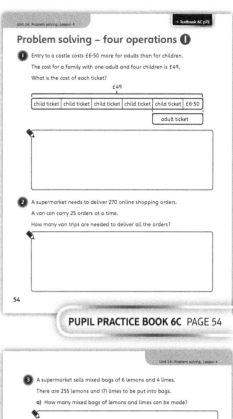

PUPIL PRACTICE BOOK 6C PAGE 54

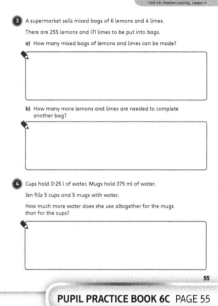

PUPIL PRACTICE BOOK 6C PAGE 55

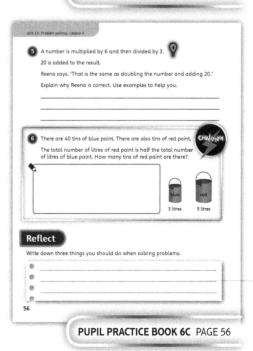

PUPIL PRACTICE BOOK 6C PAGE 56

Problem solving – four operations ❷

Learning focus

In this lesson, children will use the four operations to solve a range of non-routine problems involving missing numbers, unknown values and also problems set in the context of measurement. They will reason about the given information and decide the best starting point.

Small steps

→ Previous step: Problem solving – four operations (1)
→ **This step: Problem solving – four operations (2)**
→ Next step: Problem solving – fractions

NATIONAL CURRICULUM LINKS

Year 6 Number – Addition, Subtraction, Multiplication and Division

Solve problems involving addition, subtraction, multiplication and division.

ASSESSING MASTERY

Children can explain what a problem requires them to do and which operations they will need to use. They can reason about the most useful starting point and justify their decision.

COMMON MISCONCEPTIONS

Children often think that the first piece of information they are given is the one they should use first. Remind them that they need to look at the whole problem. In the case of diagrammatic problems, tell them to make annotations to help them make sense of the information they already know; annotating diagrams will also help children to keep track of the stages of the problem, so they do not miss anything out. Ask:

• *What do you need to find? What information do you already know? Can you write it on your diagram? How does this help you decide what to do next?*

STRENGTHENING UNDERSTANDING

Encourage children to label diagrams with information that they are given in the problem and discuss how this can be used to solve the problem posed. Discuss problems where the first piece of information given is not the most important so that children develop the ability to look at a problem in its entirety before deciding what to do.

GOING DEEPER

Give children a range of algebraic problems with unknown values. Ask them to explain the similarities between these problems and the problems they have been solving in this lesson. Challenge children to express some of the problems from this lesson in algebraic form.

KEY LANGUAGE

In lesson: adding, base, multiplication

Other language used by the teacher: multiply, divide, multiple, diameter, subtract, equivalent

RESOURCES

Optional: copies of diagrams for children to annotate

 In the eTextbook of this lesson, you will find interactive links to a selection of teaching tools.

Before you teach

• Can children explain what a problem is asking them to do?
• Can they explain what steps are required and the operations needed?
• Can they reason about a useful starting point and explain their thinking?

Discover

ASK

- Question ① a): *What is the total of the column? What is the total of the row?*
- Question ① a): *What can you tell me about the value of the triangle compared to the hexagon? How do you know?*
- Question ① b): *Why does Lexi think this? What do you think?*
- Question ① b): *What if the totals are halved, to 60? What might Lexi say now?*

IN FOCUS Question ① a) exposes children to a non-routine problem as they reason about the value of unknown shapes. Question ① b) requires them to reason about the relationship between the totals of the row and column and the values of the individual shapes, using Lexi's statement as a starting point.

PRACTICAL TIPS Give children copies of the puzzle so they can annotate them with information they find.

ANSWERS

Question ① a): ⬡ = 50
△ = 25

Question ① b): Lexi is correct because doubling the totals is the same as adding the values in the row or column twice.

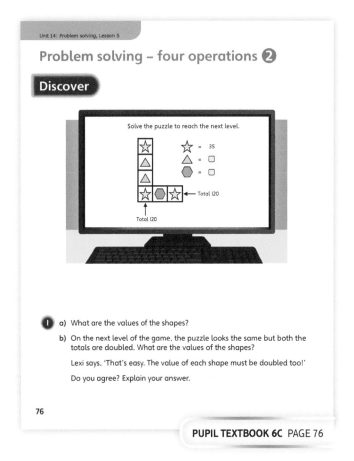

Problem solving – four operations ②

Discover

Solve the puzzle to reach the next level.

☆ = 35
△ = ☐
⬡ = ☐

Total 120
Total 120

① a) What are the values of the shapes?

b) On the next level of the game, the puzzle looks the same but both the totals are doubled. What are the values of the shapes?

Lexi says, 'That's easy. The value of each shape must be doubled too!'

Do you agree? Explain your answer.

76

PUPIL TEXTBOOK 6C PAGE 76

Share

ASK

- Question ① a): *Why has Dexter chosen to look at the row first?*
- Question ① a): *How do you know that the value of the triangle must be half the value of the hexagon?*
- Question ① a): *Many people give the value of the triangle as 50. What mistake have they made?*
- Question ① b): *What is doubling the same as?*
- Question ① b): *Is there another strategy you could use to find the values?*

IN FOCUS In question ① a), children may forget the last step of the problem when finding the value of the triangle, i.e. giving the answer as 50 and not halving it to give the value of one triangle. Check the values are correct using the calculations $25 × 2 + 35 × 2 = 50 + 70 = 120$ for the column and $35 × 2 + 50 = 120$ for the row.

STRENGTHEN For question ① b), write the doubled values in a copy of the diagram so children can check the totals. Agree that this is the same as adding the original values twice.

DEEPEN Ask children to think about halving the totals and to explain why the value of each shape must also be halved. Then consider what they could say about the value of the shapes if the totals were 10 times smaller.

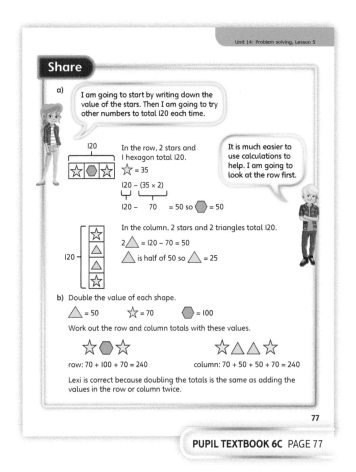

Share

a) I am going to start by writing down the value of the stars. Then I am going to try other numbers to total 120 each time.

It is much easier to use calculations to help. I am going to look at the row first.

120

In the row, 2 stars and 1 hexagon total 120.
☆ = 35
$120 – (35 × 2)$
$120 – 70 = 50$ so ⬡ = 50

120

In the column, 2 stars and 2 triangles total 120.
$2△ = 120 – 70 = 50$
△ is half of 50 so △ = 25

b) Double the value of each shape.
△ = 50   ☆ = 70   ⬡ = 100

Work out the row and column totals with these values.

☆⬡☆
row: 70 + 100 + 70 = 240

☆△△☆
column: 70 + 50 + 50 + 70 = 240

Lexi is correct because doubling the totals is the same as adding the values in the row or column twice.

77

PUPIL TEXTBOOK 6C PAGE 77

Think together

Whole class teacher led (I do, We do, You do)

ASK

- Question ❶: *What information do you already know? What operations will you need to use?*
- Question ❷: *What measurements can you add to the diagram? How does this help?*
- Question ❷: *What calculations do you need to do to solve the problem?*
- Question ❸: *How do you know what the last digit (the ones digit) will be?*
- Question ❹: *What is the same and what is different about each side of the balance?*
- Question ❹: *How can you show this information in a number sentence? Why can you multiply 448 by 5 instead of 6?*

IN FOCUS Questions ❶ and ❷ require children to apply their reasoning to measurement as they find missing dimensions. In each case, they need to decide what they should do first.

Question ❹ gives children an opportunity to explore equivalence and a balancing equation. The question has been chosen because there is also a box on the side with the tins so the seven tins must balance five boxes. The calculation provides an opportunity to look at strategies to multiply by 5 or to decide on the order of the calculation, for example $448 \times 5 \div 7$ or $448 \div 7 \times 5$, where 448 can easily be partitioned as two multiples of 7 (420 + 28). Encourage children to make estimates before calculating.

STRENGTHEN For question ❶, model the question using a bar model, drawing attention to the similarity between the bar model and the diagram in the question. Suggest that children draw their own bar model for question ❹. Encourage children to use the inverse to check their calculations are correct.

DEEPEN Look at the order of the calculation in question ❶. The answer can be found using the calculation $90 \times 4 \div 3$. Ask children to explain why the calculation could also be completed as $90 \div 3 \times 4$ and why someone might choose to do this.

ASSESSMENT CHECKPOINT Use questions ❶ and ❷ to assess whether children can apply reasoning to different contexts. Check that they can select the operation(s) required. Use question ❸ to assess whether children can reason about the characteristics of numbers and their behaviours when they are added or multiplied, for example odd + even = odd.

ANSWERS

Question ❶: The width of the hexagon is 120 mm.

Question ❷: The height of the triangle is 108 mm.

Question ❸: A, D, E

Question ❹: The mass of one tin is 320 g.

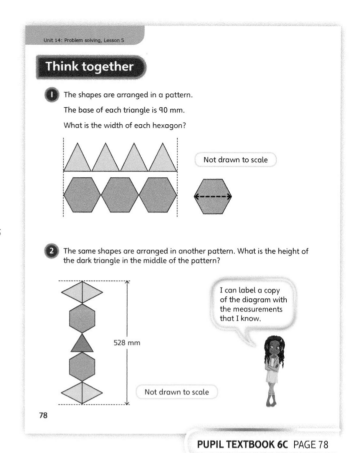

PUPIL TEXTBOOK 6C PAGE 78

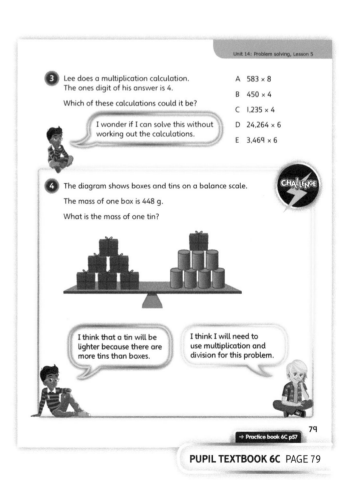

PUPIL TEXTBOOK 6C PAGE 79

Practice

WAYS OF WORKING Independent thinking

IN FOCUS Question **1** requires children to apply the strategies used in the lesson to the context of money. They should think carefully about the information they know and decide what to do first. Children may forget to include the price of the lace.

Encourage children to annotate the diagram in question **2** to aid their thinking.

STRENGTHEN Model the answer to question **1**, emphasising the importance of working systematically and writing down every step clearly:

lace + 2 plain beads + 3 spotty beads = £1·30
25p + (18p × 2) + 3 spotty beads = £1·30
3 spotty beads = £1·30 – 25p – 36p = 69p
1 spotty bead = 69p ÷ 3 = 23p

DEEPEN Ask children to reason about the diameters of the circles in question **5** if the measurement given for the two circles on the first row is doubled to 48 cm. Ask them to explain whether the diameter of every circle will double.

THINK DIFFERENTLY Question **4** requires children to reason about the results of addition and multiplication, drawing on knowledge of odds, evens and number bonds to achieve an answer with 5 ones, for example 2 + 3, 7 + 8, etc.

ASSESSMENT CHECKPOINT Use questions **1**, **2** and **3** to assess whether children can complete multi-step problems. Check that they can keep track of the calculations already completed and recognise when the answer has/ has not been reached. Use question **4** to assess whether children can predict the ones digit in the product of a multiplication, recognising that the whole calculation need not be completed.

ANSWERS Answers for the **Practice** part of the lesson appear in the separate **Practice and Reflect answer guide**.

Reflect

WAYS OF WORKING Pair work

IN FOCUS In discussing the strategies used to solve question **3** b), children should draw on previous lessons and think about different ways to find the difference; for example (720 × 10) – (450 × 10) or simply (720 – 450) × 10.

ASSESSMENT CHECKPOINT Check that children understand why different strategies can be used and why the second strategy above would not work if they had been asked to find the difference between 10 large bottles and 9 small bottles.

ANSWERS Answers for the **Reflect** part of the lesson appear in the separate **Practice and Reflect answer guide**.

After the lesson ⏸

- Can children explain what information has been given in a problem and how this will help them?
- Can they use a range of strategies for calculations, both written and mental?
- Can children explain which operations they should use and how they might reorder a calculation to make it easier?

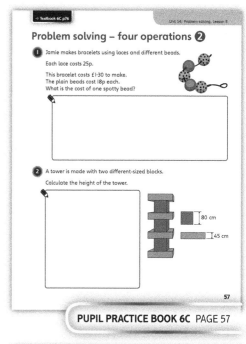

PUPIL PRACTICE BOOK 6C PAGE 57

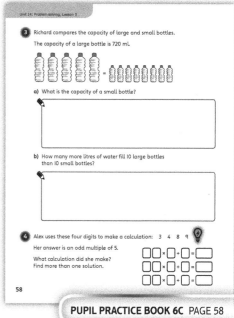

PUPIL PRACTICE BOOK 6C PAGE 58

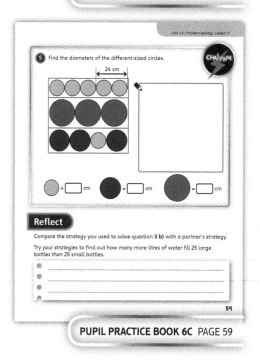

PUPIL PRACTICE BOOK 6C PAGE 59

Problem solving – fractions

Learning focus

In this lesson, children will apply their understanding of fractions to help them identify, compare and calculate. They will draw on knowledge of equivalent fractions to help solve problems and use reasoning skills to make decisions.

Small steps

→ Previous step: Problem solving – four operations (2)
→ **This step: Problem solving – fractions**
→ Next step: Problem solving – decimals

NATIONAL CURRICULUM LINKS

Year 6 Number – Fractions (Including Decimals and Percentages)

Recall and use equivalences between simple fractions, decimals and percentages, including in different contexts.

ASSESSING MASTERY

Children can solve a range of problems about fractions by drawing on their understanding of equivalence and knowledge of the number line. They can find fractions of amounts and apply this to the context of money and measure.

COMMON MISCONCEPTIONS

When asked to compare and order fractions, children may not reason about the characteristics of the fractions before converting the fractions to a common denominator. Ask:

- *What can you tell me about these fractions? Do any fractions have the same denominator? … the same numerator? How can you tell which fraction is larger?*
- *Which fractions are more than $\frac{1}{2}$? … less than $\frac{1}{2}$?*

STRENGTHENING UNDERSTANDING

Look together at different representations of fractions of shapes, agreeing which are equivalent and which are not – for example, a shape with 8 out of 20 equal pieces shaded and a shape with 6 out of 15 equal pieces shaded. Revisit comparing fractions, reasoning about shared numerators and denominators.

GOING DEEPER

Give children a range of problems or calculations that require them to make use of equivalent fractions. Ask them to sort problems into groups such as calculations that are easier to solve using equivalent fractions and those that are not, for example solving $\frac{5}{8} \div 2$ using $\frac{10}{16} \div 2$.

KEY LANGUAGE

In lesson: fraction, numerator, denominator

Other language to be used by the teacher: equivalent

STRUCTURES AND REPRESENTATIONS

number line, bar model, fraction strip

RESOURCES

Optional: multiplication grid, digit cards

 In the eTextbook of this lesson, you will find interactive links to a selection of teaching tools.

Before you teach

- Can children explain whether a fraction is smaller or greater than $\frac{1}{2}$?
- Can they explain when fractions are equivalent and when they are not?
- Can they order a set of fractions that share the same denominator?

Discover

WAYS OF WORKING Pair work

ASK

- Question **1** a): *How do you know that none of the children have completely filled their buckets with water?*
- Question **1** a): *What will you do to help order the fractions? Which fraction do you think is largest? Why?*
- Question **1** b): *How do you know that Olivia and Bella did not collect 10 litres or more of water together?*
- Question **1** b): *What do you need to do to solve this problem?*

IN FOCUS The fractions in question **1** a) have been chosen so that children can reason about them rather than simply converting to a common denominator.

PRACTICAL TIPS Draw a number line on the board and ask children to estimate the position of each fraction. This will encourage them to think about a fraction's proximity to other fractions they know.

ANSWERS

Question **1** a): Bella won the race because $\frac{5}{6} > \frac{5}{8} > \frac{2}{5} > \frac{3}{8}$.

Question **1** b): Olivia and Bella collected 5,800 ml of water in total.

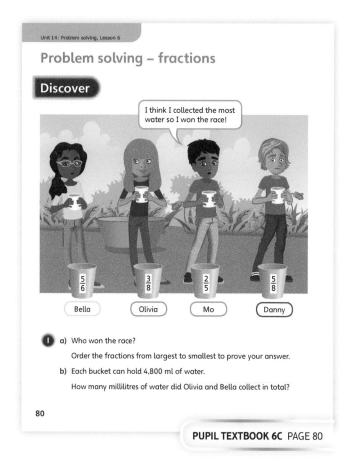

PUPIL TEXTBOOK 6C PAGE 80

Share

WAYS OF WORKING Whole class teacher led

ASK

Question **1** a): *What has Astrid noticed about the fractions? How does this help?*

Question **1** a): *What do you notice about each of the five parts when comparing $\frac{5}{6}$ and $\frac{5}{8}$?*

Question **1** a): *How can you prove that $\frac{2}{5}$ is less than $\frac{1}{2}$ and $\frac{5}{8}$ is more than $\frac{1}{2}$?*

Question **1** b): *Why do both the methods work? Which do you prefer? Why?*

IN FOCUS In question **1** a), the fraction strips help children to visually compare fractions that share the same numerator by showing that when a whole is split into more equal parts, each part is smaller. Question **1** b) encourages children to think about different strategies to solve the same problem.

STRENGTHEN For question **1** a) use equivalent fractions to prove $\frac{5}{8}$ is more than $\frac{1}{2}$, for example use $\frac{4}{8}$ for $\frac{1}{2}$ so that children can clearly see that $\frac{5}{8}$ is $\frac{1}{8}$ more. Similarly, use $\frac{5}{10}$ for $\frac{1}{2}$ and $\frac{4}{10}$ for $\frac{2}{5}$ to compare $\frac{2}{5}$ and $\frac{1}{2}$. Ask children to reason about the fraction $\frac{7}{12}$ or $\frac{5}{12}$ in the same way.

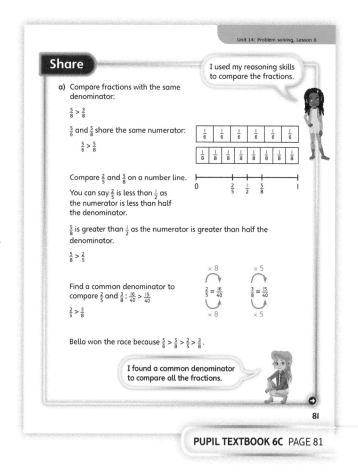

PUPIL TEXTBOOK 6C PAGE 81

Think together

Unit 14: Problem solving, Lesson 6

WAYS OF WORKING Whole class teacher led (I do, We do, You do)

ASK

- Question ❶: *What does the question require you to do? What common denominator could you use?*
- Question ❷: *What fraction of a bucket does Mo collect? How can you find half of $\frac{3}{4}$?*
- Question ❸: *How many equal parts is each shape divided into? How can you use equivalent fractions to help?*
- Question ❹: *What fraction of the whole do the lemons and sugar represent altogether? How do you know?*
- Question ❹: *How can you represent the problem using a bar model?*

IN FOCUS Question ❷ looks at the relationship between dividing by 2 and multiplying by $\frac{1}{2}$. Children can calculate either $\frac{5}{8} \div 2$ or $\frac{5}{8} \times \frac{1}{2}$ ($\frac{1}{2}$ of $\frac{5}{8}$). Look at solving the problem in both ways, to help children make sense of division methods such as 'turn the fraction upside down and multiply'. Question ❸ presents children with different images to represent fractions of a shape. Children often look for familiar representations when working with fractions, rather than thinking about the properties of the fraction. They must first identify the number of equal parts (which may not look the same in the shape) and then use knowledge of equivalent fractions to compare. Question ❹ has been designed so children can reason about the information they are given and work out how this relates to the whole: $\frac{3}{5}$ is left so the total of £2·20 and £2·80 represents $\frac{2}{5}$ of the whole.

STRENGTHEN Encourage children to think flexibly about the information they are given each time and how equivalent fractions might help them to solve the problems in questions ❶, ❷ and ❸. Use a multiplication grid to explore strings of equivalent fractions by scaling the numerator and denominator each time as they move from column to column.

DEEPEN Look at question ❹. Ask children to explain how their bar model and solution would change if the fraction of the money left was $\frac{2}{5}$.

ASSESSMENT CHECKPOINT Use questions ❶ and ❷ to assess whether children can calculate with fractions in a context. Check that they can use equivalent fractions to find a common denominator. Use question ❸ to assess whether children can identify a fraction of a shape, even when the equal parts do not look the same. Use question ❹ to assess whether children can represent a problem and understand how given information relates to the answer.

ANSWERS

Question ❶: Bella collected $\frac{13}{30}$ of a bucket more.

Question ❷: Danny collected $\frac{3}{8}$ of a bucket.

Question ❸: Shape B

Question ❹: Olivia had £12·50 to start with.

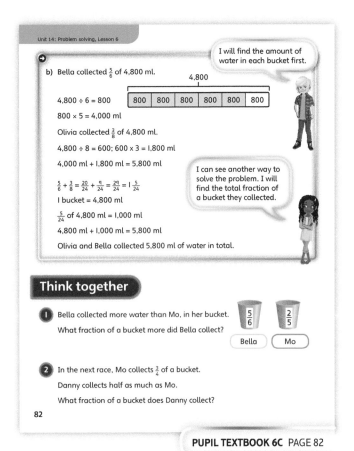

PUPIL TEXTBOOK 6C PAGE 82

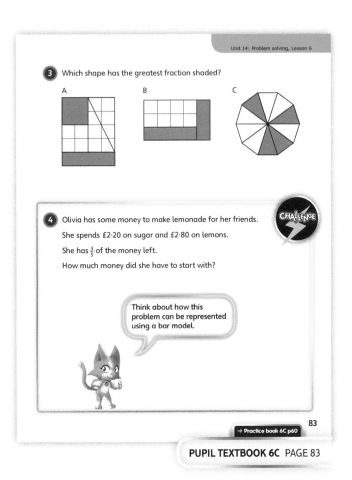

PUPIL TEXTBOOK 6C PAGE 83

Practice

Independent thinking

IN FOCUS Question ❶ has been designed for children to reason about fractions compared to $\frac{1}{2}$. They need to consider equivalent fractions and may also think about using an improper fraction for a solution. Question ❷ b) requires children to think about pairs of fractions that total one whole, recognising that 1 can be written as $\frac{9}{9}$. Question ❻ encourages children to reason about the effect of the size of a fraction when carrying out different calculations, and to consider which fractions will give the largest result each time.

STRENGTHEN For question ❺, encourage children to sketch a bar model to help make sense of the information they know and how this relates to the whole. If necessary, model a similar question and then ask them to apply the same strategy to question ❺.

DEEPEN Provide children with the digit cards 2, 4, 6, 9 and ask them to find a set of answers that will complete the statement in question ❶, using $\frac{1}{4}$ instead of $\frac{1}{2}$. Then ask children to choose four different digit cards for a partner to solve the problem.

ASSESSMENT CHECKPOINT Use question ❷ to assess whether children can confidently add and subtract fractions in context. Check that they recognise the operations needed to solve the problems.

ANSWERS Answers for the **Practice** part of the lesson appear in the separate **Practice and Reflect answer guide**.

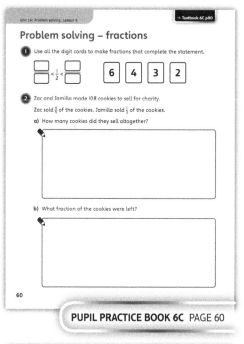

PUPIL PRACTICE BOOK 6C PAGE 60

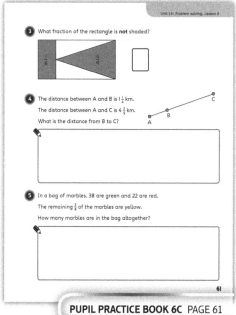

PUPIL PRACTICE BOOK 6C PAGE 61

Reflect

Pair work

IN FOCUS Children work with a partner to reason about a set of fractions, using the learning applied throughout the lesson to help make decisions.

ASSESSMENT CHECKPOINT Check that children understand how they can use equivalent fractions to help them compare fractions.

ANSWERS Answers for the **Reflect** part of the lesson appear in the separate **Practice and Reflect answer guide**.

After the lesson ⏸

- Can children explain how they have used equivalent fractions to solve problems?
- Can they confidently calculate with fractions, using equivalence to help find common denominators or to simplify a fraction?
- Can they represent a problem, explaining what they know and what they need to find out?

PUPIL PRACTICE BOOK 6C PAGE 62

Problem solving – decimals

Learning focus

In this lesson, children will work with decimals to solve problems with and without a context. They will use representations to help make sense of problems and decide which operations to use.

Small steps

→ Previous step: Problem solving – fractions
→ **This step: Problem solving – decimals**
→ Next step: Problem solving – percentages

NATIONAL CURRICULUM LINKS

Year 6 Number – Fractions (Including Decimals and Percentages)

Recall and use equivalences between simple fractions, decimals and percentages, including in different contexts.

ASSESSING MASTERY

Children can confidently work with decimals using knowledge of place value to help them calculate accurately. They can solve a range of problems, flexibly applying mental or written strategies to carry out the calculations.

COMMON MISCONCEPTIONS

Children may incorrectly apply their knowledge of writing 1·2 with measures (for example, 1·2 kg or 1·2 m) to write 1·2 in the context of money as £1·2. Show children prices written to two decimal places and ask:
• *How many decimal places do you use to write an amount in pounds and pence? How can you write 1·2 as a decimal to two decimal places? What equivalent fractions can you use to help?* ($\frac{2}{10}$ and $\frac{20}{100}$)

STRENGTHENING UNDERSTANDING

Use place value counters to support work with decimals, using arrays to work with multiplication as required. Represent each problem using a bar model to help children decide what calculations are needed.

GOING DEEPER

Explore the effect of a multiplication followed by a division, for example × 2 and then ÷ 3, relating this to finding $\frac{2}{3}$.
Ask: *How does this differ when the calculation is × 3 and then ÷ 2?*

KEY LANGUAGE

In lesson: convert

Other language used by the teacher: decimal, equivalent

STRUCTURES AND REPRESENTATIONS

number line, bar model

RESOURCES

Optional: place value counters, toy coins

 In the eTextbook of this lesson, you will find interactive links to a selection of teaching tools.

Before you teach

• Can children give the value of each digit in numbers up to three decimal places?
• Can they solve a range of two-step and multi-step problems with whole numbers?
• Can they work with decimals in the context of money and measurement?

Discover

WAYS OF WORKING Pair work

ASK

- Question ❶ a): *How can you find the price of a child ticket when you only know the price of an adult ticket?*
- Question ❶ a): *What method will you use to find the cost of two adult tickets? Is this the same as doubling £6·45?*
- Question ❶ b): *What would be a good estimate for the cost of 48 adult tickets? Will the actual amount be more or less than this?*
- Question ❶ b): *I think the problem can be solved in more than one way. How could you solve the problem?*

IN FOCUS Question ❶ a) requires children to recognise that the cost of three child tickets is equal to the cost of two adult tickets. Look for children using a written method to multiply by 2 rather than simply doubling.

PRACTICAL TIPS Use place value counters or toy coins to model the problem. Use these to support doubling £6·45 and dividing £12·90 by 3.

ANSWERS

Question ❶ a): The price of one child ticket is £4·30.

Question ❶ b): The cinema takes £103·20 more when the front row is filled with adults.

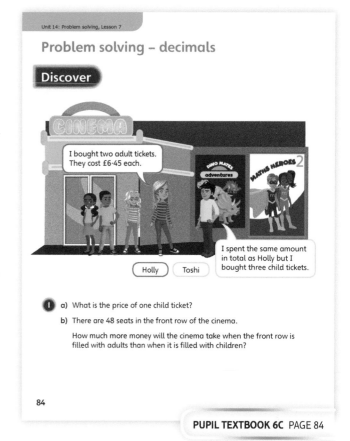

Share

WAYS OF WORKING Whole class teacher led

ASK

- Question ❶ a): *How do you know that the bar model matches the problem?*
- Question ❶ a): *What method can you use to divide £12·90 by 3? Why have you chosen this method?*
- Question ❶ b): *What method can you use to multiply by 48? Why might you choose to round and adjust?*
- Question ❶ b): *Will Flo's method give the correct answer? Which method do you prefer? Why?*

IN FOCUS Question ❶ a) uses a bar model to represent the relationship between the adult and child tickets. Make sure children recognise that they need to multiply by 2 and then divide by 3. In question ❶ b), children could look at mental strategies of rounding and adjusting to multiply by 48 (multiply by 50 and subtract 2 × the number).

STRENGTHEN Use toy coins to represent decimals in the context of money, for example 4·3 as £4·30 and not £4·3.

DEEPEN For question ❶ a) ask children to explore and explain why the answer £4·30 can also be found by carrying out the calculation $\frac{2}{3}$ of £6·45 or $\frac{2}{3}$ × £6·45.

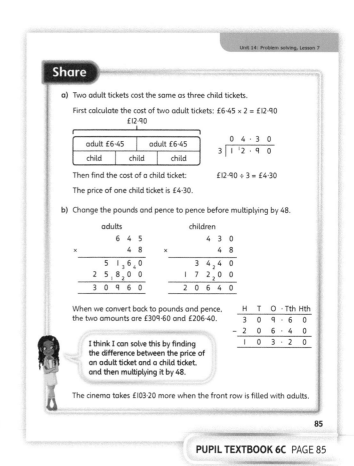

Think together

WAYS OF WORKING Whole class teacher led (I do, We do, You do)

ASK

- Question ❶: *What do you need to do first? Why?*
- Question ❷: *Why is the answer not the product of 48 × 0·6 m?*
- Question ❸: *Where should you position each number on the number line? How do you know?*
- Question ❸: *Who thinks that 0·48 is furthest from 0·4 because 48 is much larger than 4? Is that correct?*
- Question ❹: *How do you know that the two numbers cannot be whole numbers?*

IN FOCUS Question ❶ is a two-step problem that requires subtraction first; this is different from question ❶ b) in **Share**. Question ❷ provides an opportunity for children to interpret a diagram to help make sense of the problem. Children often forget to complete all steps in a problem, so encourage them to check that they have answered the question fully.

Question ❸ requires children to apply their understanding of place value to find the number closest to 0·4. They may make an error by relating these decimal numbers to whole numbers, thinking that 0·48 is much larger than 0·4 because 48 is much larger than 4.

Question ❹ has been chosen so that the numbers are required to meet two criteria. With this type of problem, many children will find a solution to suit one criterion but not the other. The answers are to two decimal places even though the difference is only to one decimal place.

STRENGTHEN Encourage children to draw bar models to support problem solving and to explain what each step of the problem requires.

DEEPEN For question ❷, ask children to reason about the length of the front row if each seat was 5 cm wider. Ask them whether they need to calculate 48 × 0·67 etc. or whether they can start with their existing answer.

ASSESSMENT CHECKPOINT Use questions ❶ and ❷ to assess whether children can use decimal numbers in context and carry out all steps of the problem. Use question ❸ to assess whether children can apply understanding of decimal place value. Use question ❹ to assess whether children can work with more than one criterion when solving problems.

ANSWERS

Question ❶: Each carton has a mass of 0·78 kg.

Question ❷: The row is 30·05 m long.

Question ❸: 0·35 is closest to 0·4.

Question ❹: The two numbers are 3·15 and 3·85.

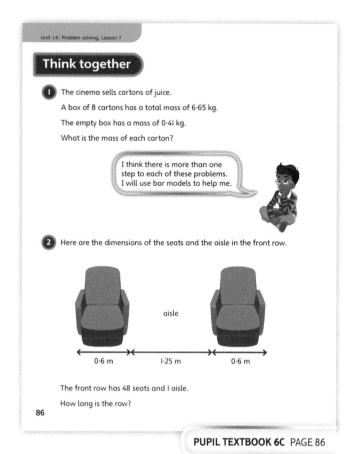

PUPIL TEXTBOOK 6C PAGE 86

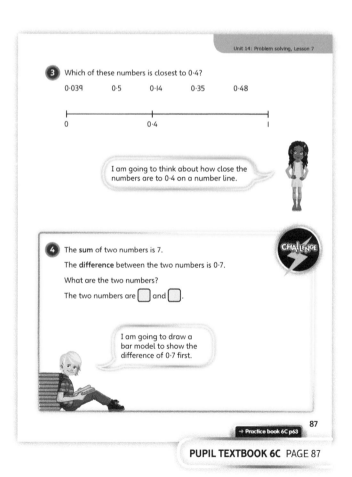

PUPIL TEXTBOOK 6C PAGE 87

Practice

→ Textbook 6C p84

WAYS OF WORKING Independent thinking

IN FOCUS Question **2** b) provides an opportunity to try different strategies, for example finding the cost of 8 bags of popcorn by doubling the cost of 4 bags and then finding the cost of 8 cartons before finding the difference; or finding the difference between the cost of one carton and one bag of popcorn before multiplying by 8.

Question **3** has been chosen as a decontextualised problem where children must first identify the scale that has been used. Children may incorrectly give 3·9 as the missing number in the first box, using the pattern 3·9, 4 and 4·1 from the scale.

Question **4** requires children to interpret a balanced scale, recognising that 8 chocolate bars are equal in mass to 6 tins of nuts. Some children may reason that 4 chocolate bars must be equal to 3 tins of nuts and carry out the calculations accordingly.

Question **5** requires children to think flexibly about adding three decimal numbers. They can use estimation to quickly discard combinations and look at the tenths digit to reason about number bonds. Some children may realise that the total for each column/row is equal to the sum of all the numbers divided by 3.

STRENGTHEN For question **5**, encourage children to look at the whole numbers first and find sets of these numbers where the whole numbers add to the same value. They can then swap the numbers as needed to find sets of three decimals that sum to the same value.

DEEPEN For question **4**, ask children to look at a method of rounding and adjusting to multiply by 0·2.

ASSESSMENT CHECKPOINT Use questions **1** and **2** to assess whether children can solve multi-step problems involving decimals. Check that they can use calculation methods accurately. Use question **3** to assess whether children can apply understanding of place value to interpret the scale on a number line. Use question **4** to assess whether they can make sense of a balancing problem and interpret a diagram correctly.

ANSWERS Answers for the **Practice** part of the lesson appear in the separate **Practice and Reflect answer guide**.

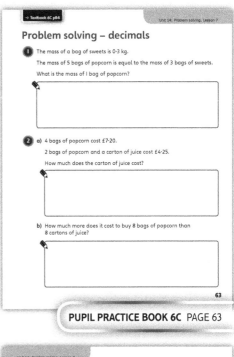

PUPIL PRACTICE BOOK 6C PAGE 63

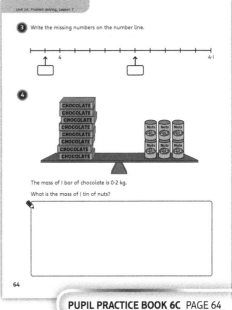

PUPIL PRACTICE BOOK 6C PAGE 64

Reflect

WAYS OF WORKING Independent thinking

IN FOCUS Children are required to use their knowledge of place value to explain which number is closest to 0·9. They may also find it useful to draw a number line.

ASSESSMENT CHECKPOINT Check that children understand and can explain why 0·87 is closer to 0·9 than 0·95.

ANSWERS Answers for the **Reflect** part of the lesson appear in the separate **Practice and Reflect answer guide**.

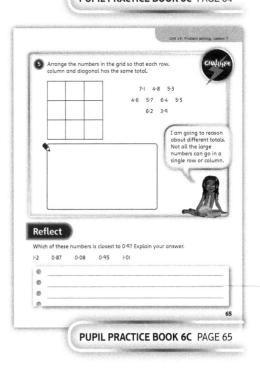

PUPIL PRACTICE BOOK 6C PAGE 65

After the lesson ⏸

- Can children confidently calculate with decimals, using place value accurately?
- Can they solve a range of problems, representing them as necessary, and explain what calculations need to be carried out?

Problem solving – percentages

Learning focus

In this lesson, children will work with percentages to solve a range of problems. They will use what they know about percentage and fraction equivalence to make decisions about calculating and to help them recognise representations.

Small steps

→ Previous step: Problem solving – decimals
→ **This step: Problem solving – percentages**
→ Next step: Problem solving – ratio and proportion

NATIONAL CURRICULUM LINKS

Year 6 Number – Fractions (Including Decimals and Percentages)

Recall and use equivalences between simple fractions, decimals and percentages, including in different contexts.

ASSESSING MASTERY

Children can calculate a percentage of a quantity or amount using what they know about fractions to help them. They can also find the value of the whole when given the percentage discount and the discounted price.

COMMON MISCONCEPTIONS

Children may take what they know about the equivalence of 10% and $\frac{1}{10}$ and assume that 20% is $\frac{1}{20}$ or 5% is $\frac{1}{5}$. Ask:
* *What is 20% as a fraction with the denominator 100? What is the simplest form of this fraction? What is the simplest form of the fraction for 5%?*
* *What is 20% relative to 10%? Think about the calculation $2 \times \frac{1}{10} = \frac{2}{10}$: what is $\frac{2}{10}$ in its simplest form?*

STRENGTHENING UNDERSTANDING

Revisit fraction and percentage equivalents. Practise finding 10% by dividing by 10, using a place value grid for support.

GOING DEEPER

Explore finding different percentages of amounts in different ways, for example:
* finding 75% by subtracting 25% from the whole or finding the total of 50% and 25% of the whole
* finding 95% by subtracting 5% from the whole.

Ask children to draw a table to summarise the various ways they can find different percentages.

KEY LANGUAGE

In lesson: percentage, equivalent, fraction

Other language to be used by the teacher: denominator

STRUCTURES AND REPRESENTATIONS

bar model

RESOURCES

Optional: examples of products, prices and discounts

 In the eTextbook of this lesson, you will find interactive links to a selection of teaching tools.

Before you teach

* Can children find 10% of a quantity by finding $\frac{1}{10}$?
* Can they write a percentage as a fraction with the denominator 100?
* Can they use a bar model to represent a problem involving percentages?

Discover

WAYS OF WORKING Pair work

ASK

- Question ❶ a): *How can you find 20% of an amount? How can finding 10% help?*
- Question ❶ a): *How does place value help you to find 10%? What fraction is the same as 10%?*
- Question ❶ b): *How does this problem differ from part a)?*
- Question ❶ b): *What is 25% as a fraction? How does this help?*
- Question ❶ b): *What fraction or percentage of the whole price does £330 represent?*

IN FOCUS These questions require children to use percentages in different ways and to apply knowledge of equivalence to help them. In question ❶ a) children find a percentage of an amount, whereas in ❶ b) they are given a percentage of an amount and must calculate the whole.

PRACTICAL TIPS Role play the scenario by setting up a 'shop' using cards to show products with prices and discounts.

ANSWERS

Question ❶ a): Jen pays £360 for her computer.

Question ❶ b): The full price of Amal's television is £440.

Problem solving – percentages

Discover

The full price of my computer is £450.

One day sale!

25% off

20% off

I paid £330 for my television after the discount.

Amal

Jen

❶ a) How much does Jen pay for her computer?

b) What is the full price of Amal's television?

88

PUPIL TEXTBOOK 6C PAGE 88

Share

WAYS OF WORKING Whole class teacher led

ASK

- Question ❶ a): *Where can you see the 20% discount in the bar model? What percentage of the full price does Jen have to pay?*
- Question ❶ a): *20% is equivalent to 0·2 or $\frac{1}{5}$. How can you find $\frac{1}{5}$ of £450?*
- Question ❶ a): *Can you explain how Flo's method works?*
- Question ❶ b): *Why does £330 only represent three parts on the bar model?*
- Question ❶ b): *What discount in pounds did Amal receive?*

IN FOCUS Children are required to work flexibly, recognising how bar models can represent the problems but with the information used differently to solve each one. In question ❶ a), children may give the answer as £90, forgetting that this is the discount and so must be subtracted from the full amount. In question ❶ b), children may find 25% of £330 because a value and a percentage have been given, without recognising that £330 does not represent the full price.

STRENGTHEN Explore Flo's idea for part a). Refer to the bar model to agree that Jen only pays 80%, which can be calculated using 8 × £45 (8 times 10%) rather than finding 20% and subtracting this from the whole.

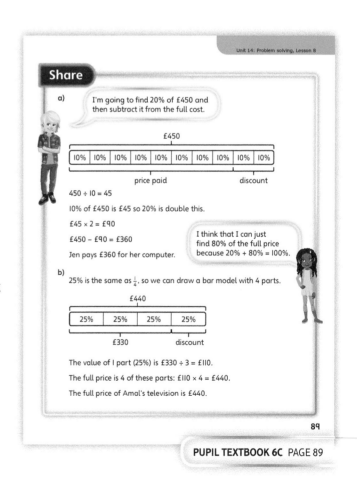

Share

a) I'm going to find 20% of £450 and then subtract it from the full cost.

£450

| 10% | 10% | 10% | 10% | 10% | 10% | 10% | 10% | 10% | 10% |

price paid   discount

450 ÷ 10 = 45

10% of £450 is £45 so 20% is double this.

£45 × 2 = £90

£450 – £90 = £360

Jen pays £360 for her computer.

I think that I can just find 80% of the full price because 20% + 80% = 100%.

b) 25% is the same as $\frac{1}{4}$, so we can draw a bar model with 4 parts.

£440

| 25% | 25% | 25% | 25% |

£330   discount

The value of 1 part (25%) is £330 ÷ 3 = £110.

The full price is 4 of these parts: £110 × 4 = £440.

The full price of Amal's television is £440.

89

PUPIL TEXTBOOK 6C PAGE 89

Think together

WAYS OF WORKING Whole class teacher led (I do, We do, You do)

ASK

- Question **1**: *What percentage of the full price does £42 represent? How do you know?*
- Question **2**: *What percentage of the whole do the children represent? How do you know?*
- Question **2**: *How can you calculate the number of adults?*
- Question **3**: *How many equal parts is each grid divided into? How does this help?*
- Question **4**: *What is $\frac{1}{5}$ as a percentage?*

IN FOCUS Question **2** provides an opportunity for children to reason about the information they are given in a table and to use this to find missing information. Question **3** shows pictorial representations of percentages, so children are first required to interpret the fraction of the whole each pattern represents. They must then use fraction and percentage equivalents to solve the problem. Similarly, question **4** requires knowledge of fraction and percentage equivalents. Look for children who incorrectly identify $\frac{1}{5}$ as 5%.

STRENGTHEN For question **2**, ensure children recognise that the whole is 100% and the children represent 40% of the customers because adults represent 60%. Provide tables with different numbers and percentages for them to practise this skill.

DEEPEN Ask children to make up their own percentage problems where the answer is £200. Challenge them to create questions where £200 is the discounted price and where £200 is the full price.

ASSESSMENT CHECKPOINT Use questions **1** and **2** to assess whether children can solve percentage problems where they need to work out the whole. Check they can interpret a table and recognise that 60% + 40% is equal to the whole 100%. Use questions **3** and **4** to assess whether children can use fraction and percentage equivalents to solve problems.

ANSWERS

Question **1**: The full price of the computer case was £60.

Question **2**: 40% (children), 1,050 (adults)

Question **3** a): B

Question **3** b): 25% of grid B is white.

Question **4**: The winner got 40% of the votes (Jamie).

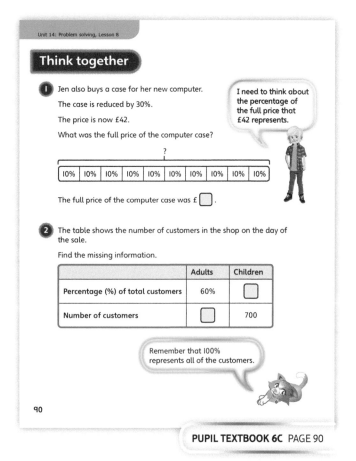

PUPIL TEXTBOOK 6C PAGE 90

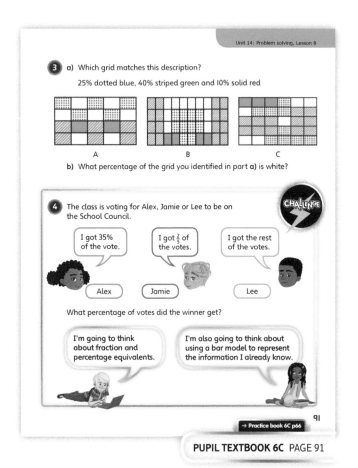

PUPIL TEXTBOOK 6C PAGE 91

Practice

WAYS OF WORKING Independent thinking

IN FOCUS Question ❷ has been chosen so that children can explore different strategies to solve the problem. For example, they can work out how many children cycle to school and come by car and subtract the total from 120, or they can recognise that the percentage who walk must be 35% and so calculate 35% of 120. Question ❸ requires children to interpret information given in a table, and then apply their knowledge of the whole as 100% to calculate what percentage of the whole a value represents.

STRENGTHEN For question ❷, encourage children to think through what they need to do to find how many children walk to school. Ask them what 30% and 20% of 120 is? Now what do they need to do with these numbers?

DEEPEN Ask children to work in pairs to make up a problem similar to question ❸. They can then swap problems with another pair.

ASSESSMENT CHECKPOINT Use questions ❶, ❷ and ❸ to assess whether children can work flexibly with percentages, knowing how to use the given information to solve the problem. Check that they understand when they are given the whole and need to work out a percentage, and when they are given a percentage and need to find the whole.

ANSWERS Answers for the **Practice** part of the lesson appear in the separate **Practice and Reflect answer guide**.

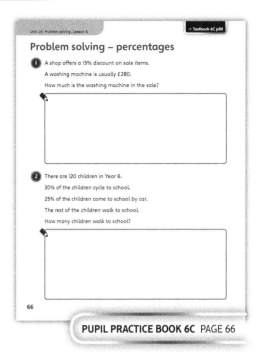

PUPIL PRACTICE BOOK 6C PAGE 66

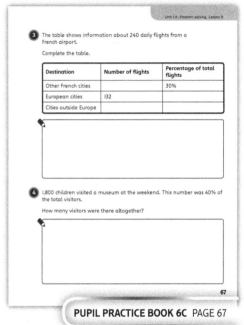

PUPIL PRACTICE BOOK 6C PAGE 67

Reflect

WAYS OF WORKING Independent thinking

IN FOCUS The shapes have been chosen so they are less familiar and not all equal parts are immediately obvious.

ASSESSMENT CHECKPOINT Check that children can use their knowledge of equivalent fractions and percentages to explain why the shaded part of each shape is 60%.

ANSWERS Answers for the **Reflect** part of the lesson appear in the separate **Practice and Reflect answer guide**.

After the lesson ⏸

- Can children explain when they are required to find a percentage of a whole and when they are required to find the whole?
- Can they solve a range of problems, representing them as necessary, and explain what calculations need to be carried out?

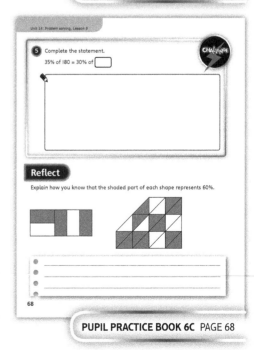

PUPIL PRACTICE BOOK 6C PAGE 68

Problem solving – ratio and proportion

Learning focus

In this lesson, children will further explore ratio as a relationship between parts to help solve problems in different contexts. They will use representations to show a ratio and make use of multiplication facts to help scale quantities.

Small steps

→ Previous step: Problem solving – percentages
→ **This step: Problem solving – ratio and proportion**
→ Next step: Problem solving – time (1)

NATIONAL CURRICULUM LINKS

Year 6 Ratio and Proportion
- Solve problems involving unequal sharing and grouping using knowledge of fractions and multiples.
- Solve problems involving the relative sizes of two quantities where missing values can be found by using integer multiplication and division facts.

ASSESSING MASTERY

Children can use the language of 'for every' to talk about ratio and use the colon notation. They can use bar models to solve problems involving ratio and proportion, explaining what each part represents.

COMMON MISCONCEPTIONS

When dealing with the number of parts in a problem, children may forget to find the total number of parts. For example, in the question, 'In a class of 32 children, there are 5 girls for every 3 boys. How many girls are there?' children may divide 32 by 5 rather than 8. Use bar models to support this concept. Ask:
- *How can you show the number of girls on the bar model? ... the number of boys? How many parts in total? What is each part worth?*

STRENGTHENING UNDERSTANDING

To work with ratio, children need to be secure in their understanding of multiplication as scaling. They also need to be confident with the idea of equivalence – for example, recognising that '2 oranges for every 3 apples' can be scaled up to '4 oranges for every 6 apples' etc., remembering that the relationship between the number of oranges and apples remains the same. Represent the scaling up of simple ratios with counters or cubes. Look at the relationship between the values each time as the numbers are scaled twice, three times, four times etc.

GOING DEEPER

Look in greater depth at the difference between a ratio and a proportion. Ask children to use sticks of cubes to represent a given ratio or proportion. Ask them to describe the stick using ratio, then proportion. Encourage children to reason about other lengths of sticks with the same ratio. Ask: *What patterns do you notice?*

KEY LANGUAGE

In lesson: ratio, scaling, relationship

Other language to be used by the teacher: fraction, similar, proportion

STRUCTURES AND REPRESENTATIONS

bar model

RESOURCES

Optional: counters, cubes

 In the eTextbook of this lesson, you will find interactive links to a selection of teaching tools.

Before you teach

- Can children recall and use multiplication and division facts?
- Can they solve simple ratio problems using multiplication as scaling?
- Can they explain how many parts in total for a given ratio?

Discover

WAYS OF WORKING Pair work

ASK

- Question ❶ a): *What do you notice about the number of car stickers compared to the number of train stickers each time? (double)*
- Question ❶ a): *How can you describe the relationship between the number of car stickers and train stickers as a ratio?*
- Question ❶ a): *What can you tell me about the number of each type of sticker and the total number of stickers in two packets?*
- Question ❶ b): *What diagram can you draw to represent this problem?*
- Question ❶ b): *How many more car stickers than train stickers are there in each packet? … in two packets? … in ten packets?*

IN FOCUS These questions require children to solve ratio problems by reasoning. The ratio of 4 car stickers to every 2 train stickers is not given in its simplest form. The children should notice that this is the same relationship as 2 car stickers for every 1 train sticker, so the number of car stickers is always double the number of train stickers.

PRACTICAL TIPS Use counters or cubes to represent the ratio, building these in rows to show the scaling for one packet, two packets etc.

ANSWERS

Question ❶ a): Andy has 48 stickers in total.

Question ❶ b): There are 25 packets of stickers in each box.

Problem solving – ratio and proportion

Discover

Get 4 car stickers and 2 train stickers in every packet!

Andy   Emma

❶ a) Andy buys some packets of stickers.
   He has 32 car stickers.
   How many stickers does he have in total?

   b) There are 50 more car stickers than train stickers in a box.
   How many packets of stickers are in a box?

92

PUPIL TEXTBOOK 6C PAGE 92

Share

WAYS OF WORKING Whole class teacher led

ASK

- Question ❶ a): *Can you explain how the bar model represents the problem?*
- Question ❶ a): *Why does the scaling show 1 packet, 2 packets, 4 packets and 8 packets, but not the other numbers of packets in between (for example, 3 packets)?*
- Question ❶ b): *Can you explain how the bar model represents the problem this time?*
- Question ❶ b): *How can you prove that each part on the bar model represents 25 stickers?*

IN FOCUS Question ❶ a) has been chosen to encourage children to explore the ratio between the car stickers and train stickers and to consider how this relates to the total amount. Look for children who recognise that, because there are 6 stickers (or parts) in each packet (2 + 4), the total number of stickers will always be a multiple of 6. Question ❶ b) has been chosen to explore the difference between the number of car stickers and train stickers rather than the total number of stickers. Look for children who mistake 50 for the number of car/train stickers rather than the difference between them.

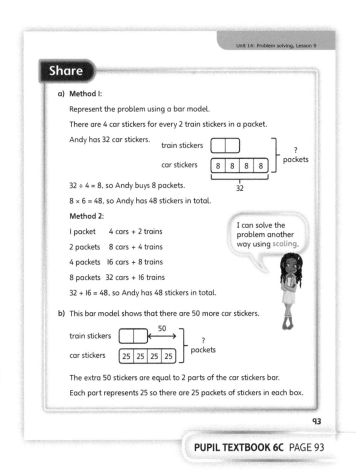

Share

a) **Method 1:**
   Represent the problem using a bar model.
   There are 4 car stickers for every 2 train stickers in a packet.
   Andy has 32 car stickers.

   train stickers / car stickers | 8 | 8 | 8 | 8 | ? packets

   $32 \div 4 = 8$, so Andy buys 8 packets.
   $8 \times 6 = 48$, so Andy has 48 stickers in total.

   Method 2:
1 packet	4 cars + 2 trains
2 packets	8 cars + 4 trains
4 packets	16 cars + 8 trains
8 packets	32 cars + 16 trains

   $32 + 16 = 48$, so Andy has 48 stickers in total.

   I can solve the problem another way using scaling.

b) This bar model shows that there are 50 more car stickers.

   train stickers / car stickers | 25 | 25 | 25 | 25 | ? packets

   The extra 50 stickers are equal to 2 parts of the car stickers bar.
   Each part represents 25 so there are 25 packets of stickers in each box.

93

PUPIL TEXTBOOK 6C PAGE 93

Think together

WAYS OF WORKING Whole class teacher led (I do, We do, You do)

ASK

- Question **1** a): *You know that 1 cm on the sticker represents 2·5 m. How does this help?*
- Question **1** b): *Which operation will you need to use?*
- Question **2**: *How many grams of fruit are needed for 1 spoon of honey? … 2 spoons? … 8 spoons?*
- Question **3**: *How many squares is the diameter of the large circle compared to the small circle? How can you describe this as a ratio?*
- Question **4**: *What is 4·8 m in centimetres? How many times will the 160 cm pattern be repeated in 480 cm? How can you find out?*

IN FOCUS These questions are designed to show ratio in different contexts: scales, recipes and measurement, geometry. For each part of question **1**, children need to work out whether they should multiply or divide. In question **2**, children may notice that double 240 g is 480 g and only another 120 g (half of 240 g) is needed to total 600 g. Therefore, the amount of honey needed is 8 spoons (double 4 spoons) plus 2 spoons (half of 4 spoons), which is 10 spoons. Alternatively, some children may choose to find the unitary value (i.e. 1 spoon for 60 g) and then divide 600 g by 60.

STRENGTHEN For question **1**, look at scaling the length of the train on the sticker to its real measurement, for example:
1 cm   2·5 m
2 cm   5 m
4 cm   10 m etc.

DEEPEN For question **3**, discuss how the relationship can also be described as 'the diameter of the small circle is $\frac{2}{5}$ of the diameter of the large circle' or 'the large circle is $\frac{5}{2}$ or $2\frac{1}{2}$ times the diameter of the small circle'.

For question **4**, ask children to work out the number of each size slab for different lengths of path, for example a 9·6 m path. Then ask questions based on the number of slabs, for example: *The same pattern is used for another path. Toshi and Sofia use 56 small slabs. How long is the path? How many large slabs do they use?*

ASSESSMENT CHECKPOINT Use question **1** to assess whether children recognise when they need to multiply and when they need to divide to solve a ratio problem. Use questions **1**, **2** and **4** to assess whether they can use what they know about ratio to solve problems involving units of measurement. Use question **4** to assess whether they can solve ratio problems that involve more than one step.

ANSWERS

Question **1** a): The train is 15 m long in real life.

Question **1** b): The sticker is 8 cm long.

Question **2**: 10 spoons of honey are needed for 600 g of fruit.

Question **3**: a : b = 2 : 5

Question **4**: They use 24 small rectangular slabs and 9 large square slabs.

PUPIL TEXTBOOK 6C PAGE 94

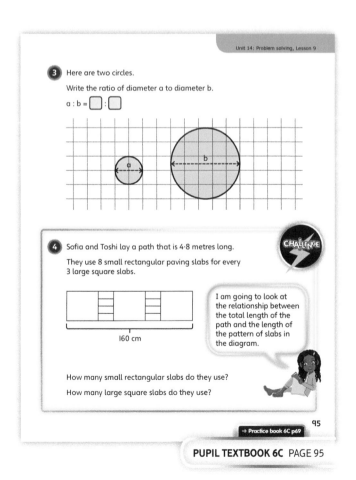

PUPIL TEXTBOOK 6C PAGE 95

Practice

WAYS OF WORKING Independent thinking

IN FOCUS Question ❶ has been chosen to explore proportion. Children should notice that proportions are written as fractions and show a part compared to the whole, for example 3 out of 8 so $\frac{3}{8}$.

Question ❷ requires children to scale a recipe for 6 cakes. In part b) they need to scale the recipe for 15 cakes; 15 is not a multiple of 6, so they could think about 15 as 12 + 3 (a multiple of 6 plus half of 6).

In question ❺, children must express a proportion as a ratio. Look for children who show the ratio as 3 boys to every 8 girls because they have incorrectly interpreted the meaning of the fraction. There are 8 parts in the whole, so if boys represent 3 parts, girls must represent 5 parts.

STRENGTHEN For question ❺, use a stick of 8 cubes to represent the fraction of boys, for example 3 yellow cubes and 5 red. Discuss what the stick is showing: 8 equal parts and 3 of them represent the boys. Ask children to explain what the other 5 cubes represent. Agree that the stick shows that there are 3 boys for every 5 girls.

DEEPEN Look at different strategies for solving question ❷ b): for example, finding the ingredients for 1 cake (unitary value) and then multiplying by 15; finding the ingredients for 3 cakes by halving the ingredients for 6 cakes and then multiplying by 5 as 5 × 3 = 15; using doubling for 12 cakes and halving for 3, then adding.

ASSESSMENT CHECKPOINT Use questions ❶ and ❷ to check whether children can use scaling to solve ratio problems. Use questions ❶ and ❹ to assess whether children can interpret a proportion. Use question ❸ to assess whether children can interpret a ratio shown in the context of geometry and represent it using the colon notation (:). Check whether children recognise when a ratio can be shown in its simplest form, for example 3 : 1 rather than 9 : 3.

ANSWERS Answers for the **Practice** part of the lesson appear in the separate **Practice and Reflect answer guide**.

Reflect

WAYS OF WORKING Independent thinking

IN FOCUS Children are required to show that they understand how to solve problems involving ratio. Encourage them to show the correct way to write a ratio using a colon and explain what it means.

ASSESSMENT CHECKPOINT Check that children can clearly explain the steps they need to take to solve the problem. If they can do this, it is likely they have mastered the topic.

ANSWERS Answers for the **Reflect** part of the lesson appear in the separate **Practice and Reflect answer guide**.

After the lesson ⏸

- Can children solve a range of different ratio problems, applying multiplication or division facts as required?
- Can they explain how scaling can be used to solve ratio problems, explaining how the relationship stays the same?
- Can children interpret a fraction as a proportion, recognising that the denominator describes the total number of equal parts? Can they describe it as a ratio?

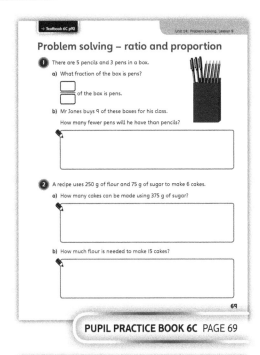

PUPIL PRACTICE BOOK 6C PAGE 69

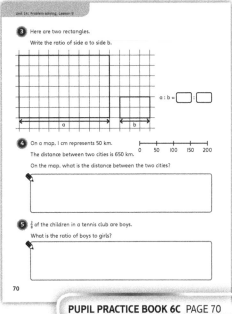

PUPIL PRACTICE BOOK 6C PAGE 70

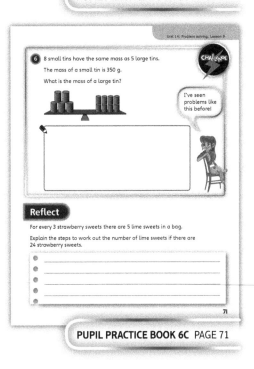

PUPIL PRACTICE BOOK 6C PAGE 71

127

Problem solving – time ❶

Learning focus

In this lesson, children will calculate time intervals and convert between units of time to solve problems. They will interpret and make use of number lines as time lines.

Small steps

→ Previous step: Problem solving – ratio and proportion
→ **This step: Problem solving – time (1)**
→ Next step: Problem solving – time (2)

NATIONAL CURRICULUM LINKS

Year 6 Measurement

Use, read, write and convert between standard units, converting measurements of length, mass, volume and time from a smaller unit of measure to a larger unit, and vice versa, using decimal notation to up to three decimal places.

ASSESSING MASTERY

Children can solve a range of problems using time conversions. They can calculate an interval or use a given interval to identify a specific time.

COMMON MISCONCEPTIONS

When calculating time intervals, children may revert to familiar methods of adding and subtracting quantities, which are incorrect when working with time. Look together at a range of time lines, counting on in hours and minutes and counting up or back to the next or previous hour. Ask:
• *What is the time now? How many minutes have passed? What was the time 40 minutes ago?*

STRENGTHENING UNDERSTANDING

Use a geared clock with a time line to show the jumps moving from one time to the next on the time line. Model a problem that involves times on a 24-hour clock.

GOING DEEPER

Look at calculating time intervals as part of line graphs. Ask children to explain why the processes are the same as those used within the lesson.

KEY LANGUAGE

In lesson: hour, minute, day, week, month, am, pm, time line

Other language to be used by the teacher: second, 24-hour clock, 12-hour clock

STRUCTURES AND REPRESENTATIONS

number line, time line, calendar

RESOURCES

Optional: geared clock, calendar

 In the eTextbook of this lesson, you will find interactive links to a selection of teaching tools.

Before you teach

• Can children convert between hours and minutes?
• Can they represent or calculate an interval using a number line?
• Can they convert between the 12-hour and 24-hour clock?

Discover

WAYS OF WORKING Pair work

ASK

- Question ❶ a): *What do you need to do first?*
- Question ❶ a): *Why do you need to know about the dentist's 20-minute breaks in the morning and afternoon?*
- Question ❶ b): *How many weeks is the same as 28 days?*
- Question ❶ b): *Why do you need to know the number of days in April?*

IN FOCUS Question ❶ a) requires children to reason about the number of 15-minute appointments in the morning and afternoon sessions. They need to calculate time intervals and make allowances for the dentist's 20-minute breaks. Question ❶ b) has been chosen as children will need to apply several known facts and skills: the number of days in a week, the number of days in April, and counting backwards over a month boundary.

PRACTICAL TIPS Use a calendar to explore counting over month boundaries and showing the same count of weeks or days on a number line.

ANSWERS

Question ❶ a): 3 more appointments can be made in the afternoon than in the morning.

Question ❶ b): The date of the previous dentist clinic was 14 April.

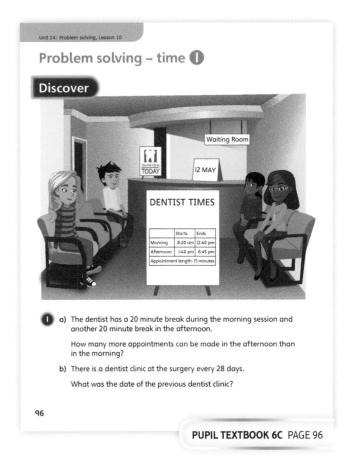

Problem solving – time ❶

Discover

❶ a) The dentist has a 20 minute break during the morning session and another 20 minute break in the afternoon.

How many more appointments can be made in the afternoon than in the morning?

b) There is a dentist clinic at the surgery every 28 days.

What was the date of the previous dentist clinic?

96

PUPIL TEXTBOOK 6C PAGE 96

Share

WAYS OF WORKING Whole class teacher led

ASK

- Question ❶ a): *How has the time line been used to calculate time intervals? What jumps can you see? Could you have made different jumps and still calculated the intervals as 4 hours 20 minutes and 5 hours 5 minutes?*
- Question ❶ a): *Can you tell me a different way to solve the problem?*
- Question ❶ b): *How do you know that 14 April and 12 May are both on the same day of the week?*

IN FOCUS Number lines (referred to as time lines) have been used to solve both problems. In question ❶ a), children are given the start and end times and must calculate a time interval. In question ❶ b), children are given an end date and a time interval, and must calculate a start date. Use a calendar to support children counting back in weeks from May into April.

STRENGTHEN For question ❶ a) discuss why they do not need to work out the number of 15-minute sessions in 4 hours and again in 4 hours 45 minutes to find the difference. Although this is a credible method, it takes much longer.

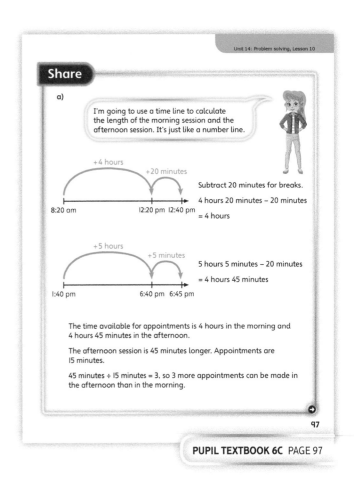

Share

a)

I'm going to use a time line to calculate the length of the morning session and the afternoon session. It's just like a number line.

Subtract 20 minutes for breaks.
4 hours 20 minutes – 20 minutes
= 4 hours

5 hours 5 minutes – 20 minutes
= 4 hours 45 minutes

The time available for appointments is 4 hours in the morning and 4 hours 45 minutes in the afternoon.

The afternoon session is 45 minutes longer. Appointments are 15 minutes.

45 minutes ÷ 15 minutes = 3, so 3 more appointments can be made in the afternoon than in the morning.

97

PUPIL TEXTBOOK 6C PAGE 97

Think together

Whole class teacher led (I do, We do, You do)

ASK

• Question ❶ a): *What time is Mr Nash's appointment? When does Miss Ana's appointment end? How can you use this information?*
• Question ❷: *How many minutes did Jamilla take to run her laps?*
• Question ❷: *What do you notice about the number of laps completed by Max compared with the number completed by Jamilla?*
• Question ❸: *How can you use a number line to help?*
• Question ❹: *Why might it be useful to make a timetable for each bus?*

IN FOCUS In question ❶, children need to interpret a time line to answer two different problems relating to intervals of time. Not all information is given on the time line so they will need to use what they know about the length of each appointment.

Question ❸ requires children to calculate a time interval in months and then multiply this by the cost of electricity per month. Children may forget to carry out the second step of the problem.

Question ❹ has been chosen so that children work with two different sets of information to find the next time when the bus departures coincide. Ash prompts them to think about other times in the day when the buses should leave together.

STRENGTHEN Remind children to use time lines to help solve the problems. Explore the effect of using different jumps on the time line, encouraging children to work with jumps that are manageable for them, breaking numbers across boundaries as appropriate to avoid errors.

DEEPEN For question ❹ ask children to reason about other times in the day when the buses depart at the same time. Challenge them to identify any patterns that could help.

ASSESSMENT CHECKPOINT Use question ❶ to assess whether children can interpret and use a time line. Use question ❷ to assess whether children look for relationships within the given information to help them. Check that they can work with the 24-hour clock notation and that they can convert between hours and minutes. Use question ❸ to assess whether children can work with units of months and years, recognising that there are 12 months in each year.

ANSWERS

Question ❶ a): They spend 55 minutes at the surgery.

Question ❶ b): Mr Wye leaves the surgery at 11:50 am.

Question ❷: Jamilla is faster.

Question ❸: They spend £10,780 in total.

Question ❹: The buses will next depart together at 11:45 am.

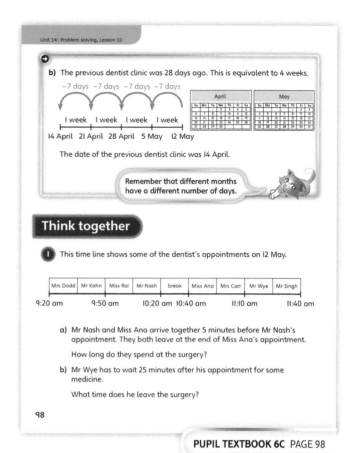

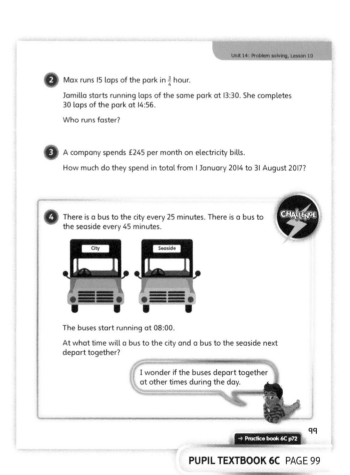

Practice

WAYS OF WORKING Independent thinking

IN FOCUS Question **1** a) requires children to convert between 12-hour and 24-hour notation. Children may mistakenly record the answer as 4 hours 25 minutes by misinterpreting 18:45 as 8:45 pm. Question **3** is a two-step problem: children must first find the length of time for which Olivia walked and then calculate the amount of money raised.

Question **4** has been designed to allow children to use different strategies to find 12 intervals of 45 minutes, for example: multiplying 45 by 12 and then dividing by 60 to find the number of hours; rounding 45 minutes to 1 hour and then subtracting 12 lots of 15 minutes from 12 hours; or looking at 6 lots of $1\frac{1}{2}$ hours or 3 lots of 3 hours. Question **5** requires another conversion, but this time from hours to days. Children will also need to use knowledge of the calendar to find when the puppy was born.

STRENGTHEN For question **2** encourage children to use a number line as a time line and mark the different appointments and breaks for Tuesday. They can then add this to the number of appointments on Wednesday to work out the total.

DEEPEN Ask children to calculate how many weeks/minutes/seconds the puppy in question **5** has been alive for. Then ask them to work out how old it will be on the upcoming New Year's Eve.

ASSESSMENT CHECKPOINT Use questions **1** and **2** to assess whether children can calculate and work flexibly with time intervals. Use questions **4** and **5** to assess whether children can accurately convert between units of time. Use question **4** to check that children understand how to compare a duration of minutes with a fraction of a day.

ANSWERS Answers for the **Practice** part of the lesson appear in the separate **Practice and Reflect answer guide**.

Reflect

WAYS OF WORKING Independent thinking

IN FOCUS Children first need to work out a time, given the starting time and a time interval. They then need to write this answer in three ways: using the 12-hour and 24-hour clocks and in words. They should notice that the time is in the evening rather than the morning.

ASSESSMENT CHECKPOINT Check that children can add a time interval to a given time, crossing the hour boundary correctly. Check that they can write the time using the 12-hour and 24-hour clock notation, explaining how to convert from one to the other. Check that they correctly use pm to show an evening time in 12-hour clock notation.

ANSWERS Answers for the **Reflect** part of the lesson appear in the separate **Practice and Reflect answer guide**.

After the lesson ⏸

- Can children interpret time lines to help work with and calculate time intervals?
- Can they confidently convert between different units of time, including between 12-hour and 24-hour clock notation?
- Can they work with time to solve a range of problems?

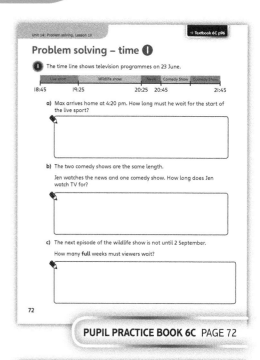

PUPIL PRACTICE BOOK 6C PAGE 72

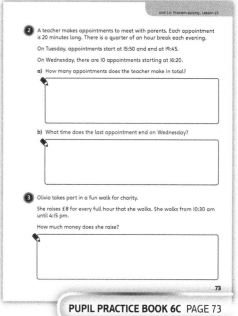

PUPIL PRACTICE BOOK 6C PAGE 73

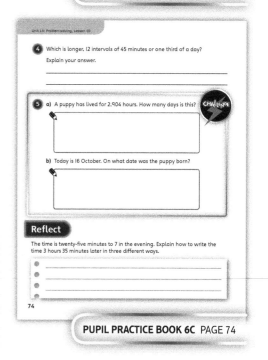

PUPIL PRACTICE BOOK 6C PAGE 74

Problem solving – time ②

Learning focus

In this lesson, children will solve more complex problems about time involving two or more steps. They will convert between units of time to calculate and compare. They will also draw on understanding of timetables, the number line, measurement and statistics.

Small steps

→ Previous step: Problem solving – time (1)
→ **This step: Problem solving – time (2)**
→ Next step: Problem solving – position and direction

NATIONAL CURRICULUM LINKS

Year 6 Measurement

Use, read, write and convert between standard units, converting measurements of length, mass, volume and time from a smaller unit of measure to a larger unit, and vice versa, using decimal notation to up to three decimal places.

ASSESSING MASTERY

Children can solve a set of contextualised problems that involve several steps. They can draw on time conversions to interpret and work with timetables, line graphs and other representations.

COMMON MISCONCEPTIONS

Children may fail to check the notation (12-hour or 24-hour) that has been used to represent a time. They should recognise that timetables usually use 24-hour notation, understanding why this is the case. Similarly, they may not check units before comparing. Ask:

- *Do these times include am/pm? What does that tell you?*
- *What do you need to do before comparing these times?*

STRENGTHENING UNDERSTANDING

Model using a number line to calculate a time interval. Discuss how the axis on a time graph can be seen as a number line and interpreted in the same way.

GOING DEEPER

Look at a range of problems involving time. Ask children to sort them into those that require a time conversion and those that do not. Include some that require conversion between 12- and 24-hour times, but not between units of time.

KEY LANGUAGE

In lesson: hour, minute, 24-hour time, pm

Other language to be used by the teacher: second, 12-hour time, am

STRUCTURES AND REPRESENTATIONS

number line, timetable, line graph

 In the eTextbook of this lesson, you will find interactive links to a selection of teaching tools.

Before you teach

- Can children convert between 12- and 24-hour times?
- Can they represent or calculate a time interval using a number line?
- Can they explain why timetables usually use the 24-hour clock?

Discover

WAYS OF WORKING Pair work

ASK

- Question **1** a): *Sofia has just missed a train. How many minutes before 11:43 did this train depart?*
- Question **1** a): *What time train must she catch now? How do you know that she will arrive in Stanton in time?*
- Question **1** b): *What steps do you need to take to solve this problem?*
- Question **1** b): *How do you know that the length of the train journey from Winbeech to Stanton is always the same?*
- Question **1** b): *How many minutes earlier does the bus arrive in Stanton than the train?*

IN FOCUS Children are required to interpret a train timetable, using given information to help make decisions and to calculate. Both questions involve times after midday so children may wish to convert the times to the 12-hour clock to make sense of the problem, particularly as Sofia uses this notation to give the time she needs to be in Stanton. In part b) children may forget to complete the final step, giving the answer as 2 hours 16 minutes; alternatively, they may calculate the departure time based on the arrival time of the train, rather than the bus.

PRACTICAL TIPS Draw number lines to help children to work with time intervals. Remind them that they can use number lines to count on or to count back. Model the first train in the timetable on a time line.

ANSWERS

Question **1** a): Sofia will have to wait 22 minutes for her train.

Question **1** b): The bus leaves Winbeech at 10:54.

Share

WAYS OF WORKING Whole class teacher led

ASK

- Question **1** a): *Is 13:25 the same as 3:25 pm? Why not?*
- Question **1** a): *Why is the first jump on the time line only 17 minutes?*
- Question **1** b): *On the time line, why has 16 minutes been partitioned into 10-minute and 6-minute jumps?*

IN FOCUS Question **1** a) has been chosen so children first carry out a straightforward time conversion and calculation of a time interval. Question **1** b) is more complex as it requires several steps. Both parts have been approached using time lines, partitioning time intervals as necessary to count across an hour boundary.

STRENGTHEN Look together at partitioning across hour boundaries to help calculate accurately. Discuss how partitioning can be used to count on or back over a boundary.

DEEPEN Ask children to explain how much earlier Sofia would have needed to arrive at Winbeech to catch the 10:54 bus.

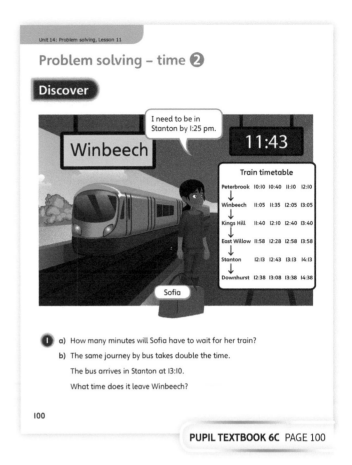

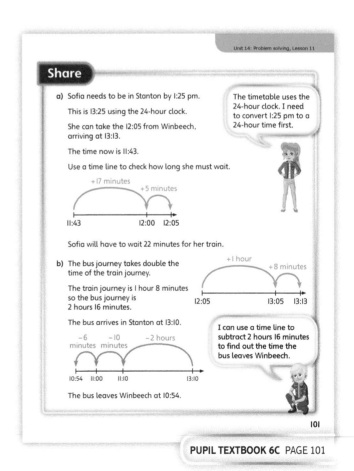

133

Think together

Whole class teacher led (I do, We do, You do)

ASK

- Question **1**: *There is a lot of information here. What do you need to find out first? Why?*
- Question **2** a): *Why do you need to check the length of each lesson before calculating? How can you calculate this?*
- Question **3** b): *At what time did the number of visitors reach 1,000? At what time did the number of visitors drop again to under 1,000? How does this help?*
- Question **4**: *What do you notice about the relationship between Holly and Toshi's times?*

IN FOCUS Question **2** features a different structure for a timetable. For part b), children can consider different strategies to calculate, for example: finding the total time available for hire each day and working out the difference; or comparing the time available each day by looking at what is the same and what is different.

For question **4**, children may think that Toshi was faster because he swam for longer or Holly was faster because she swam lengths. The numbers have been chosen so children can explore the relationship between the times to reason about who was faster, working out how far they each swam in 45 minutes.

STRENGTHEN For question **1**, encourage children to think about the number of 20-minute intervals in an hour and the number in 40 minutes. Consider strategies for calculating 5 × £2·95, for example, rounding to £3 and then adjusting, or multiplying by 10 (£29·50) and then halving (£14·75).

DEEPEN For question **4**, ask children to look at different strategies, for example: for Toshi, find 80 × 16 for $1\frac{1}{2}$ hours and then divide by 2 to compare the same amount of time with Holly; or halve 80 widths in $1\frac{1}{2}$ hours to 40 widths in 45 minutes and then calculate 40 × 16 metres. They could also reason about other relationships, for example a length of the pool is 3 m longer than two widths of the pool; the number of widths swum by Toshi is just over 4 times the number of lengths swum by Holly, etc.

ASSESSMENT CHECKPOINT Use questions **1** and **4** to assess whether children can solve more complex multi-step problems. Use questions **2** and **4** to assess whether children look for relationships within the given information to help them. Use question **3** to assess whether children can interpret a scale showing measurement and can identify a specific time or calculate a time interval using the scale.

ANSWERS

Question **1**: They paid £19·95 together in total.

Question **2** a): The courts are used for lessons for 6 hours and 45 minutes..

Question **2** b): The courts are available 3 hours longer on Saturday.

Question **3** a): There were 750 visitors at 08:30 and 12:00.

Question **3** b): There were 1,000 or more visitors at the sports centre for 135 minutes.

Question **4**: Toshi is faster.

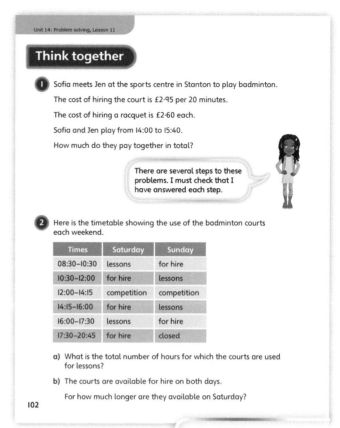

PUPIL TEXTBOOK 6C PAGE 102

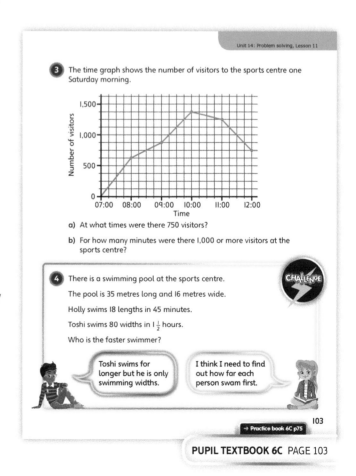

PUPIL TEXTBOOK 6C PAGE 103

Practice

WAYS OF WORKING Independent thinking

IN FOCUS Question ❶ provides an opportunity for children to independently interpret a timetable. The buses do not always stop at all of the stations so children should think carefully before calculating each time. For part a), some children may notice that both buses leave at 12 minutes past the hour but the 15:12 bus arrives 45 minutes after the hour compared with 42 minutes past for the 16:12.

Question ❸ has been designed to provide another opportunity for children to interpret scales on a line graph. They must reason about the 'story' of the graph to find when Mr Lopez stopped for lunch.

STRENGTHEN For question ❸, encourage children to tell the story of the graph to a partner, explaining what was happening at different intervals and how they know.

DEEPEN For question ❸, ask children to describe Mr Lopez's journey home and show this on a line graph. Remind them that the line will go down again as he gets nearer home.

ASSESSMENT CHECKPOINT Use questions ❶ and ❷ to assess whether children can complete multi-step problems with time intervals. Use question ❸ to assess whether children can work with two different scales on a line graph.

ANSWERS Answers for the **Practice** part of the lesson appear in the separate **Practice and Reflect answer guide**.

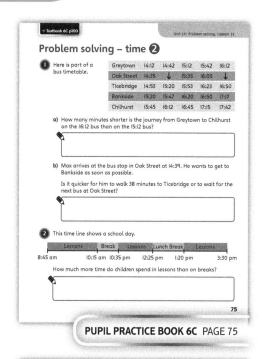

PUPIL PRACTICE BOOK 6C PAGE 75

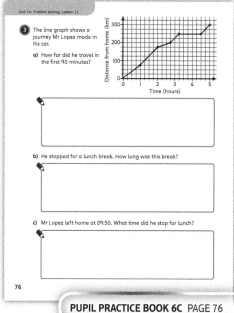

PUPIL PRACTICE BOOK 6C PAGE 76

Reflect

WAYS OF WORKING Pair work

IN FOCUS Children are required to explain the mistake Lexi has made when calculating what time it will be in 1 hour 55 minutes. They should notice that she has not added 55 minutes to 45 minutes correctly. 55 minutes is only 5 minutes less than an hour, so the time will be nearly 2 hours later.

ASSESSMENT CHECKPOINT Check that children understand the 24-hour clock; that 12.45 is quarter to 1.

ANSWERS Answers for the **Reflect** part of the lesson appear in the separate **Practice and Reflect answer guide**.

After the lesson ⏸

- Can children work with time and other aspects of measurement to solve a range of multi-step problems?
- Can they interpret time lines as part of a line graph, reading the scale accurately and calculating intervals?
- Can they explain the relationship they may find between given numbers or measurements and how this can be used to help solve the problem?

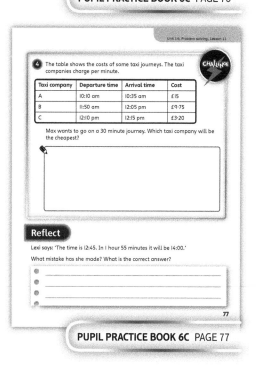

PUPIL PRACTICE BOOK 6C PAGE 77

Problem solving – position and direction

Learning focus

In this lesson, children will solve problems using coordinates in all four quadrants. They will apply their knowledge of the properties of shapes to reason about the coordinates of an unlabelled or unknown vertex, including following a translation or reflection. They will also find half-way points, using the structure of the grid.

Small steps

→ Previous step: Problem solving – time (2)
→ **This step: Problem solving – position and direction**
→ Next step: Problem solving – properties of shapes (1)

NATIONAL CURRICULUM LINKS

Year 6 Geometry – Position and Direction

Describe positions on the full coordinate grid (all four quadrants).

ASSESSING MASTERY

Children can identify and use coordinates in all four quadrants. They can use the structure of the grid to reason about plotted sequences, vertices of shapes or inside shapes. They can use reflections and translations.

COMMON MISCONCEPTIONS

Children may not make the link between the axes and the number line as it crosses 0, recognising the position of negative values in relation to 0 (for example, ⁻20 is smaller than ⁻2 so it is further away from 0). Ask:
• *Can you count down the x-axis from 5? What happens when you reach 0? What is the next number?*

STRENGTHENING UNDERSTANDING

Children often find it more difficult to identify coordinates on a blank grid with few or no labels on the axes. Draw axes and a shape on the board, labelling the vertices. Ask children to take turns to add labels to the axes, explaining how they know these values.

GOING DEEPER

Give children a range of questions that require them to think flexibly about properties of shape so that they have to reason to a deeper level about the coordinates of vertices following a transformation – for example: a shape shown in a more unusual orientation; a reflection where the mirror line goes through the shape.

KEY LANGUAGE

In lesson: coordinates, x-axis, y-axis, reflected, translated, mirror line, vertex, vertices, square, rectangle, parallelogram, isosceles

Other language to be used by the teacher: axes, rhombus, trapezium, half-way

STRUCTURES AND REPRESENTATIONS

coordinate grid

RESOURCES

Optional: squared paper, set squares or protractors, tracing paper

 In the eTextbook of this lesson, you will find interactive links to a selection of teaching tools.

Before you teach

• Can children plot or identify coordinates in all four quadrants?
• Can they explain what is the same and what is different about a shape following a reflection?
• Can they explain what is the same and what is different about a shape following a translation?

Discover

Unit 14: Problem solving, Lesson 12

WAYS OF WORKING Pair work

ASK

- Question ① a): *How can you use what you know about the coordinates (4, 15) to help you find the x-coordinate for vertex A?*
- Question ① a): *Which coordinate can you use to help you find out about the y-coordinate for vertex A? Why?*
- Question ① b): *What can you tell me about reflecting a shape? What stays the same and what changes?*
- Question ① b): *What is the length and width of the original rectangle? How does this help?*

IN FOCUS Children must reason about the coordinates of the vertices of a rectangle before and after a reflection. In question ① b), children need to use the fact that the reflected rectangle is the same size as the original rectangle.

PRACTICAL TIPS Draw the diagram on the board and annotate the coordinate grid. Use the given coordinates to add labels on the axes, for example 4, 10 and 18 on the x-axis.

ANSWERS

Question ① a): Vertex A is (4, 5). Vertex B is (10, 15).

Question ① b): (24, 15), (18, 5), (24, 5)

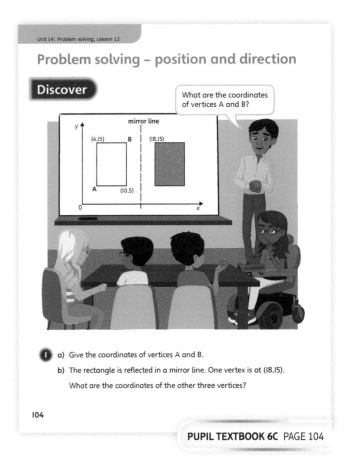

Problem solving – position and direction

Discover

What are the coordinates of vertices A and B?

① a) Give the coordinates of vertices A and B.

b) The rectangle is reflected in a mirror line. One vertex is at (18,15). What are the coordinates of the other three vertices?

104

PUPIL TEXTBOOK 6C PAGE 104

Share

WAYS OF WORKING Whole class teacher led

ASK

- Question ① a): *Why is it important to know about the properties of a rectangle here?*
- Question ① a): *Why has the grid been annotated with lines that pass through the x- and y-axes?*
- Question ① b): *How do you know that the y-coordinates must stay the same for the reflected vertices?*
- Question ① b): *Is there another way you could find the vertices of the reflected rectangle?*

IN FOCUS Question ① a) has been chosen so that children can see how coordinate problems can be solved even when the grid and labels are missing, by using the structure of the grid. Question ① b) shows how to apply understanding of the properties of a rectangle and of a reflection. Some children may suggest an alternative strategy of reflecting each vertex of the rectangle in the mirror line. They need to remember that the reflection is the same distance from the mirror line as the original shape.

STRENGTHEN Revisit reflections, reminding children that the reflection is the same size and shape as the original but is 'flipped' – this is not obvious here so it is useful to label the reflected vertices A and B as A^1 (24, 5) and B^1 (18, 15) to show this. Model reflections of scalene triangles to emphasise the properties of reflection. Ensure children understand that the reflection is the same distance from the mirror line as the original shape.

DEEPEN Ask children to explain where the mirror line passes through the x-axis, using the grid to help them.

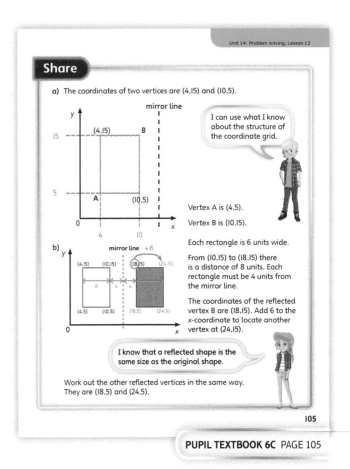

Share

a) The coordinates of two vertices are (4,15) and (10,5).

I can use what I know about the structure of the coordinate grid.

Vertex A is (4,5).
Vertex B is (10,15).

Each rectangle is 6 units wide.

From (10,15) to (18,15) there is a distance of 8 units. Each rectangle must be 4 units from the mirror line.

The coordinates of the reflected vertex B are (18,15). Add 6 to the x-coordinate to locate another vertex at (24,15).

I know that a reflected shape is the same size as the original shape.

Work out the other reflected vertices in the same way. They are (18,5) and (24,5).

105

PUPIL TEXTBOOK 6C PAGE 105

Think together

WAYS OF WORKING Whole class teacher led (I do, We do, You do)

ASK

- Question **1** a): *What do you know about the properties of an isosceles triangle? How does this help?*
- Question **2**: *How can you work out the x-coordinate for point P by using what you know about the x-coordinates for N and S?*
- Question **3** b): *What do you know about a shape following a translation?*
- Question **4** a): *You know the length of one side of the square. How does this help you to reason about the possible positions of the other vertices?*

IN FOCUS Question **2** has been chosen to allow children to reason about given information, spotting patterns in the linear sequence. This includes recognising that point N must have the coordinates (0, 0) even though it is not labelled. Question **3** b) uses a translation, requiring children to know that the translated parallelogram will be the same size, shape and orientation as the original. For question **4** b), children need to think about all possible solutions for part a), using reasoning skills to explain their answer without drawing all the squares.

STRENGTHEN Provide children with squared paper so they can draw diagrams to check their solutions. For question **3** a), discuss why it is important to know the length of the horizontal sides to find the coordinate of the fourth vertex.

DEEPEN For question **4**, ask children to reason about coordinates that will not be in any of the squares. Ask them to explain why no sets of coordinates can be inside more than one square (although some of the vertices are shared).

ASSESSMENT CHECKPOINT Use questions **1** and **3** to assess whether children can reason about shapes following a reflection or translation. Use questions **1**, **3** and **4** to assess whether they can apply knowledge of the properties of shapes to reason about coordinates. Use question **2** to assess whether they look for relationships within the information provided.

ANSWERS

Question **1** a): The other two vertices are (⁻14, 9) and (⁻10, 19).

Question **1** b): A (6, 9), B (10, 19), C (14, 9)

Question **2**: P (20, 12), T (60, 36)

Question **3** a): D (6, ⁻6)

Question **3** b): The new coordinates of vertex C are (⁻4, ⁻1).

Question **4** a): (10, 15), (15, 15), (15, 10); (5, 10), (5, 15), (10, 15); (5, 10), (5, 5), (10, 5); (15, 10), (15, 5), (10, 5)

Question **4** b): The coordinates (8, 12) will only be inside the square with vertices (10, 10), (5, 10), (5, 15) and (10, 15). It cannot be inside any other squares with x-coordinates that are 10 or more. It cannot be inside any other squares with y-coordinates that are 10 or less.

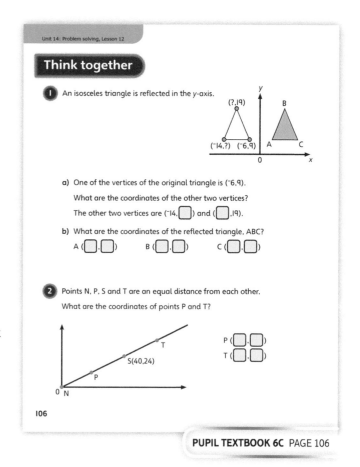

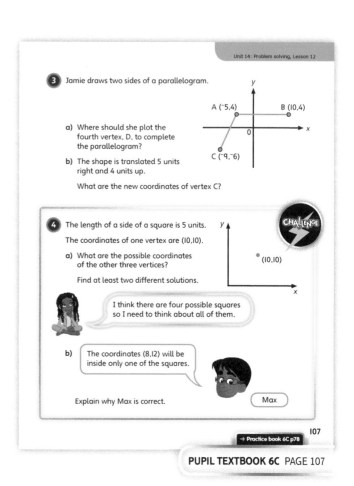

138

Practice

WAYS OF WORKING Independent thinking

IN FOCUS The line in question ❶ has been chosen so that children need to think about positive and negative values for the *x*-coordinates. In question ❸, the point where the mirror line passes through the *y*-axis is not labelled, so children must look at the information given and use it to make decisions. For example, the reflection of vertex (32, 22) is at (32, 14); since the mirror line is half-way between the *y*-coordinates 22 and 14, it must have the *y*-value 18.

Question ❹ requires children to reason about four possibilities for a missing vertex, drawing on their understanding of right-angled triangles. They may find it useful to use a set square, a protractor or tracing paper to reason about the triangles that are not immediately obvious, for example tracing one of these triangles and repositioning it on the grid.

STRENGTHEN For question ❸ c), encourage children to estimate and draw the position of each of the coordinates to find the pair that is inside the shape. Then discuss how they can reason about this, thinking about how far along each axis the vertices of the reflected shape are and how this can help them to discard coordinates that do not fit in these ranges. Encourage them to reason about any other coordinates that will be inside the shape.

DEEPEN For question ❹, ask children to investigate the different positions of the third vertex for an isosceles triangle.

ASSESSMENT CHECKPOINT Use question ❶ to assess whether children can use the structure of the coordinate grid to reason about points on a straight line. Use question ❷ to assess whether they can complete a reflection and give the new coordinates. Use questions ❸ and ❹ to assess whether children can use knowledge of the properties of shape to solve problems.

ANSWERS Answers for the **Practice** part of the lesson appear in the separate **Practice and Reflect answer guide**.

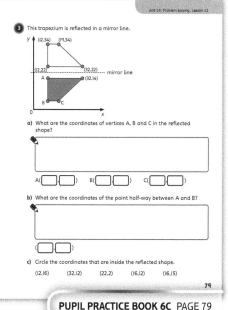

PUPIL PRACTICE BOOK 6C PAGE 78

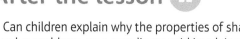

PUPIL PRACTICE BOOK 6C PAGE 79

Reflect

WAYS OF WORKING Independent thinking

IN FOCUS Children are required to explain how to find the half-way point between two coordinates. Some children may choose to draw the points on a coordinate grid, while others sketch the axes and points.

ASSESSMENT CHECKPOINT Ensure children notice that the two given points have the same *x*-coordinate, so the half-way point must also have the same *x*-value.

ANSWERS Answers for the **Reflect** part of the lesson appear in the separate **Practice and Reflect answer guide**.

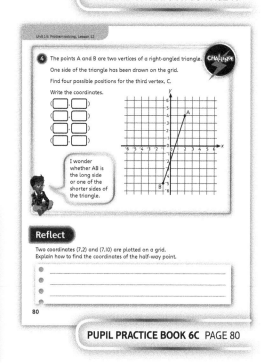

PUPIL PRACTICE BOOK 6C PAGE 80

After the lesson ⏸

- Can children explain why the properties of shapes help them to solve problems on a coordinate grid involving an unknown vertex or a transformation?
- Can they confidently plot or identify a given coordinate given information and the structure of the grid?
- Can they find half-way points between two given coordinates?

Problem solving – properties of shapes ❶

Learning focus

In this lesson, children will use knowledge of the notation used to label a right angle, the angle sum of triangles and quadrilaterals, angles on a straight line or at a point and vertically opposite angles to reason about missing angles.

Small steps

→ Previous step: Problem solving – position and direction
→ **This step: Problem solving – properties of shapes (1)**
→ Next step: Problem solving – properties of shapes (2)

NATIONAL CURRICULUM LINKS

Year 6 Geometry – Properties of Shapes
• Recognise angles where they meet at a point, are on a straight line, or are vertically opposite, and find missing angles.
• Compare and classify geometric shapes based on their properties and sizes and find unknown angles in any triangles, quadrilaterals, and regular polygons.

ASSESSING MASTERY

Children can flexibly apply what they know about interior angles in shapes to help find missing values. They can explain and use what they know about the sum of angles on a straight line or at a point to solve problems.

COMMON MISCONCEPTIONS

Children may think that they always need to use a protractor to solve missing angle problems. Remind them that diagrams are not always drawn to scale. Ask:
• *What does 'Not drawn to scale' mean? What information does the diagram show? What angle facts do you know about triangles/ quadrilaterals/straight lines/etc.?*

You could look at some examples where there is not sufficient information and a protractor must be used.

STRENGTHENING UNDERSTANDING

Look together at angles that meet at a point or on a straight line. Relate this to two right angles on a straight line and to four right angles meeting at a point. Label each of the right angles. Discuss how to use the right angles to prove the angle sum on a straight line and at a point.

GOING DEEPER

Encourage children to reason about and explore different quadrilaterals. Ask them to draw a quadrilateral with:
• three obtuse angles and one acute angle
• two obtuse angles and two acute angles
• three acute angles and one obtuse angle.

Ask them to explain why a quadrilateral cannot have four obtuse angles or four acute angles.

KEY LANGUAGE

In lesson: angle, right angle, straight line, point, obtuse, acute, isosceles, scalene

Other language used by the teacher: sum of interior angles, vertically opposite

RESOURCES

Optional: protractors

 In the eTextbook of this lesson, you will find interactive links to a selection of teaching tools.

Before you teach

• Can children recall the sum of the interior angles in a triangle or quadrilateral?
• Can they find the missing angle on a straight line when they know the other angles?
• Can they use properties of shape to reason about the size of angles?

Discover

Unit 14: Problem solving, Lesson 13

WAYS OF WORKING Pair work

ASK

- Question ❶ a): *You know that the triangle is isosceles. How does this help?*
- Question ❶ a): *How do you know that one of the angles in the shaded triangle makes a right angle with angle a? How can you use this information to calculate the size of angle a?*
- Question ❶ b): *How can you estimate the size of angle b? Is it acute or obtuse?*
- Question ❶ b): *You don't know the size of any of the angles on the straight line with b. How can you find out their sizes?*

IN FOCUS Children are required to draw on knowledge of the sum of the interior angles in a triangle and to use what they know about right angles or angles that meet on a straight line. Children should recognise that the two unlabelled angles in the isosceles triangle must be equal. Some children may forget that the triangle is drawn inside a rectangle, whose interior angles are all 90°.

PRACTICAL TIPS Encourage children to annotate diagrams with information they know and to add angles as they work them out. This will help them to work towards the solution.

ANSWERS

Question ❶ a): Angle a is 58°.

Question ❶ b): Angle b is 116°.

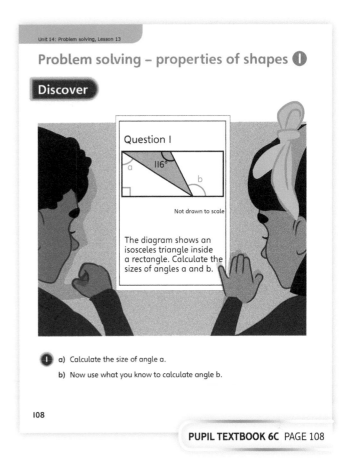

Problem solving – properties of shapes ❶

Discover

Question 1

116°

Not drawn to scale

The diagram shows an isosceles triangle inside a rectangle. Calculate the sizes of angles a and b.

❶ a) Calculate the size of angle a.

b) Now use what you know to calculate angle b.

108

PUPIL TEXTBOOK 6C PAGE 108

Share

WAYS OF WORKING Whole class teacher led

ASK

- Question ❶ a): *How do Dexter's annotations help you to reason about the size of angle a?*
- Question ❶ a): *Why is the calculation 180° – 116° written in brackets? Why do you need to divide by 2?*
- Question ❶ b): *How do Dexter's annotations help you to reason about the size of angle b?*

IN FOCUS Both problems require several steps, emphasising the need for a systematic approach. Question ❶ a) starts by demonstrating what is known about angle a, establishing that children must first find the missing angles in the isosceles triangle. Question ❶ b) requires children to recognise that another triangle has been formed when the shaded triangle was drawn inside the rectangle.

STRENGTHEN For question ❶ b), ask children to explain why the third angle in the triangle could have been calculated simply by finding 90° – 58° rather than 180° – 90° – 58°. Discuss why this method is possible for this triangle but would not be possible for a triangle with known angles 35° and 100°.

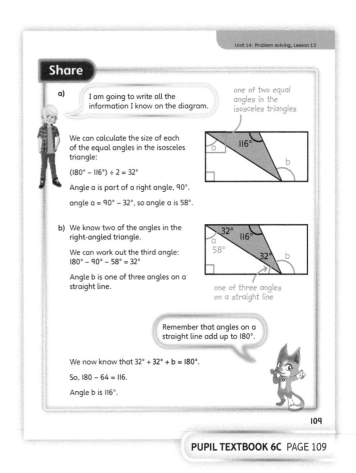

Share

a)   I am going to write all the information I know on the diagram.

one of two equal angles in the isosceles triangles

We can calculate the size of each of the equal angles in the isosceles triangle:

(180° – 116°) ÷ 2 = 32°

Angle a is part of a right angle, 90°.

angle a = 90° – 32°, so angle a is 58°.

b) We know two of the angles in the right-angled triangle.

We can work out the third angle:
180° – 90° – 58° = 32°

Angle b is one of three angles on a straight line.

one of three angles on a straight line

Remember that angles on a straight line add up to 180°.

We now know that 32° + 32° + b = 180°.

So, 180 – 64 = 116.

Angle b is 116°.

109

PUPIL TEXTBOOK 6C PAGE 109

Think together

Whole class teacher led (I do, We do, You do)

ASK

- Question ❶: *None of the angles in the isosceles triangle are known. Can you use what you know about vertically opposite angles?*
- Question ❷: *You only know the size of one angle in the triangle so you can't use the sum of the internal angles. What else do you know?*
- Question ❷: *What type of angle is n? How do you know?*
- Question ❸: *What do you know about obtuse angles? So what do you know about angle a? What is the range of possible sizes for angle b? How do you know?*
- Question ❹: *The two lines are the diagonals in the rectangle. How does this help?*

IN FOCUS These questions encourage children to use a chain of reasoning, establishing what they need to find out before finding the angle asked for.

Question ❶ requires children to reason about both vertically opposite angles and properties of an isosceles triangle. Check that they can explain why angles c and d are equal. Question ❷ involves a reflex angle, n. Children may try to subtract from 180° rather than 360° – they may assume that, because the angle is connected to the triangle, they must still use what they know about the sum of angles in a triangle. Question ❸ is an abstract problem that requires children to apply what they know about the size of acute and obtuse angles.

For question ❹, children must draw upon other aspects of geometry, recognising that the lines within the rectangle are the diagonals, so creating isosceles triangles.

STRENGTHEN For question ❸, discuss which angle children can work out immediately (c). Encourage them to make lists of possible angles for a and b, using what they know about angle c to help them: a and b must sum to 285°. They must then find a pair of values that suit both criteria – sum to 285° where one angle is double the size of the other. Children can model the problem using a bar model.

DEEPEN For question ❸, revisit ratio. Ask children to give the ratio of a to b. Challenge them to use this information to find the solution.

ASSESSMENT CHECKPOINT Use questions ❶ to ❹ to assess whether children can use a chain of reasoning to find unknown angles. Use questions ❶, ❷ and ❹ to check that children can apply knowledge of the sum of the interior angles in a triangle. Use questions ❶ and ❹ to check that children recognise that vertically opposite angles are equal.

ANSWERS

Question ❶ a): Angles a and b are both 47°.

Question ❶ b): Angles c and d are both 94°.

Question ❷: Angle m is 73°. Angle n is 285°.

Question ❸: Angle a = 95°, angle b = 190°, angle c = 75°

Question ❹: Angle x = 96°, angle y = 48°, angle z = 48°

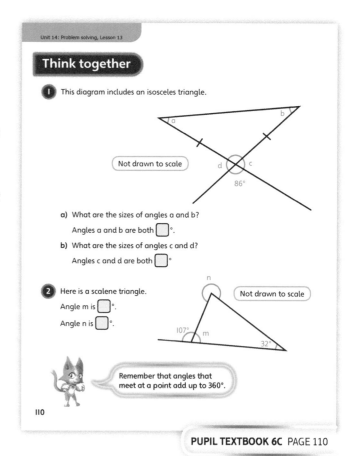

Think together

❶ This diagram includes an isosceles triangle.

Not drawn to scale

86°

a) What are the sizes of angles a and b?

Angles a and b are both ☐°.

b) What are the sizes of angles c and d?

Angles c and d are both ☐°

❷ Here is a scalene triangle.

Angle m is ☐°.

Angle n is ☐°.

Not drawn to scale

107°   m   32°

Remember that angles that meet at a point add up to 360°.

110

PUPIL TEXTBOOK 6C PAGE 110

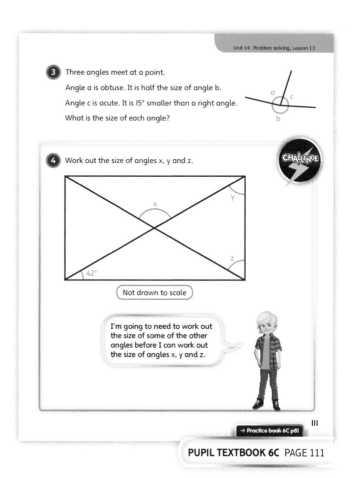

❸ Three angles meet at a point.

Angle a is obtuse. It is half the size of angle b.

Angle c is acute. It is 15° smaller than a right angle.

What is the size of each angle?

❹ Work out the size of angles x, y and z.

CHALLENGE

x   y

z

42°

Not drawn to scale

I'm going to need to work out the size of some of the other angles before I can work out the size of angles x, y and z.

→ Practice book 6C p81

III

PUPIL TEXTBOOK 6C PAGE 111

Practice

WAYS OF WORKING Independent thinking

IN FOCUS Question ❶ requires children to interpret the notation used to show a right angle so that they can take account of this 90° when finding the missing angle. Question ❷ has been chosen as it requires children to find missing angles in a triangle and a quadrilateral. They must use a chain of reasoning to find the required angles.

In question ❸, children need to apply their knowledge about the angles in a square to reason about missing angles. Children may find this question more challenging because the right angles are not labelled. Question ❺ requires children to follow a chain of reasoning, applying understanding of right angles in shapes, the sum of interior angles in a quadrilateral, angles on a straight line and vertically opposite angles.

STRENGTHEN In question ❷ b), children need to explain how they will find the size of two angles. Encourage them to annotate the diagram with the information they know from part a) to help them. Look together at the correct terminology, for example 'vertically opposite', 'angles on a straight line', 'equal' etc. to help children who may find it difficult to construct an explanation. Write these terms on the board to help children write their explanation.

DEEPEN Ask children to make up problems similar to question ❹ for a partner to solve. Encourage them to include relationships such as double, one third, half, difference, sum etc. The problems could be related to angles that are on a straight line or make a right angle. They should include terminology such as acute and obtuse.

THINK DIFFERENTLY Question ❹ is an abstract problem, requiring children to reason about the relationships between the angles. They may find it useful to draw bar models to help them explore the relationships.

ASSESSMENT CHECKPOINT Use questions ❶, ❷ and ❸ to assess whether children can apply what they know about the sum of the interior angles of a triangle to find missing angles. Use questions ❷, ❹ and ❺ to assess whether they can reason about angles that meet at a point or on a straight line. Check that children can use all notation or given angles to make decisions.

ANSWERS Answers for the **Practice** part of the lesson appear in the separate **Practice and Reflect answer guide**.

Reflect

WAYS OF WORKING Independent thinking

IN FOCUS This question has been chosen as there is more than one solution to the problem.

ASSESSMENT CHECKPOINT Children should recognise that the unknown angles must sum to 92° as this is the difference between the known angle and 180°.

ANSWERS Answers for the **Reflect** part of the lesson appear in the separate **Practice and Reflect answer guide**.

After the lesson ⏸

- Can children use a chain of reasoning to identify unknown angles?
- Do they make use of notations and of properties of shapes to help solve problems?
- Can they use correct terminology to explain and reason about missing angles (for example, vertically opposite)?

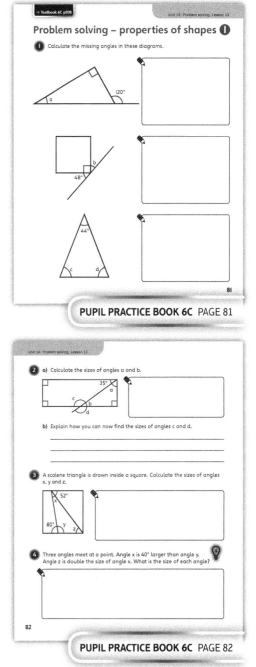

PUPIL PRACTICE BOOK 6C PAGE 81

PUPIL PRACTICE BOOK 6C PAGE 82

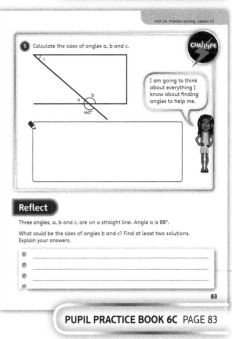

PUPIL PRACTICE BOOK 6C PAGE 83

Problem solving – properties of shapes ❷

Learning focus

In this lesson, children will continue to reason about the sum of interior angles in triangles and quadrilaterals, and angles on a straight line and at a point. They will revisit calculating the sum of the interior angles in regular polygons to identify the size of each angle. They will continue to apply their understanding to find missing angles.

Small steps

→ Previous step: Problem solving – properties of shapes (1)
→ **This step: Problem solving – properties of shapes (2)**
→ Next step: The mean (1)

NATIONAL CURRICULUM LINKS

Year 6 Geometry – Properties of Shapes
- Recognise angles where they meet at a point, are on a straight line, or are vertically opposite, and find missing angles.
- Compare and classify geometric shapes based on their properties and sizes and find unknown angles in any triangles, quadrilaterals, and regular polygons.

ASSESSING MASTERY

Children can recall and calculate the sum of the interior angles in a polygon and use this to find the size of each angle. They can solve problems that involve a chain of reasoning to find the size of an unknown angle.

COMMON MISCONCEPTIONS

Children may think that irregular polygons do not have the same sum of interior angles as regular polygons, because the angles are not all the same size. Use a protractor to check the size of angles in irregular pentagons, hexagons and octagons, finding the sum each time. Ask:
- *What do the angles in a regular pentagon/hexagon/octagon add up to? What do the angles in this irregular pentagon/hexagon/octagon add up to? What is the same and what is different about the shapes?*

STRENGTHENING UNDERSTANDING

Give children regular pentagons or hexagons to cut up into triangles. Ask them to measure and label the angles. Reassemble the regular shape and add the angles of the triangles that make up each vertex, agreeing that they sum to 108° for the pentagon and 120° for the hexagon.

GOING DEEPER

Give children a set of 2D shapes including regular and irregular polygons. Ask them to arrange them in different ways, reasoning about the size of any angles they make. Ask them to explain when they may need to measure at least one of the angles in a shape to get started, and to identify situations in which they can just calculate the angles.

KEY LANGUAGE

In lesson: angle, straight line, regular, irregular, polygon, equilateral, quadrilateral, pentagon, hexagon

Other language to be used by the teacher: sum of interior angles, point, right angle, octagon

RESOURCES

Optional: protractors, 2D shapes

 In the eTextbook of this lesson, you will find interactive links to a selection of teaching tools.

Before you teach

- Can children recall the size of each angle in an equilateral triangle?
- Can they find a missing angle at a point?
- Can they use properties of shape to reason about the sizes of angles?

Discover

ASK

- Question **1** a): *What do you know about each angle in a regular shape?*
- Question **1** a): *Do you remember the size of each angle in a regular pentagon? How can you work it out?*
- Question **1** b): *What do you notice about angle b?*
- Question **1** b): *The pentagon is inside a rectangle. How does this help?*

IN FOCUS Children need to reason about the sizes of angles that have been formed by placing a regular pentagon inside a rectangle. In question **1** a), they are asked to find the size of each angle in the pentagon. In 1b), children should recognise that each of the unknown angles is on a straight line with an angle in the pentagon.

PRACTICAL TIPS Provide paper versions of the image for children to annotate or cut up to help them make sense of the problem.

ANSWERS

Question **1** a): Each angle in a regular pentagon is 108°.

Question **1** b): Angle a is 72°, angle b is 36°.

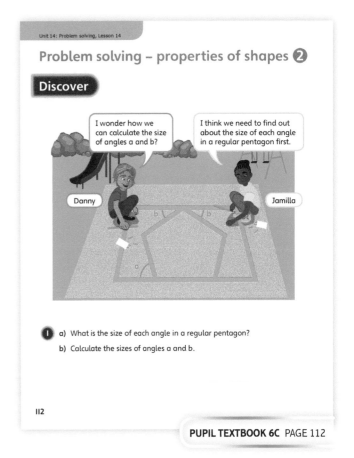

PUPIL TEXTBOOK 6C PAGE 112

Share

WAYS OF WORKING Whole class teacher led

ASK

- Question **1** a): *How does splitting the regular shape into triangles help?*
- Question **1** a): *Why do you need to divide 540° by 5 and not 3 to match the number of triangles?*
- Question **1** b): *What do you know about angles on a straight line?*
- Question **1** b): *Why do you have to divide 72° by 2 to find the size of angle b?*

IN FOCUS Question **1** a) enables children to revisit a method for finding the sum of the interior angles in a regular polygon and to use this to find the size of each angle. Question **1** b) requires children to recognise that the unknown angles are on a straight line with angles within the pentagon. Make sure children understand that angle b is not 72° (180 – 108°) since two equal angles of size b make up this amount.

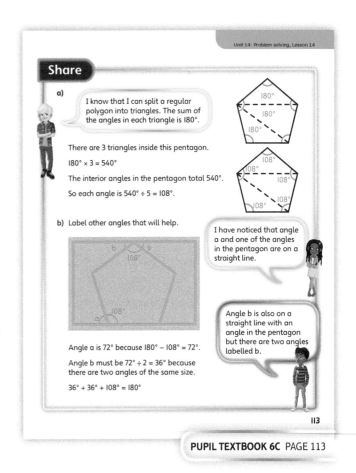

PUPIL TEXTBOOK 6C PAGE 113

Think together

WAYS OF WORKING Whole class teacher led (I do, We do, You do)

ASK

- Question ❶: *What do you need to find first? How can you do this?*
- Question ❷: *Do you agree with Dexter? Why?*
- Question ❸: *What are the names of the two quadrilaterals? What do you know about their properties?*
- Question ❹: *What is the size of each angle in an equilateral triangle? How can you check?*

IN FOCUS Question ❶ has been chosen because it requires children to recall or calculate the size of each interior angle in a regular hexagon. Children may divide the sum of the interior angles by 5 rather than 6 as this was the calculation used in **Share**.

Question ❷ helps children to reason about the similarities and differences between a regular pentagon and an irregular pentagon, recognising that the sum of the interior angles is the same for both (although the angles in an irregular shape are not equal).

STRENGTHEN For question ❶, begin to formulate a rule to help children calculate the size of each interior angle in a regular polygon: they have to divide the sum each time by the number of equal angles.

DEEPEN For question ❶, children could further develop the rule for finding the size of angles in a regular polygon by looking at the number of triangles that can be made each time in relation to the number of sides in the shape: the number of triangles is two less than the number of sides. They could explore heptagons, nonagons and decagons to check this.

ASSESSMENT CHECKPOINT Use questions ❶ to ❹ to assess whether children can use their knowledge of angles in polygons and angles on a straight line. Use question ❶ to assess whether they can calculate the size of each angle in a regular polygon; use questions ❷ and ❸ to assess whether they can apply this understanding of the sum of interior angles to irregular shapes, recognising that the total is the same as for regular shapes.

ANSWERS

Question ❶: Angle x = 60°, angle y = 30°

Question ❷: Angle a = 26°

Question ❸: Angle a in the parallelogram must be 50° because the interior angles in a quadrilateral sum to 360°. Two of the angles total 260° so the remaining two angles must total 100°, meaning each one is 50°.
Angle a in the trapezium is also 50° as the sum of the interior angles is again 360°. Two right angles make 180° and 130° and 50° make up the remaining 180°.

Question ❹: Angle a = 12°

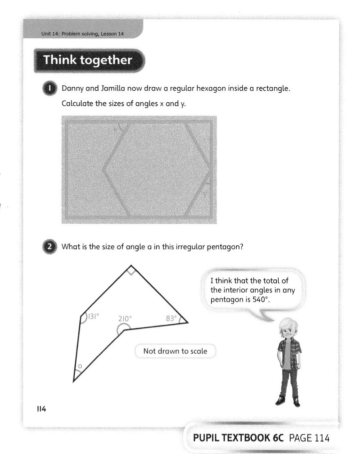

Think together

❶ Danny and Jamilla now draw a regular hexagon inside a rectangle.
Calculate the sizes of angles x and y.

❷ What is the size of angle a in this irregular pentagon?

131° 210° 83°
a

Not drawn to scale

I think that the total of the interior angles in any pentagon is 540°.

114

PUPIL TEXTBOOK 6C PAGE 114

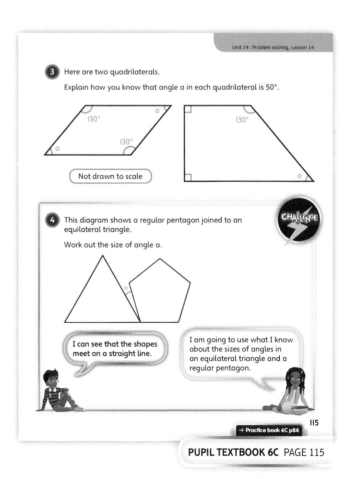

❸ Here are two quadrilaterals.
Explain how you know that angle a in each quadrilateral is 50°.

130° a
a 130°

Not drawn to scale

130°
a

❹ This diagram shows a regular pentagon joined to an equilateral triangle.
Work out the size of angle a.

CHALLENGE

a

I can see that the shapes meet on a straight line.

I am going to use what I know about the sizes of angles in an equilateral triangle and a regular pentagon.

➔ Practice book 6C p84

115

PUPIL TEXTBOOK 6C PAGE 115

Practice

WAYS OF WORKING Independent thinking

IN FOCUS Question ② has been chosen as it requires children to reason about a range of different polygons. One of the criteria focuses on the sum of the interior angles, hence the inclusion of different quadrilaterals.

Questions ③ and ④ both combine angles meeting at a point and the sum of interior angles in a regular polygon. Question ④ also includes the properties of a parallelogram (equal diagonally opposite angles). Children may also notice that the missing angle a sums to 180° with 60°.

STRENGTHEN With question ⑤, discuss with children how they could represent the problem using bar models. Ensure children understand that the sum of the interior angles in an irregular hexagon is the same as in a regular hexagon.

DEEPEN Ask children to reason about other sets of regular shapes that will meet at a point like the hexagons in question ③. Ask them to look at tessellations of squares and equilateral triangles and explain why these also meet at a point (all have angles that are factors of 360°). Challenge them to make a pattern of more than one regular shape meeting at a point (for example, two octagons and a square)

ASSESSMENT CHECKPOINT Use question ① to assess whether children can calculate the size of each interior angle in a regular polygon. Use question ② to assess whether they can apply knowledge of properties of different shapes to categorise them accurately. Use questions ④ and ⑤ to assess whether they can use known and derived information flexibly to reason about missing angles.

ANSWERS Answers for the **Practice** part of the lesson appear in the separate **Practice and Reflect answer guide**.

Reflect

WAYS OF WORKING Independent thinking

IN FOCUS This question has been chosen so that children make decisions about which method to use to prove that three angles in a regular pentagon cannot add up to 330°. Although the question does not state that the three angles are equal, children can make this assumption as otherwise the pentagon would obviously not be regular. So they can either compare one interior angle of a regular pentagon with 110°, or multiply the interior angle by 3 to compare with 330°.

ASSESSMENT CHECKPOINT Check that children understand how to find the interior angle in a regular pentagon.

ANSWERS Answers for the **Reflect** part of the lesson appear in the separate **Practice and Reflect answer guide**.

After the lesson ⏸

- Can children recall or calculate the size of each angle and the sum of angles in a regular polygon?
- Do they make use of notations and properties of shapes to help solve problems?
- Can they reason about angles that meet at a point or on a straight line to help find missing angles?

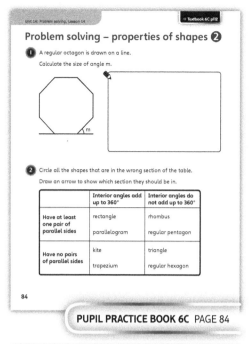

PUPIL PRACTICE BOOK 6C PAGE 84

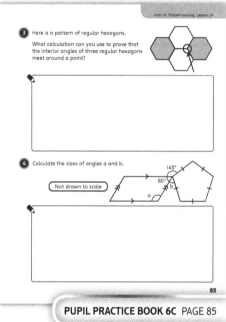

PUPIL PRACTICE BOOK 6C PAGE 85

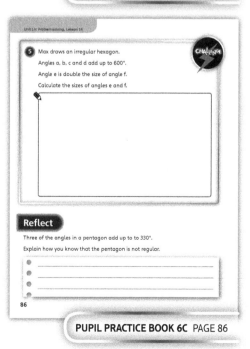

PUPIL PRACTICE BOOK 6C PAGE 86

End of unit check

Don't forget the *Power Maths* unit assessment grid on p26.

Don't forget the *Power Maths* unit assessment grid on p26.

WAYS OF WORKING Group work adult led

IN FOCUS All the questions are SATs-style questions to draw out the range of skills taught across the unit. There are also more questions than in other *Power Maths* textbooks.

- Many of the problems can be represented using bar models (questions **4**, **5**, **6**, **7**, **8**, **9**) or solved using number lines (questions **1**, **2**, **10**), although children may choose to use different approaches.
- Questions **4**, **7** and **8** have been written using numbers that will give children opportunities to think flexibly about the order in which they approach the calculations.
- Question **5** is set in the structure of a bar model. Children need to notice that the two given fractions and the unknown value total one, and use their knowledge of equivalent fractions to add the given fractions.

ANSWERS AND COMMENTARY

Children who have mastered this unit will fluently apply their understanding of number, measurement and geometry to a range of problems. They will reason about the relationships between known and unknown information, representing this as required. They will calculate flexibly, choosing a mental or written method depending on the numbers involved.

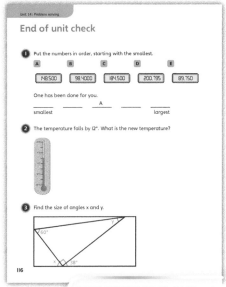

PUPIL TEXTBOOK 6C PAGE 116

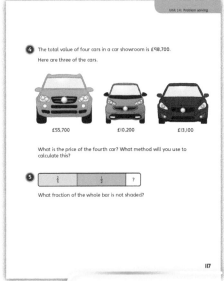

PUPIL TEXTBOOK 6C PAGE 117

Q	A	WRONG ANSWERS AND MISCONCEPTIONS	STRENGTHENING UNDERSTANDING
1	E, B, A, C, D	Children may think that, say, 89,750 is larger than 148,500 because it starts with the digit 8.	Suggest that children use a place value grid to help order the numbers.
2	$^-7°C$	Children may add rather than subtract 12 or they may miscalculate as they cross 0.	Encourage children to stop at 0, partitioning the number to help complete the calculation.
3	$x = 52°$, $y = 30°$	Children may overlook the notation for the right angle and conclude that they have insufficient information.	Encourage children to annotate diagrams with any known information, including labelling right angles as 90°.
4	£19,700	Children may not complete all steps, for example they may find the total of the known values, but not subtract this from £98,700.	Revisit the use of a bar model to represent problems so children are secure with the number of steps required.
5	$\frac{1}{10}$	Children may find $\frac{1}{2} + \frac{2}{5}$ but not complete the last step. As 5 is not a multiple of 2, they may struggle to find a common denominator.	Look at other calculations involving fractions where one denominator is not a multiple of the other and remind children how to find equivalent fractions in these cases.

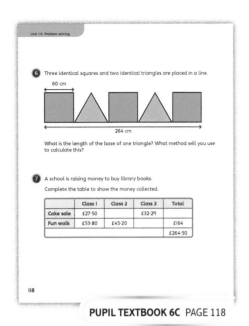

PUPIL TEXTBOOK 6C PAGE 118

PUPIL TEXTBOOK 6C PAGE 119

Q	A	WRONG ANSWERS AND MISCONCEPTIONS	STRENGTHENING UNDERSTANDING
6	42 cm	Children may give as the answer the total length of the bases for the two triangles, rather than dividing by 2.	Encourage children to check their answers, summing the values to check that they total 264 cm.
7	top row: £40·71, £100·50; bottom row: £65	Some children may struggle to interpret the relationships between the pieces of information in the table.	Explore retrieving information and finding missing information in a range of tables and charts.
8	320 g	Children may find the total mass of strawberries and cherries but not use this to find the mass of raspberries.	Explore different strategies to solve this problem, for example using bar models to make relationships explicit.
9	30	Children may not recognise that the number of story books has been scaled by 6 so the total number of books must also be scaled by 6.	Use bar models or counters to explore ratios, emphasising the relationship between the parts and the whole.
10	35 minutes	Children may misread 14:10 as 4:10 pm rather than correctly interpreting the 24-hour clock notation.	Practise converting between the 12-hour and 24-hour clock notation.

My journal

WAYS OF WORKING   Independent thinking

ANSWERS AND COMMENTARY

Toshi will save £7,776 in 3 years.

This problem draws on children's knowledge of money, percentages, fractions, ratio and proportion. Encourage children to read the question carefully and to approach it one step at a time. Ask:

• *What is the first thing you need to do? How will you find 25% of £1,200?*

For the next step, ensure children understand that they then need to find $\frac{3}{10}$ of the original amount (£1,200), not $\frac{3}{10}$ of the amount they just calculated. Ask:

• *How will you find $\frac{3}{10}$ of £1,200? What is $\frac{3}{10}$ as a percentage?*

If children get stuck, encourage the use of a bar model at this stage. It should help them to understand that Toshi spends 25% of his monthly income on rent and 30% on food and entertainment, so he has 45% left for bills and savings.

Children then need to determine the proportion of £540 (45% of £1,200) Toshi saves each month. Ask:

• *How can you express the amount Toshi saves per month as a ratio? What is this as a fraction? As a percentage?*

Ensure children then complete the question by calculating how much Toshi saves over 3 years, not just the one month.

PUPIL PRACTICE BOOK 6C PAGE 87

Power check

WAYS OF WORKING   Independent thinking

ASK

• *In what different ways have you used bar models and number lines? How have they helped?*

• *How confident are you about identifying the calculation(s) needed to solve a word problem?*

• *What is the same and what is different about finding fractions of amounts and percentages of amounts?*

• *What can you tell me about the sum of the interior angles in different shapes?*

Power play

WAYS OF WORKING Pair work

IN FOCUS This draws on aspects of multiplication, fractions, money and time. Children need to make use of and draw on the relationships between the given information to decide what is being asked and what they need to do first. The information they may need to use first is not given until the end of the problem, so they need to look at the problem as a whole. They are required to represent their solution in a table so they must decide what goes where.

ANSWERS AND COMMENTARY

	Money spent	Arrival time	Departure time
Jamie	£7·50	13:00	14:15
Max	£2·50	10:30	13:00
Zac	£10	11:15	13:15

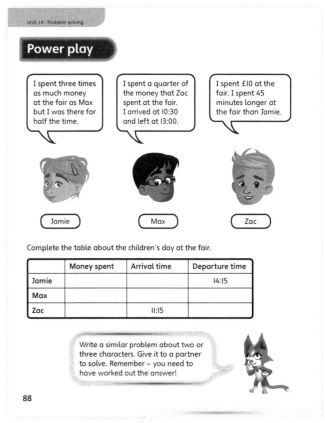

After the unit

How well did the prompts and questions promote learning and what were children's responses to them?

Are children ready to move on with their learning? Following on from the end of unit assessment, how confident are they in representing and solving a range of problems in different contexts?

Strengthen and **Deepen** activities for this unit can be found in the *Power Maths* online subscription.

Unit 15
Statistics

Don't forget to watch the Unit 15 video!

Mastery Expert tip! "I found that this unit provided a great opportunity for cross-curricular links and real-life situations. Children can use data from science experiments such as growing plants and measuring shadows to draw and create line graphs. PE can provide the data for calculating the mean, for example children can record the distances of a long jump and calculate the mean."

WHY THIS UNIT IS IMPORTANT

In this unit children learn what the mathematical mean is and how to calculate it and they consider when using the mean is particularly useful, for example when comparing sets of data of different sizes. Children learn what a pie chart is and how to interpret one, they compare tally charts and bar charts and learn when a pie chart is the best way to display data. Children develop their ability to interpret and create line graphs.

WHERE THIS UNIT FITS

→ Unit 14: Problem solving
→ **Unit 15: Statistics**

This unit builds on the skills children have gained in Year 5 interpreting and using line graphs. They learn what the mathematic mean is and how to calculate it and are introduced to pie charts.

Before they start this unit, it is expected that children:
- can plot and interpret simple line graphs
- are confident with dividing 2- and 3-digit numbers by a 1-digit number
- understand about angles of a circle
- can identify and calculate fractions of a circle
- can do calculations with percentages.

ASSESSING MASTERY

Children who have mastered this unit can calculate the mean of sets of data and can compare sets of data by calculating the mean. They should also be able to use the mean to identify missing data. Also in this unit, children will learn to read and interpret pie charts, and will calculate fractions and percentages of data as a whole. At the end of the unit, children will show mastery if they can interpret and create line graphs.

COMMON MISCONCEPTIONS	STRENGTHENING UNDERSTANDING	GOING DEEPER
Some children may find the word 'mean' confusing as it is a homonym.	Explain that in maths 'mean' is the mathematical average. Ask: *What is the mean number of marshmallows on a stick?*	Challenge children to write a definition of the mathematical 'mean' or explain what the mean is and how to calculate it for other children.
Children may mistake the number of sections in a pie chart as the fraction, for example they may say that as there are 3 sections, each is $\frac{1}{3}$.	Recap fractions of circles with the children. Provide circles and ask the children to shade $\frac{1}{2}$, $\frac{1}{4}$, $\frac{1}{3}$, $\frac{3}{4}$ etc. This will help the children to visualise the fractions.	Discuss and compare different pie charts.
Children may confuse the x-axis and y-axis when interpreting line graphs and may read/interpret the scales used incorrectly.	Discuss the line graphs in detail and practise reading simple points from the graph. Begin with marked points and progress to unmarked points.	Explore different shaped line graphs – curved and straight. Challenge children to create stories to explain what is happening in a line graph.

WAYS OF WORKING

Recap on percentages, fractions and angles, especially in circles. Children will need to be able to calculate and convert these to understand the work on pie charts. Children will also be looking at line graphs again, so it would be worthwhile reminding them about these, and how to read them.

STRUCTURES AND REPRESENTATIONS

Bar model: These help children to work out the mean, showing how groups of different numbers can be made equal, so showing the mean. They are also useful to demonstrate the whole, or total, represented in a pie chart, and how the sections represent different percentages or fractions of the whole.

30				

5	6	5	4	10

6	6	6	6	6

KEY LANGUAGE

There is some key language that children will need to know as part of the learning in this unit:

→ average, mean, set, share
→ pie chart, segment, whole, section, degree, angle, right angle
→ tally chart, bar chart
→ fraction, percentage
→ line graph, axis/axes, estimate, accurate, interpret, increase, above, below, zero (0), value, x-axis, y-axis, minus (−), between, plot, point, vertical, horizontal, construct, convert/conversion, straight, equivalent, predict, curve
→ more, equal, even, size, total, share, great(er/est), calculate, divide, highest, compare, lowest, group, data, represent, balance, odd, different/difference, least, inverse, operation, advantages, disadvantages, largest, half, scale, quarter, frequency, smallest, part, same, more, category, results, exact

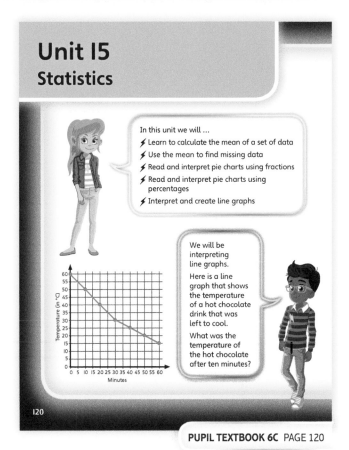

PUPIL TEXTBOOK 6C PAGE 120

PUPIL TEXTBOOK 6C PAGE 121

153

The mean ❶

Learning focus

In this lesson, children learn to use the mathematical term 'mean' when referring to the average. The children consider two methods for calculating the mean of a set of numbers.

Small steps

→ Previous step: Problem solving – properties of shapes (2)
→ **This step: The mean (1)**
→ Next step: The mean (2)

NATIONAL CURRICULUM LINKS

Year 6 Statistics

Calculate and interpret the mean as an average.

ASSESSING MASTERY

Children can calculate the mean of a set of objects or numbers by sharing the amount equally. Children can share sets of objects practically and then progress to finding the mean of a set of numbers using division. Children can confidently use, explain and understand the mathematical term 'mean' as calculating the average of a set of numbers by sharing the amounts equally.

COMMON MISCONCEPTIONS

Some children may find the word 'mean' confusing as it is a homonym. Discuss the different meanings of the word 'mean': mathematical average (for example: 'What is the mean number of marshmallows on a stick?'), to be nasty or unkind (for example: 'It was mean to pull your sister's hair.'), and to represent something (for example: 'What does that mean?').

Another common misconception is that the greater the number of 'groups' in a set then the greater the mean. Ask:
• *Which is the set with the greatest mean? A: 4, 1, 1, 2; B: 2, 0, 0, 2; or C: 2, 0, 1, 0, 1, 0, 0, 0.*

STRENGTHENING UNDERSTANDING

Provide children with counters, cubes, marshmallows and other manipulatives to share sets of objects and find the average practically.

GOING DEEPER

Focus on finding sets of numbers by dividing. Explore a variety of sets of numbers from real-life situations such as how tall sunflowers have grown, how many mini-beasts children have found, how much sponsor money children have collected, how many cars drive past school each day.

KEY LANGUAGE

In lesson: mean, average, more, equal, even, size, set, total, share, greatest
Other language to be used by the teacher: calculate, divide

STRUCTURES AND REPRESENTATIONS

bar model, number lines

RESOURCES

Mandatory: counters, cubes

Optional: marshmallows

 In the eTextbook of this lesson, you will find interactive links to a selection of teaching tools.

Before you teach ⏸

• Are children secure in dividing 2-digit numbers?
• Are there any children who would benefit from pre-teaching the new vocabulary (mean) as a mathematical term?

Discover

WAYS OF WORKING Pair work

ASK

- Question ① a): *What does the term 'average' mean mathematically?*
- Question ① a): *Do the children have an equal amount of marshmallows? Is this fair?*
- Question ① a): *How many marshmallows are there in total? How many children are there?*
- Question ① b): *What if you shared the marshmallows equally?*

IN FOCUS The questions introduce children to the term 'average'. Children should discuss the term and what it might mean mathematically. They can explore how to divide the marshmallows so that everyone has the same amount.

PRACTICAL TIPS Provide children with counters or cubes to represent marshmallows and sort practically.

ANSWERS

Question ① a): The mean (average) number of marshmallows on a stick is 9.

Question ① b): The mean (average) number of marshmallows on a stick would be 11.

PUPIL TEXTBOOK 6C PAGE 122

Share

WAYS OF WORKING Whole class teacher led

ASK

- Question ① a): *What new language have you learnt? What does the term 'mean' mean mathematically?*
- Question ① a): *How can you share the marshmallows equally? (27 divided by 3 = 9)*
- Question ① b): *What two different ways can you use to find the 'mean'?*

IN FOCUS Question ① a) shows children how to rearrange the groups of marshmallows so that everyone has an equal amount. This requires an understanding of sharing objects equally. Ask: *Can you explain to a partner how to make the groups equal?* Question ① b) asks children to consider what would happen if there were 6 more marshmallows and how this would affect the mean. Two methods are presented. Ask: *Which method do you prefer?*

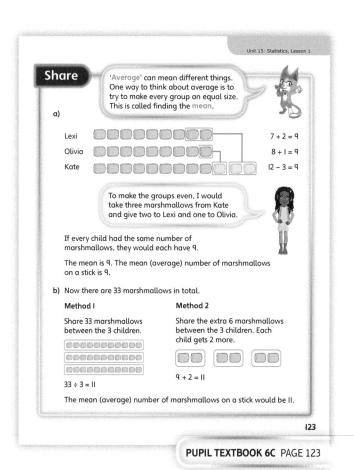

PUPIL TEXTBOOK 6C PAGE 123

155

Think together

WAYS OF WORKING Whole class teacher led (I do, We do, You do)

ASK

- Question **1**: *What does 'mean' mean mathematically?*
- Question **2**: *How many marshmallows are there altogether?*
- Question **3**: *How many towers/children are there?*

IN FOCUS Question **1** introduces a more varied number of marshmallows per person. Kate has many more than Bella, who has only 1. Children need to understand that to find the mean they need to make all the groups equal and will discover that they don't always have to take away from each group. Kate has the most, so most of the marshmallows will be taken from her and given to Bella. Question **3** introduces the idea that some methods of finding the mean are better for different problems. Children are asked to discuss two methods to see what is different about them, then choose one to work out question **3** b).

STRENGTHEN For question **1** provide children with counters and ask them to practically rearrange the counters so each person has an equal amount.

For question **2** provide children with cubes to build towers practically.

DEEPEN For question **2**, ask children to build another set of towers that is different but has the same mean. Ask: *Can you explain why the mean is the same?*

ASSESSMENT CHECKPOINT Question **1** will assess whether children understand that the mean is the average amount i.e. when all the groups in the set have the same amount. Question **2** will show whether children understand that two sets of different numbers can have the same mean if the total and number of groups are both the same. Although the towers are different sizes, there is the same amount of towers in each set and the same amount of cubes altogether.

ANSWERS

Question **1**: 7

Question **2**: The mean number of cubes in each set of towers is 6.

Question **3** a): The mean is 7. Both methods work although it is not always possible to rearrange practically for example when not dealing with concrete items or when the numbers involved are large.

Question **3** b): 120 + 150 + 120 + 130 = 520
520 ÷ 4 = 130
Children should discuss with their partners the best method to use. Obviously they cannot rearrange the heights, but they can find the total and divide.

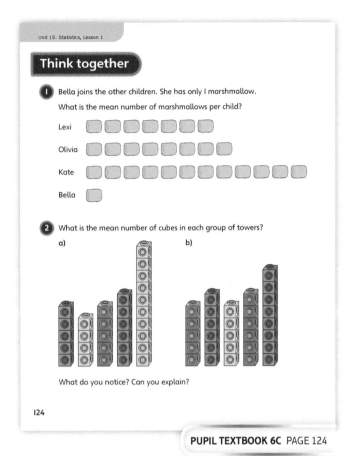

PUPIL TEXTBOOK 6C PAGE 124

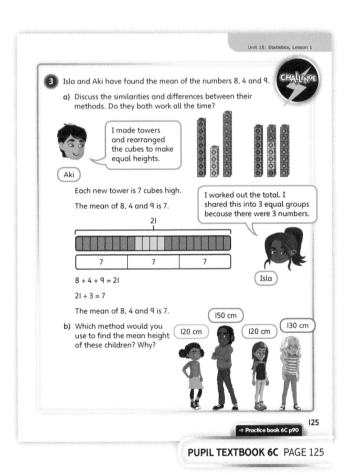

PUPIL TEXTBOOK 6C PAGE 125

Practice

WAYS OF WORKING Independent thinking

IN FOCUS Question **2** allows children to choose their method: drawing a diagram or calculating to find the mean number of marbles in a bag. In question **3** children are challenged to identify which sets have the same mean. Children will need to identify which sets have the same total and same number of dice (all the sets have the same number of dice in this example). By question **4** the children need to think about calculating the mean as the numbers involved are too big to use counters or cubes. Question **5** highlights the misconception that if there are more numbers in the set then the mean will be greater. Question **6** challenges children to find the mean of numbers on a number line. This provides a different visual representation for the children. They should recognise that they can use the same method to find the mean.

STRENGTHEN Provide children with counters and cubes to rearrange practically. This will help them to see equal groups, which they can then draw.

DEEPEN Provide children with a set of data and challenge them to find as many different sets with the same mean as they can.

ASSESSMENT CHECKPOINT Question **2** will allow you to assess whether children can select an efficient method to find the mean.

Question **3** will show which children understand how different sets can have the same mean.

Question **5** will allow you to assess whether children understand that a greater number in a set does not result in a greater mean.

ANSWERS Answers to the **Practice** part of the lesson appear in a separate **Practice and Reflect answer guide**.

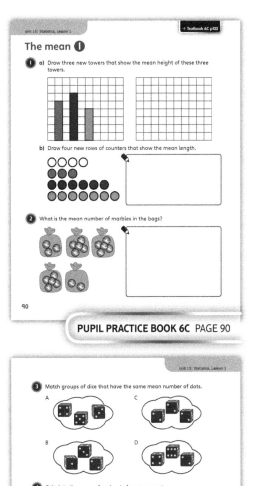

PUPIL PRACTICE BOOK 6C PAGE 90

PUPIL PRACTICE BOOK 6C PAGE 91

Reflect

WAYS OF WORKING Independent thinking

IN FOCUS Children are required to explain two different methods to find the mean. They could draw a diagram, use counters/cubes to rearrange the groups so they are equal, or they could calculate by dividing (total ÷ number of groups = mean).

ASSESSMENT CHECKPOINT Can children use and explain two different methods to find the mean of a set of numbers?

ANSWERS Answers for the **Reflect** part of the lesson appear in the separate **Practice and Reflect answer book**.

After the lesson ⏸

- What percentage of children understand the mathematical term 'mean'?
- What did the children find challenging and how could you address this next time?

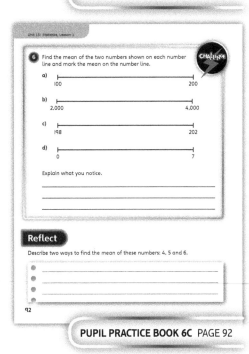

PUPIL PRACTICE BOOK 6C PAGE 92

The mean ❷

Learning focus

In this lesson, children practise calculating the mean. Children explore using bar models as a visual representation. They consider situations when the mean is useful to compare groups of data.

Small steps

→ Previous step: The mean (1)
→ **This step: The mean (2)**
→ Next step: The mean (3)

NATIONAL CURRICULUM LINKS

Year 6 Statistics

Calculate and interpret the mean as an average.

ASSESSING MASTERY

Children can calculate the mean of a group of objects or numbers using bar models. They can calculate the mean by finding the total and dividing by the amount of numbers in the group.

Children can identify and suggest situations where finding the mean is particularly useful to compare groups of data; for example when the groups don't have an equal amount of numbers.

COMMON MISCONCEPTIONS

Some children may find the word 'mean' confusing as it is a homonym, a word that is spelt and pronounced the same but has several meanings. Discuss the different meanings of 'mean': mean – mathematical average 'what is the mean number of marshmallows on a stick?'; mean – to be nasty or unkind 'it was mean to pull your sister's hair'; mean – to represent 'what does that mean?'

STRENGTHENING UNDERSTANDING

Provide children with cubes or counters and encourage them to use these to represent the different scores. This will give children a visual representation of the groups of numbers they are comparing. They can rearrange the cubes and explore whether the mean changes or stays the same.

GOING DEEPER

Give children some problems to solve, in which they can use their understanding of the mean and division.

KEY LANGUAGE

In lesson: highest, mean, compare, size, total, whole, lowest, set, greater,

Other language to be used by the teacher: average, share, even, equal, group, divide, calculate, data

STRUCTURES AND REPRESENTATIONS

bar model, towers of cubes

RESOURCES

Mandatory: counters, cubes

Optional: dice

 In the eTextbook of this lesson, you will find interactive links to a selection of teaching tools.

Before you teach

- Are children able to explain the mathematical term 'mean'?
- Are there any misconceptions from the previous lesson that need addressing?
- Are children secure in adding decimals up to 2 decimal points?

Discover

PUPIL TEXTBOOK 6C PAGE 126

WAYS OF WORKING Pair work

ASK

- Question ① a): *Do the skaters have the same number of scores? Does this make it difficult to compare them?*
- Question ① a): *Who had the highest/lowest score?*
- Question ① a): *Who do you think won the competition? Why?*
- Question ① b): *Can you think of different ways to compare the results?*

IN FOCUS In question ① a) children are asked to find the mean of two skaters' scores. Remind children of the previous lesson on finding the mean. Recap the two methods used: making the scores equal using counters or cubes to share out the scores or calculating the total and dividing by the amount of numbers in the group.

Question ① b) will remind children that the mean provides a way to compare results when there is a different amount of numbers in the groups. Encourage lots of discussion about the skaters' scores.

PRACTICAL TIPS Provide children with cubes or counters to represent the skaters' scores.

ANSWERS

Question ① a): Jamie had the highest mean score at 6·5.

Question ① b): This is an open-ended question that requires the children's opinion. Possible answers include: who had the highest and lowest mark? Who was the most consistent? What was the most common mark? Encourage children to give reasons for their answer.

Share

WAYS OF WORKING Whole class teacher led

ASK

- Question ① a): *Do you agree with the comments in the speech bubbles?*
- Question ① a): *What method did you use to find the mean?*
- Question ① a): *What do the bar models representing the results show you?*

IN FOCUS For question ① a) children need to add the two groups of scores to find the total and divide by the amount of numbers in the groups. Discuss the bar model used, explaining what it shows. Establish that it is difficult to compare the results as there is not the same number of scores in each group but that finding the mean provides a way to compare the results.

For question ① b) discuss the comments comparing the skating results in detail.

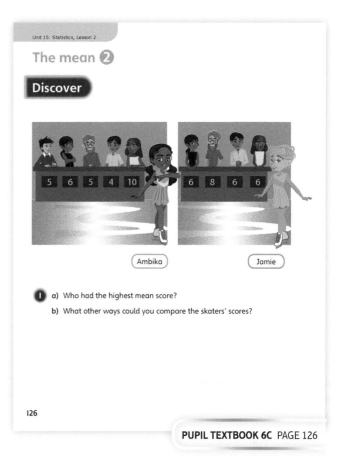

The mean ❷

Discover

① a) Who had the highest mean score?

b) What other ways could you compare the skaters' scores?

126

PUPIL TEXTBOOK 6C PAGE 126

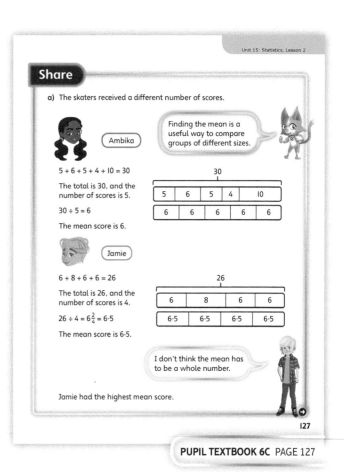

Share

a) The skaters received a different number of scores.

Ambika

Finding the mean is a useful way to compare groups of different sizes.

$5 + 6 + 5 + 4 + 10 = 30$

The total is 30, and the number of scores is 5.

$30 \div 5 = 6$

The mean score is 6.

Jamie

$6 + 8 + 6 + 6 = 26$

The total is 26, and the number of scores is 4.

$26 \div 4 = 6\frac{2}{4} = 6\cdot5$

The mean score is 6·5.

I don't think the mean has to be a whole number.

Jamie had the highest mean score.

127

PUPIL TEXTBOOK 6C PAGE 127

Think together

Whole class teacher led (I do, We do, You do)

ASK

- *What does 'mean' mean mathematically?*
- *Can different groups of data have the same mean?*
- *Can you give an example where the mean is particularly useful to compare groups of data?*

IN FOCUS Question ❶ asks children to compare scores by finding the mean. Question ❷ will show whether children are able to calculate the mean of a group of data. Question ❸ provides an opportunity to discuss that different groups of data can have the same mean. Explain that the mean is particularly useful in comparing groups of data that are not the same size or do not have the same amount of numbers in a group.

STRENGTHEN Provide children with counters and ask them to practically rearrange the counters so each person has an equal amount. Support children to draw a bar model for each question/group of data to provide a visual model.

DEEPEN Give children groups of data and ask them to create a second group with the same mean.

Group of data 1	Mean	Group of data 2 (with the same mean)
3, 4, 3, 4, 1	15 ÷ 5 = 3	Example: 5, 5, 5
10, 11, 9, 10		
1·5, 1·5, 1·2, 1·3		
6, 6, 7, 8, 2, 2		

ASSESSMENT CHECKPOINT Question ❷ will allow you to check that children understand mean is the average amount, i.e. when all the sets have the same amount of numbers in a group. Assess whether children are secure in calculating the mean.

Question ❸ will show whether children recognise that different groups of data can have the same mean.

ANSWERS

Question ❶: Aki: 6 + 7 + 7 + 8 = 28   28 ÷ 4 = 7
Lee: 6 + 4 + 7 + 8 + 2 + 6 = 33 33 ÷ 6 = 5·5
Aki has the highest mean score.

Question ❷: Emma: 1·4 + 2·1 + 1 = 4·5   4·5 ÷ 3 = 1·5 m
Lee: 1·55 + 1·1 + 1·1 = 3·75   3·75 ÷ 3 = 1·25 m
Luis: 2 + 1·2 = 3·2   3·2 ÷ 2 = 1·6 m
Luis has the highest mean height.

Question ❸: These groups of numbers all have a mean of 2. This shows that different groups of numbers can have the same mean.

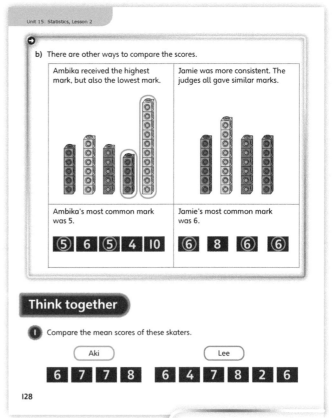

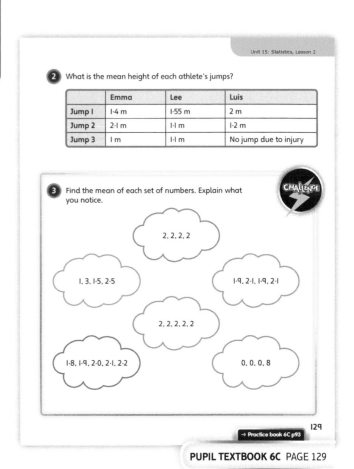

160

Practice

WAYS OF WORKING Independent thinking

IN FOCUS Question ❶ develops children's ability to calculate the mean of groups of data. Encourage children to use the bar models. Ask: *Can you describe the bar models and explain what they represent?*

The other questions will help children to realise that finding the mean is particularly useful when you need to compare groups of data of different sizes.

STRENGTHEN Support children to draw bar models. Provide templates for bar models if necessary.

DEEPEN Ask children to work in pairs or small groups. They roll a dice 5 times each, recording the results to create groups of data. Then they can swap with a partner to calculate the mean.

ASSESSMENT CHECKPOINT These questions will give you the opportunity to assess whether children recognise when it is useful to use the mean to compare groups of data. Ask: *Can you calculate the mean by dividing? Do you understand different groups can have the same mean?*

ANSWERS Answers to the **Practice** part of the lesson appear in a separate **Practice and Reflect answer guide**.

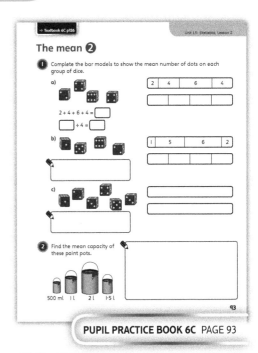

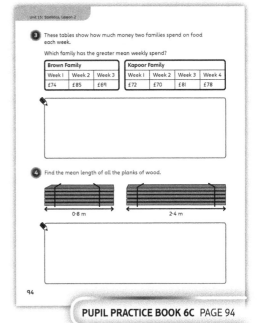

Reflect

WAYS OF WORKING Independent thinking

IN FOCUS Children explain a method to find the mean. Children should confidently be able to write a clear step-by-step explanation of a method to find the mean of a group of numbers.

ASSESSMENT CHECKPOINT Look for explanations that include drawing a bar model to represent the data and calculating the mean by dividing.

ANSWERS Answers for the **Reflect** part of the lesson appear in the separate **Practice and Reflect answer book**.

After the lesson ⏸

- What percentage of children understand the mathematical term 'mean'?
- What did the children find challenging and how could you address this next time?
- Are there any misconceptions you need to pick up on before next lesson?

The mean ③

Learning focus

In this lesson, children solve problems involving the mean of a group of data. They learn to use the mean to calculate missing parts of data. Children secure their knowledge and understanding of finding the mean of a group of data.

Small steps

→ Previous step: The mean (2)
→ **This step: The mean (3)**
→ Next step: Introducing pie charts

NATIONAL CURRICULUM LINKS

Year 6 Statistics

Calculate and interpret the mean as an average.

ASSESSING MASTERY

Children can calculate the mean of a group of objects. Children use a given mean to find a missing part of the data group. They use diagrams and bar models to visually represent problems involving the mean. Children can solve problems involving the mean of a group of data.

COMMON MISCONCEPTIONS

Some children may confuse finding the mean and the total for example finding the different ways 3 numbers can total 11 rather than have a mean of 11. Ask:
• *What are you being asked to find?*

STRENGTHENING UNDERSTANDING

Explore simple missing number problems to begin with and look at how the same method is used when dealing with the mean.

$2 + 5 + 4 + 6 + ? = 24$; $2 + 5 + 4 + 6 + ? =$ mean of 4; $2 + 5 + 4 + 6 + ? = 6 \times 4$

Provide children with string or ribbon and encourage them to represent the different lengths of the snakes using the string or ribbon. This will give children a practical representation of the groups they are comparing.

GOING DEEPER

Focus on finding groups of numbers that involve more difficult division skills. Explore a variety of groups of numbers from real-life situations.

KEY LANGUAGE

In lesson: mean, represent, balance, even, odd, difference, greatest, least, whole, set

Other language to be used by the teacher: average, divide, share, equal, data, inverse, operation

STRUCTURES AND REPRESENTATIONS

bar model

RESOURCES

Mandatory: counters, cubes

Optional: string or ribbon

 In the eTextbook of this lesson, you will find interactive links to a selection of teaching tools.

Before you teach ⏸

• Are there any misconceptions from the previous lesson that need addressing?
• Are children secure in multiplication facts?
• Can children use their understanding of the inverse to find missing numbers?

Discover

WAYS OF WORKING Pair work

ASK

- Question ① a): *How many snakes are there?*
- Question ① a): *How long are the snakes?*
- Question ① a): *Can you draw a bar model or diagram to represent the problem?*
- Question ① a): *Can you explain to a partner what the mean is?*
- Question ① a): *What methods did you use last lesson to find the mean?*

IN FOCUS Question ① a) asks children to find a missing piece of data in a group that they know the mean of. Children begin to explore problems involving the mean. Discuss the steps they need to take to work out the length of the fifth snake.

PRACTICAL TIPS Provide children with string, ribbon or cubes to practically represent the length of the snakes.

ANSWERS

Question ① a): 15 cm

Question ① b): 26 cm

Share

WAYS OF WORKING Whole class teacher led

ASK

- Question ① a): *What does the diagram show you?*
- Question ① a): *Did anyone use a diagram to solve the problem presented in the **Discover** section?*
- Question ① a): *Would this method work for other questions?*
- Question ① b): *How can you check your answer to question ① b)?*
- Question ① b): *Can you check your answer by adding the length of the snakes together?*

IN FOCUS In question ① a) the visual representation shows children how to calculate the missing piece of data using the mean. Discuss what the diagram shows. Children could draw their own diagrams on individual white boards to show the problem and explain to a partner.

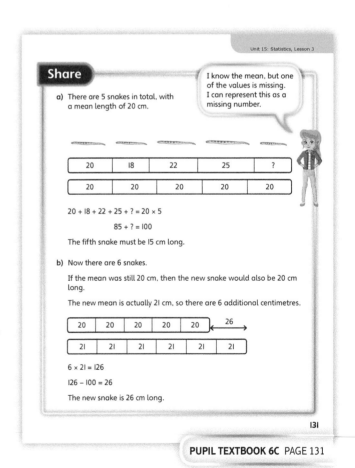

163

Think together

Whole class teacher led (I do, We do, You do)

ASK

- Question ❶: *How do the bar models help you?*
- Question ❷: *How many items are in the group?*
- Question ❷: *What do you need to find out first?*

IN FOCUS Question ❶ introduces data in the form of a bar chart. Children have the opportunity to recap on reading bar charts. Support children to use the bar model.

$$2 + 5 + 4 + 6 + 1 + ? = 6 \times 4 \qquad 18 + ? = 24$$

Question ❷ practises finding a missing number when you know the mean. The bar model has less scaffolding, but children should be able to use this to work out the missing number.

$$1.1 + 1.7 + 2.1 + ? = 1.5 \times 4 \qquad 4.9 + ? = 6$$

Question ❸ has many different solutions. Children should compare their solutions with their partner to help them understand the fact that different groups of numbers can have the same mean.

STRENGTHEN To strengthen understanding, practise simple missing number problems to ensure children are familiar with the method and can select the inverse operation.

$$34 + ? = 67 \qquad ? + 28 = 54 \qquad 83 + ? = 112$$

DEEPEN Give children groups of data (with one part missing) and the mean – challenge them to calculate the missing piece.

Group of data	Mean
3, 4, 5, 1, 1, ?	3
10, 3, 2, 8, ?	6
15, 12, 17, 3, ?	10

ASSESSMENT CHECKPOINT Questions ❶ and ❷ will give you another opportunity to check that children are able to solve problems involving the mean.

Question ❸ can be used to check that children realise different groups of numbers can have the same mean. Prompt discussion by pointing out Ash's comment.

ANSWERS

Question ❶: 6

Question ❷: 1·1 kg

Question ❸: There are several solutions to each set of numbers. For example, for the first person, the total is 33 and the numbers could be 10, 11 and 12. For the second person, the total is 50 and the numbers could be 9, 5, 10, 10, 16. For the third person, the total is 50 and the numbers could be 18, 15, 7, 5, 5. For the fourth person, the total is 40 and the numbers could be 12, 8, 11, 9.

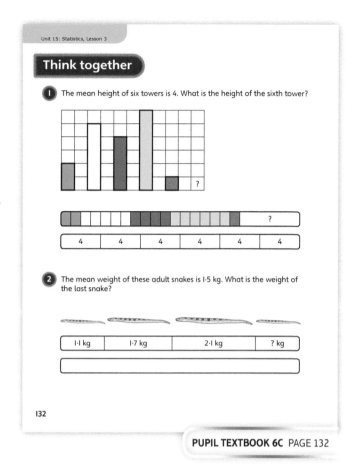

Think together

❶ The mean height of six towers is 4. What is the height of the sixth tower?

❷ The mean weight of these adult snakes is 1·5 kg. What is the weight of the last snake?

| 1·1 kg | 1·7 kg | 2·1 kg | ? kg |

132

PUPIL TEXTBOOK 6C PAGE 132

❸ Four people are thinking of numbers. What are the numbers? **CHALLENGE**

> I am thinking of three numbers. The mean is 11.

> I wonder whether there is more than one solution.

> I will choose one number to be 11, and then pick two other numbers to balance the mean.

> I am thinking of five numbers. The mean is 10.

> I am thinking of five numbers. The mean is 10, but none of the numbers is 10.

> I am thinking of four numbers. The difference between the biggest and the smallest number is 4. The mean is 10.

133

→ Practice book 6C p96

PUPIL TEXTBOOK 6C PAGE 133

Practice

WAYS OF WORKING Independent thinking

IN FOCUS Children practise using the mean to find missing numbers. Questions ❸ and ❹ introduce problems involving money and measures. Ask: *Can you apply the same methods to find the mean using numbers in these situations?*

STRENGTHEN Support the children by providing cubes to investigate possible solutions. With question ❺ discuss different ways to represent the mean – for example $\frac{1}{4}$ litre is the same as 250 ml.

Provide coins and jugs for children to explore the problems practically.

DEEPEN Ask children to find the missing number in groups of numbers using the mean. Ask: *Can you find two missing numbers? Can you find the missing number when the mean is not a whole number?*

THINK DIFFERENTLY Question ❺ asks children to calculate the possible volume of water contained in two jugs so the mean volume of five jugs is $\frac{1}{4}$ litre. This will test their ability to read different scales as well as their understanding of calculations involving a mean. Check that they find numbers appropriate to the size of the jugs.

ASSESSMENT CHECKPOINT Question ❶ assesses whether children recognise that there is often more than one solution to a problem.

Question ❹ assesses whether children can find two missing numbers in a group of data using the mean.

ANSWERS Answers to the **Practice** part of the lesson appear in a separate **Practice and Reflect answer guide**.

Reflect

WAYS OF WORKING Independent thinking

IN FOCUS Children are asked to choose two sets of numbers that have the same mean. In this problem the mean is not a whole number and therefore requires the children to use decimals and consider groups of data containing decimals. The statement doesn't specify how many numbers are in the group so there are many different solutions. Encourage the children to explore solutions with different amounts of numbers in the group.

ASSESSMENT CHECKPOINT Do children recognise there is often more than one solution to a problem? Do they recognise that different groups of data can have the same mean? Can they find the missing number when the mean is not a whole number?

ANSWERS Answers for the **Reflect** part of the lesson appear in the separate **Practice and Reflect answer book**.

After the lesson ⏸

- What percentage of children are confident using the mean to solve problems?
- Are there any misconceptions you need to pick up on before next lesson?

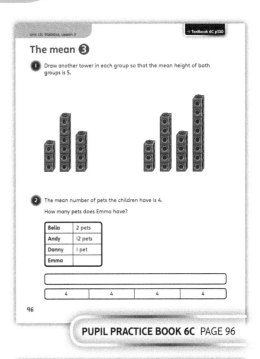

PUPIL PRACTICE BOOK 6C PAGE 96

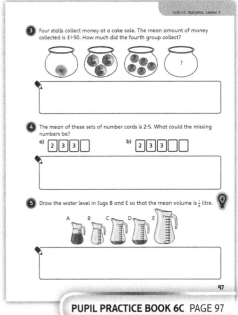

PUPIL PRACTICE BOOK 6C PAGE 97

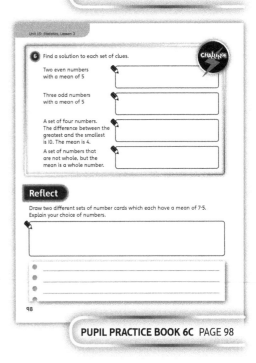

PUPIL PRACTICE BOOK 6C PAGE 98

Introducing pie charts

Learning focus

In this lesson, children are introduced to pie charts. They compare pie charts to tally charts and bar charts. Children should begin to understand that pie charts show results as a whole split into parts.

Small steps

→ Previous step: The mean (3)
→ **This step: Introducing pie charts**
→ Next step: Reading and interpreting pie charts

NATIONAL CURRICULUM LINKS

Year 6 Statistics

Interpret and construct pie charts and line graphs and use these to solve problems.

ASSESSING MASTERY

Children can recognise and name pie charts. They understand that the pie chart represents a set of data as a whole split into parts and the whole circle represents all the results together. Children can explain that a pie chart makes it easy to compare parts with a whole. They can suggest when a pie chart is more useful than other types of data representation such as tally charts or bar charts. Children can suggest types of questions that a pie chart is most suitable to answer.

COMMON MISCONCEPTIONS

Some children may not recognise that a pie chart shows the same information as a tally and bar chart. Ask:
• *What is the pie chart showing? Does it show the same thing as a tally chart or a bar chart?*

Children may find it difficult to understand that a pie chart represents the whole. Ask:
• *Could you think of a pie chart like a cake or a pie? The pie chart represents the whole and a slice or segment is a part of the whole.*

STRENGTHENING UNDERSTANDING

Provide children with circles and ask them to shade in fractions; for example, colour $\frac{1}{2}$ of the circle, colour $\frac{3}{4}$ of the circle and explain that the parts are fractions of the whole (the whole is the total number of people or data collected). Look at examples of pie charts representing data where half the children or a quarter of the children have chosen an activity or item. Ask: *Which activity or item did half the children choose? Which activity did $\frac{1}{4}$ choose?*

GOING DEEPER

Provide children with statements about different types of chart and ask them to identify which chart it is about (pie chart/bar chart/tally chart). Ask: *Can you add any statements of your own?*

You can draw the chart as you collect data.
It is simple to draw this type of chart.
You can calculate the numerical difference between parts easily.
It is easy to compare the parts with the whole with this type of chart.
It can be tricky to draw this type of chart precisely.

KEY LANGUAGE

In lesson: pie chart, advantages, disadvantages, **segment**, whole, represent, largest, section, half, data, tally chart, bar chart, compare, scale, quarter, total, frequency

Other language to be used by the teacher: smallest, percentage, fraction, part

STRUCTURES AND REPRESENTATIONS

pie charts, tally charts, bar charts

RESOURCES

Optional: paper circles, counters, cubes

 In the eTextbook of this lesson, you will find interactive links to a selection of teaching tools.

Before you teach

• Are children secure in identifying fractions of a circle such as $\frac{1}{2}, \frac{1}{4}, \frac{1}{3}$, etc.?
• Are children able to draw and use tally and bar charts accurately?

Discover

WAYS OF WORKING Pair work

ASK

- Question **1** a): *What different ways is the data represented? What are the charts called?*
- Question **1** a): *What do the charts show? Do they show the same data?*
- Question **1** a): *Which were the most popular and the least popular activities? How do you know?*
- Question **1** a): *How many children were asked in total? What would half be?*
- Question **1** b): *What is similar or different about the charts?*
- Question **1** b): *Which chart do you prefer and why?*

IN FOCUS Question **1** gives children the opportunity to discuss the different ways of representing data. Ensure children understand that the different charts represent the same data. Encourage children to discuss what is the same or different about the charts. Elicit from discussions that different charts can be better/easier to interpret in different situations or more suitable to answer certain questions. Ask children to consider how they could represent their thoughts or comparisons of the different types of chart. For example they could create a table or list.

PRACTICAL TIPS Provide children with counters or cubes which they can group to represent the different votes visually.

ANSWERS

Question **1** a): The pie chart shows most clearly.

Question **1** b): See table in **Share** section in Textbook 6C Unit 15 page 135.

Share

WAYS OF WORKING Whole class teacher led

ASK

- Question **1** b): *What is a pie chart? What are the advantages and disadvantages of a pie chart?*
- Question **1** b): *Do you agree with the advantages and disadvantages?*

IN FOCUS This is the first time children are formally introduced to pie charts. Ensure children understand that the circle represents all the results. Discuss the advantages and disadvantages of tally charts, bar charts and pie charts. Give example questions or situations and ask children to suggest which chart would be most suitable. Ask:
- *How many more children chose the beach than cooking? (Bar chart)*
- *Which is the least popular activity? (Bar chart)*
- *Which chart is the easiest to draw? (Tally)*
- *Which chart can I draw while collecting data? (Tally)*
- *Which chart shows if more or less than half chose the same activity? (Pie chart)*

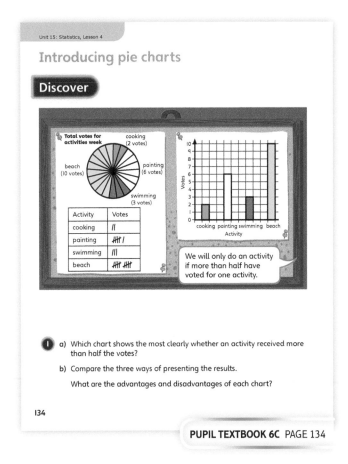

PUPIL TEXTBOOK 6C PAGE 134

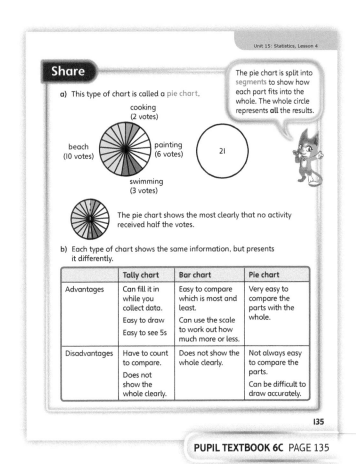

PUPIL TEXTBOOK 6C PAGE 135

Think together

WAYS OF WORKING Whole class teacher led (I do, We do, You do)

ASK

- Question ❶: *What do the different sections of the pie chart represent?*
- Question ❷: *How is a pie chart similar or different to a bar chart and a tally chart?*
- Question ❷: *Which chart is the best one to use for each question? Why?*

IN FOCUS In question ❶ children compare different types of chart to represent the same data. Encourage them to explore the usefulness of pie charts. Elicit from children that pie charts show the whole and are particularly useful when comparing one category to all of the results as a whole.

Question ❸ focusses on children's ability to match a tally chart to a pie chart showing the same information. Discuss Ash's comment. Ask: *Can you explain why the charts match or don't match?*

STRENGTHEN For question ❷ prompt children by giving examples of questions and asking them to identify which chart they would use to answer the question and discuss why. For example:

- *How many more gold medals than bronze medals were won? (Bar chart)*
- *How many silver medals were won? (Tally chart)*
- *A quarter of the medals were which colour? (Pie chart)*

DEEPEN Challenge children to draw a tally to match each pie chart in question ❸.

ASSESSMENT CHECKPOINT Use all the questions to check whether children understand that the circle of a pie chart represents all of the results and the sections represent the different categories. Ask: *Do you understand that the same data can be represented in different ways, and that different charts are more suited to answer different types of question?*

ANSWERS

Question ❶:

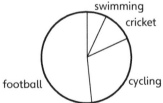

Question ❷ a): The bar chart shows best, that the team won 4 more gold medals than silver medals.

Question ❷ b): The pie chart shows best that the bronze medals were approximately a quarter of the total.

Question ❷ c): The tally chart shows best that the total number of medals won was 67.

Question ❸: Pie chart C best represents the results shown in the tally chart.

Think together

❶ Which section of the pie chart represents each activity?

cricket	///
cycling	⫽卅 ///
swimming	//
football	卅 卅 ////

Tally chart   Pie chart   Bar chart

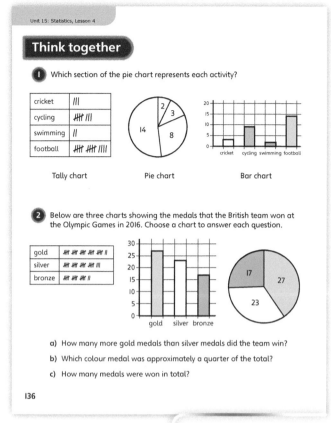

❷ Below are three charts showing the medals that the British team won at the Olympic Games in 2016. Choose a chart to answer each question.

gold	卅 卅 卅 卅 卅 //
silver	卅 卅 卅 卅 ///
bronze	卅 卅 卅 //

a) How many more gold medals than silver medals did the team win?

b) Which colour medal was approximately a quarter of the total?

c) How many medals were won in total?

136

PUPIL TEXTBOOK 6C PAGE 136

---

❸ Max spins a spinner 30 times and records the results in a tally chart.

Animal	Frequency
cat	卅 卅 ////
bird	卅 卅 /
fish	卅

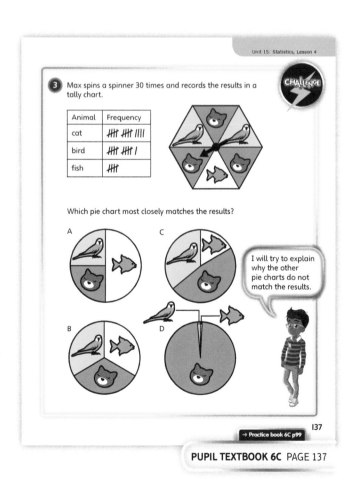

Which pie chart most closely matches the results?

I will try to explain why the other pie charts do not match the results.

137

→ Practice book 6C p99

PUPIL TEXTBOOK 6C PAGE 137

Practice

WAYS OF WORKING Independent thinking

IN FOCUS In question ❶ children compare the information in three pie charts to work out which shows a fraction of more than half. This requires them to understand that parts of a pie chart represent fractions of a whole.

STRENGTHEN If children are finding it a challenge to recognise fractions in a pie chart, provide them with circles and ask them to shade in fractions; for example, colour $\frac{1}{2}$ of the circle, colour $\frac{3}{4}$ of the circle. Explain that the parts are fractions of the whole (the whole is the total number of people/data collected).

DEEPEN Challenge children to draw a tally to match each pie chart in question ❶.

ASSESSMENT CHECKPOINT Question ❹ assesses whether children can use the data in a tally chart to create a pie chart. Ensure children understand that the same data can be represented in different ways.

Question ❺ assesses whether children recognise that different charts are more appropriate for different types of question. They should be able to provide clear explanations as to why each one is better for different questions.

ANSWERS Answers to the **Practice** part of the lesson appear in a separate **Practice and Reflect answer guide**.

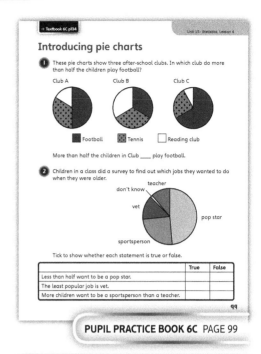

PUPIL PRACTICE BOOK 6C PAGE 99

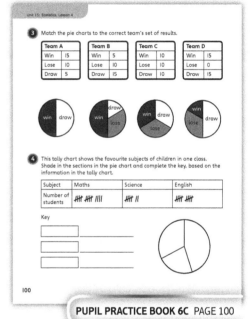

PUPIL PRACTICE BOOK 6C PAGE 100

Reflect

WAYS OF WORKING Independent thinking

IN FOCUS Children should identify that a pie chart is a circle that represents all the results with each section showing a category of data. A bar chart shows each category of data as a separate bar. Children should recognise that bar charts are more useful to compare the categories, whereas a pie chart is particularly useful when comparing a category (as a fraction) to the results (as a whole).

ASSESSMENT CHECKPOINT Do children recognise the differences/similarities between different types of chart?

Can children suggest when a pie chart is most useful?

ANSWERS Answers for the **Reflect** part of the lesson appear in the separate **Practice and Reflect answer book**.

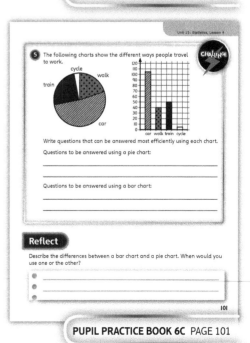

PUPIL PRACTICE BOOK 6C PAGE 101

After the lesson ⏸

- What percentage of children are confident at matching different types of chart showing the same data?
- Are there any misconceptions you need to pick up on before next lesson?

169

Reading and interpreting pie charts

Learning focus

In this lesson, children begin to read and interpret pie charts. Children can answer questions about pie charts.

Small steps

→ Previous step: Introducing pie charts
→ **This step: Reading and interpreting pie charts**
→ Next step: Fractions and pie charts (1)

NATIONAL CURRICULUM LINKS

Year 6 Statistics

Interpret and construct pie charts and line graphs and use these to solve problems.

ASSESSING MASTERY

Children can read and interpret pie charts using a key when provided.. Children can use a pie chart to answer questions about a set of data. Children are able to complete a pie chart using data in a tally chart and a key by colouring in the appropriate segmentss. Children are able to sketch simple pie charts to represent data by dividing the circle into equal parts to represent each person.

COMMON MISCONCEPTIONS

When transferring information from a tally chart to a pie chart, children may not understand they need to fill in segments, of the same vote for example, next to each other to create a category. Ask:
- *Will it be easier to understand what fraction of the whole is represented if segments of the same type are next to each other or apart?*

STRENGTHENING UNDERSTANDING

Children may find it difficult to divide a circle into equal parts. Support children by providing templates. Practise transferring sets of data in a tally chart into a pie chart by using a key and colouring a segment for each person. Ensure children understand that segments of the same colour go next to each other.

GOING DEEPER

Provide children with sets of data to transfer to a pie chart where each segment represents more than one person. For example:

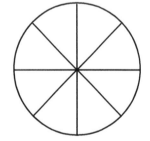

Fruit	Tally
pear	///
banana	ﬀﬀ /
orange	ﬀﬀ ////
strawberry	ﬀﬀ /

KEY LANGUAGE

In lesson: pie chart, represent, same, different, tally chart, equal, segment, section, more, same

Other language to be used by the teacher: data, bar chart, percentage, fraction, part, whole, category, results, total

STRUCTURES AND REPRESENTATIONS

tally chart , bar chart, pie chart

RESOURCES

Optional: pie charts, templates (circles split into 6, 8, 10, 12, 24), counters, cubes

 In the eTextbook of this lesson, you will find interactive links to a selection of teaching tools.

Before you teach

- Are children secure in reading and interpreting tally charts?
- Are children able to use a key confidently?
- Do children understand that the circle of the pie chart represents all of the results as a whole?

Discover

WAYS OF WORKING Pair work

ASK

- Question **1** a): *How many different categories are there?*
- Question **1** a): *How many children are at the party in total?*
- Question **1** a): *How many segments will be on the pie chart?*

IN FOCUS For question **1** a) children are required to use the picture of the fancy dress party to create a pie chart. They will need to decide how many categories there are and how many segments there will be on the pie chart. Prompt discussion about how children will fill in the pie chart and whether they will use a key to represent each category.

PRACTICAL TIPS Provide children with blank pie chart templates, in this case circles divided into 12 segments.

ANSWERS

Question **1** a): Children should recognise that each segment of the pie chart should represent one person at the fancy dress party.

Question **1** b):

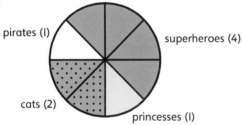

pirates (1)
superheroes (4)
cats (2)
princesses (1)

This pie chart has fewer segments; the cat section is the same size and the superhero section is bigger but the numbers are different; the same colours are used.

Share

WAYS OF WORKING Whole class teacher led

ASK

- Question **1** a): *What does each segment of the pie chart represent?*
- Question **1** a): *How many categories or sections is the pie chart split into? What does each section represent?*

IN FOCUS It is important that children understand that each segment on the pie chart represents one person at the party and that each colour represents a different fancy dress category (a section of the pie chart). The pie chart in question **1** a) is divided into 12 segments because there are 12 people. The pie chart in question **1** b) is divided into 8 segments because there are 8 people.

Reading and interpreting pie charts

Discover

1 a) How could you represent the children at the fancy dress party with a pie chart?

   b) One superhero, one cat and two pirates leave early. What would the pie chart look like now?

   What is the same and what is different about the two pie charts?

138

Share

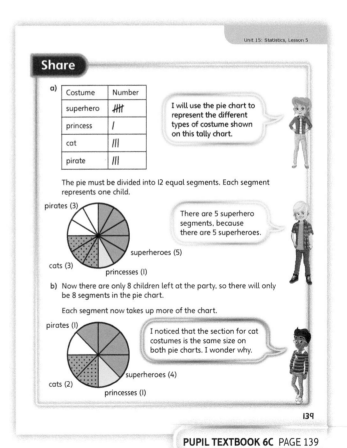

a)

Costume	Number
superhero	卌
princess	I
cat	III
pirate	III

I will use the pie chart to represent the different types of costume shown on this tally chart.

The pie must be divided into 12 equal segments. Each segment represents one child.

pirates (3)
superheroes (5)
cats (3)
princesses (1)

There are 5 superhero segments, because there are 5 superheroes.

b) Now there are only 8 children left at the party, so there will only be 8 segments in the pie chart.

Each segment now takes up more of the chart.

pirates (1)
superheroes (4)
cats (2)
princesses (1)

I noticed that the section for cat costumes is the same size on both pie charts. I wonder why.

139

Think together

WAYS OF WORKING Whole class teacher led (I do, We do, You do)

ASK

- Question ❶: *How many children are there?*
- Question ❷: *What does each coloured section represent?*

IN FOCUS In question ❷ children are asked to compare two pie charts. Ask: *Can you count the segments and identify that there were 3 children who chose rap music and now there are 5?*

In question ❸ children need to identify that there are 8 segments on the pie chart and 24 people, therefore each segment represents 3 people.

STRENGTHEN For question ❸ a), if children are finding the concept of each segment representing more than one person challenging, give them some division examples:

- *If there are 9 segments and 18 people how many people does each segment represent?*
- *If there are 4 segments and 20 people how many people does each segment represent?*

DEEPEN For question ❸ b) encourage children to consider different pie charts to represent the same data. For example, different numbers of segments. The pie chart could have 32, 16 or 8 segments. Ask: *Can you compare the pie charts?*

Children could also draw pie charts from previous questions with different numbers of segments. Children should recognise the number of segments must be a factor of the total.

ASSESSMENT CHECKPOINT Use question ❶ to check that children can compare the information in two pie charts when there are a different number of segments. Consider whether children can recognise that they will not be able to work out whether more boys or girls like singing just by comparing the size of the coloured sections.

ANSWERS

Question ❶: The statements are both wrong. The same percentage of boys and girls like singing. More girls than boys like musical statues.

Question ❷: Two children voted for rock and two voted for rap music.

Question ❸ a): 9 children danced and 3 performed magic: 9 – 3 = 6, therefore 6 more children danced than performed magic.
18 children did not sing.

Question ❸ b):

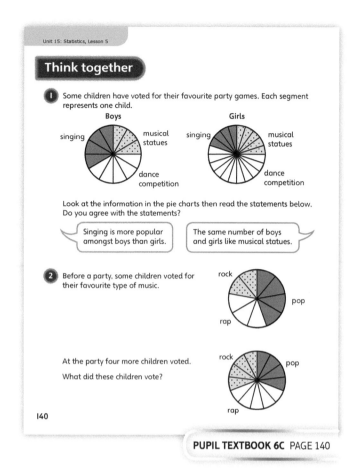

PUPIL TEXTBOOK 6C PAGE 140

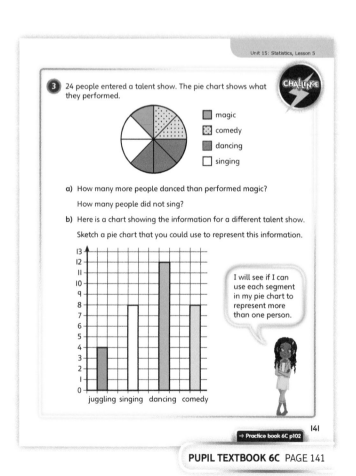

PUPIL TEXTBOOK 6C PAGE 141

Practice

WAYS OF WORKING Independent thinking

IN FOCUS In question ① children complete pie charts by transferring data from a tally chart and bar chart. Children are required to calculate how many people each segment on the pie chart represents.

In question ②, children must recognise that each section does not represent one football match; it represents a group of football matches, those either won, lost or drawn. To solve the problem children must calculate how many points each of the three sections of the pie chart represents before they can work out the total points of each team.

STRENGTHEN For question ① discuss and model how to calculate what each segment represents.

DEEPEN For question ④, challenge children to draw different representations of the same pie charts; for example, with different numbers of segments. Provide children with templates of pie charts, ready for them to work with.

ASSESSMENT CHECKPOINT Question ① gives you an opportunity to assess whether children are confident drawing pie charts to reflect information presented in different ways.

All questions allow you to assess children's understanding that a segment can represent different things, for example, people or points.

ANSWERS Answers to the **Practice** part of the lesson appear in a separate **Practice and Reflect answer guide**.

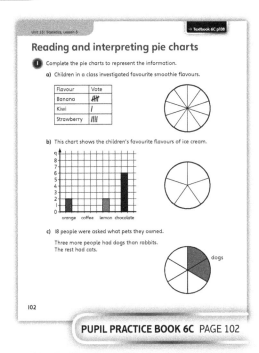

PUPIL PRACTICE BOOK 6C PAGE 102

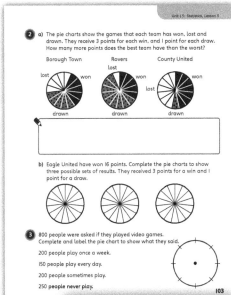

PUPIL PRACTICE BOOK 6C PAGE 103

Reflect

WAYS OF WORKING Independent thinking

IN FOCUS Children explain how to calculate what each segment of a pie chart represents. Encourage children to give examples.

ASSESSMENT CHECKPOINT Look for an explanation that shows that children understand that: the total number of people ÷ the number of segments in the pie chart = how many people each segment represents.

ANSWERS Answers for the **Reflect** part of the lesson appear in the separate **Practice and Reflect answer book**.

After the lesson ⏸

- What percentage of children are confident reading and interpreting pie charts?
- How many children can sketch a basic pie chart?
- Did all children understand that a section of a pie chart can represent more than one segment?

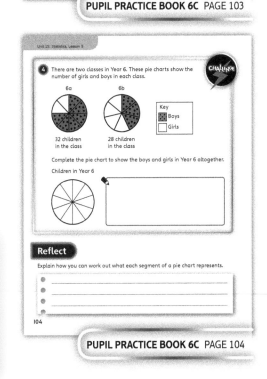

PUPIL PRACTICE BOOK 6C PAGE 104

Fractions and pie charts ❶

Learning focus

In this lesson, children calculate the fractions represented in pie charts. They compare the categories by converting them into fractions of the pie chart.

Small steps

→ Previous step: Reading and interpreting pie charts
→ **This step: Fractions and pie charts (1)**
→ Next step: Fractions and pie charts (2)

NATIONAL CURRICULUM LINKS

Year 6 Statistics

Interpret and construct pie charts and line graphs and use these to solve problems.

ASSESSING MASTERY

Children can calculate what fraction of a total each category is. They are able to say if a category is greater or less than a given fraction. They compare different pie charts taking into account the whole as well as what each section looks like. Children calculate the fractions represented by each segment. They are able to match statements to the correct pie chart.

COMMON MISCONCEPTIONS

Children can mistake the number of sections as the fraction; for example, they may say that as there are 3 sections, then each is $\frac{1}{3}$. Ask:
• *How many parts is the whole split into here?*

Children may forget that the fractions of the pie chart must add up to 1. 1 is the whole. Ask:
• *What is the whole? When do you have the total?*

STRENGTHENING UNDERSTANDING

Recap fractions of circles with the children. Provide circles and ask the children to shade $\frac{1}{2}, \frac{1}{4}, \frac{1}{3}, \frac{3}{4}$, etc. This will help the children to visualise the fractions.

GOING DEEPER

Go deeper by asking children to discuss and compare different pie charts split into different numbers of segments, and where the segments and sections represent different amounts or groups.

KEY LANGUAGE

In lesson: fraction, pie chart, segment, represent, divide, estimate

Other language to be used by the teacher: data, tally chart, bar chart, percentage, part, whole, category, results, total, section

STRUCTURES AND REPRESENTATIONS

tally chart, bar chart, pie chart

RESOURCES

Optional: circles split into fractions for children to shade given fractions, counters, cubes

 In the eTextbook of this lesson, you will find interactive links to a selection of teaching tools.

Before you teach

• Are children secure in shading and identifying fractions of circles?
• Are children able to use a key confidently?
• Do children understand the circle of the pie chart represents all of the results as a whole?

Discover

Pair work

ASK

- Question **1** a): *How many segments are in the circle? (24: there are 24 hours in a day)*
- Question **1** a): *What does each section represent? (1 hour)*

IN FOCUS In question **1**, children are required to calculate what fraction a section of a pie chart represents. Encourage children to discuss the pie chart. Ask: *How many segments does it have? What does each segment represent? What does the largest coloured section represent? Which is the smallest section?* Ask questions such as: *How many hours does Emily play for? How many hours does Emily sleep? Does Emily sleep for more or less than $\frac{1}{2}$ the day?*

PRACTICAL TIPS Provide children with images of fractions, i.e. a circle split into half, a circle split into quarters, a circle split into thirds as visual images for them to compare the pie chart to. Check that children know how many hours are in the day and recap if necessary with a 24 hour clock.

ANSWERS

Question **1** a): $\frac{14}{24} = \frac{7}{12}$; Emily sleeps for $\frac{7}{12}$ of each day.

Question **1** b): Max is not correct. $\frac{1}{6}$ of Emily's day is spent eating.

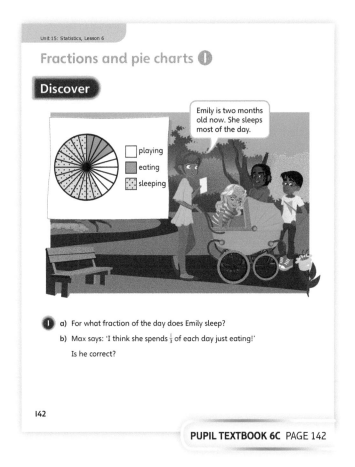

Share

Whole class teacher led

ASK

- Question **1** b): *What does each section on the pie chart represent?*
- Question **1** b): *How many hours does Emily spend eating? How can you show this as a fraction?*

IN FOCUS Question **1** b) provides a good opportunity for children to discuss fractions of circles. Ensure children understand that each segment on the pie chart represents one hour of the day and that each colour or pattern (section of segments) represents a different activity in baby Emily's day. Ask: *Can you show each activity as a fraction? Can you simplify the fractions?*

In question **1** b) Max thinks Emily eats for $\frac{1}{3}$ of the day. Point out the model of the pie chart divided into thirds (total number of segments divided by three). Ask: *How many segments are there in a third?*

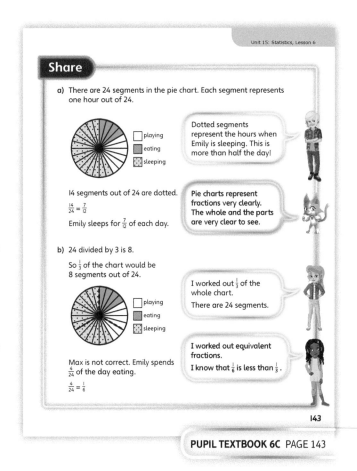

175

Think together

Whole class teacher led (I do, We do, You do)

ASK

- Question **1**: *What fraction of the whole does each colour represent? Can you simplify the fractions?*
- Question **2**: *How many segments are there?*
- Question **2**: *How many hours does a segment represent?*

IN FOCUS Check children are working out how many hours each segment represents (question **1**: each segment is an hour; question **2**: each segment is 3 hours). Ensure children are able to simplify the fractions.

Remind children that the fractions of a pie chart must add up to 1. 1 is the whole. For example: $\frac{1}{2} + \frac{1}{8} + \frac{1}{8} + \frac{1}{4} = 1$

In question **3**, children need to consider the whole when comparing the two pie charts. In a) the chart represents 80 people; in b) it represents 30. The yellow dotted section (people who give up) represents approximately 15 people in the first pie chart. In the second pie chart 15 people would be half the pie chart. Children should identify that a bigger section in a different pie chart doesn't mean more people chose that category but is dependent on the whole.

STRENGTHEN Provide children with circles divided into fractions to support children in estimating the sections in question **3**. Highlight that the fractions of a pie chart must add up to 1. 1 is the whole; for example: $\frac{1}{2} + \frac{1}{8} + \frac{1}{8} + \frac{1}{4} = 1$

DEEPEN Expand on the challenge question by asking children to compare all the sections of the two pie charts. Do they fully understand that it is important to identify what the sections represent and that a larger section in a different pie chart can represent a smaller number?

ASSESSMENT CHECKPOINT Question **1** will show whether children can calculate the fractions represented by segments in a pie chart.

Question **2** checks that children recognise that a segment represents more than I hour. Can they explain why it is important to take the whole into consideration?

Question **3** assesses children's ability to estimate fractions in a pie chart without counting individual segments.

ANSWERS

Question **1**: $\frac{1}{2}$ of Emily's time is spent sleeping, $\frac{1}{6}$ of Emily's time is spent eating, $\frac{1}{3}$ of Emily's time is spent playing.

Question **2**: $\frac{1}{8}$ of Emily's time is spent eating; $\frac{3}{8}$ of Emily's time is spent sleeping, $\frac{1}{4}$ of her time is spent playing and $\frac{1}{4}$ of her time is spent at school.

Question **3** a): Approximately $\frac{1}{2}$ ask for help, $\frac{5}{16}$ try to fix it, $\frac{2}{16}$ give up and $\frac{1}{16}$ hit the computer.

Question **3** b): A similar number of children would give up because, although the segment is bigger on the children's pie chart, not as many children were asked.

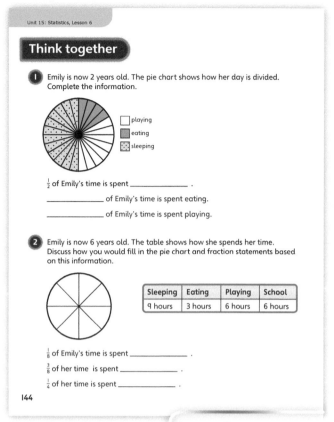

PUPIL TEXTBOOK 6C PAGE 144

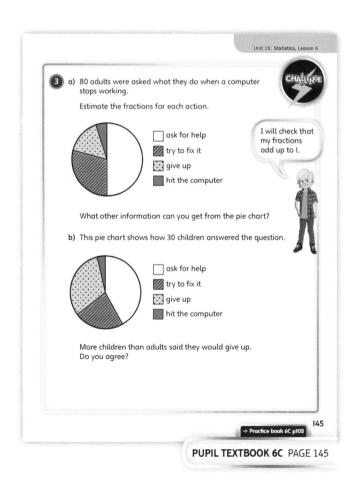

PUPIL TEXTBOOK 6C PAGE 145

Practice

WAYS OF WORKING Independent thinking

IN FOCUS For question ❶ children find the fraction represented by a shaded segment in three pie charts. They will need to remember how many hours there are in a day because this is the whole for each chart.

For question ❹ children match statements to the correct pie chart. This requires understanding the need to consider the whole of each pie chart. Then they can calculate the numbers represented by the sections.

STRENGTHEN Recap how to calculate the value of each segment and section. Ask children to sketch and shade fractions of circles on an individual white board (or chalkboard) to familiarise themselves with the visual images of $\frac{1}{4}$, $\frac{1}{2}$, $\frac{1}{8}$ and $\frac{1}{3}$ of a circle.

DEEPEN For Question ❸, challenge children to draw different representations of the same pie charts; for example, with different numbers of segments and sections.

THINK DIFFERENTLY Question ❸ requires children to compare two pie charts and work out from them which school team has lost the most games. The teams have not played the same amount of games, so children should realise that the fractions shown on each one will not be the same number. Children must explain their answer in words instead of showing it in a calculation. This should show whether they truly understand the importance of the whole.

ASSESSMENT CHECKPOINT Question ❺ requires children to show that their fraction estimates add up to 1. This will reinforce their understanding of the whole. The question also provides an opportunity to check children can calculate fractions of a 3-digit number.

ANSWERS Answers to the **Practice** part of the lesson appear in a separate **Practice and Reflect answer guide**.

Reflect

WAYS OF WORKING Independent thinking

IN FOCUS Children are asked to calculate the fraction represented by each section (group of segments). Ensure children are simplifying fractions. Make sure children recognise that the fractions of a pie chart must add up to 1 and use this understanding to check their answers. $\frac{1}{12} + \frac{3}{12} + \frac{8}{12} = 1$.

ASSESSMENT CHECKPOINT This is a good question to assess which children have mastered fractions and pie charts, and which need more support.

ANSWERS Answers for the **Reflect** part of the lesson appear in the separate **Practice and Reflect answer book**.

After the lesson ⏸

- What percentage of the children are secure calculating the fractions in a pie chart?
- How many children are able to estimate the fractions of a pie chart?
- Are there any misconceptions you need to pick up on before next lesson?

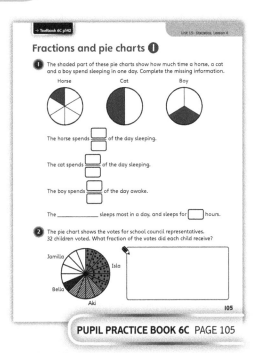

PUPIL PRACTICE BOOK 6C PAGE 105

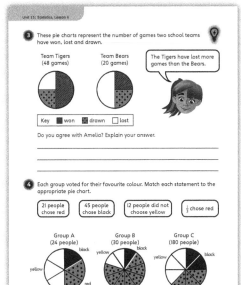

PUPIL PRACTICE BOOK 6C PAGE 106

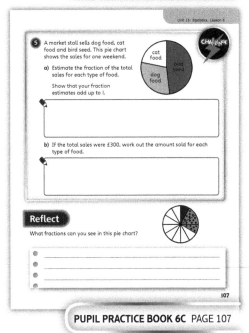

PUPIL PRACTICE BOOK 6C PAGE 107

Fractions and pie charts ❷

Learning focus

In this lesson, children use given fractions of a pie chart to calculate the amount/number of items in a category. They use the difference between two categories to identify the total or amount of items in each of the categories.

Small steps

→ Previous step: Fractions and pie charts (1)
→ **This step: Fractions and pie charts (2)**
→ Next step: Percentages and pie charts

NATIONAL CURRICULUM LINKS

Year 6 Statistics

Interpret and construct pie charts and line graphs and use these to solve problems.

ASSESSING MASTERY

Children can use known facts about a pie chart to identify or calculate further information. They can use fractions of a pie chart to calculate the number of items represented in a category. Children can use the difference between two categories to calculate the amount represented by a category. Children can confidently estimate fractions of a pie chart.

COMMON MISCONCEPTIONS

Children may mistake the number of sections as the fraction, for example they may say that as there are 3 sections, each is $\frac{1}{3}$. Ask:
• *How many sections are there?*

Children may forget that the fractions of the pie chart must add up to 1. 1 is the whole. Ask:
• *What do the sections add up to?*

STRENGTHENING UNDERSTANDING

Recap fractions of circles with the children. Provide circles and ask children to shade $\frac{1}{2}, \frac{1}{4}, \frac{1}{3}, \frac{3}{4}$, etc. This will help children to visualise the fractions.

GOING DEEPER

Discuss and compare different pie charts. Ask children to create a pie chart and write their own questions about it.

KEY LANGUAGE

In lesson: fraction, pie chart, section, right angle, exact, tally chart, segment

Other language to be used by the teacher: data, bar chart, percentage, part, whole, category, results, total

STRUCTURES AND REPRESENTATIONS

pie charts, bar models, arrays

RESOURCES

Mandatory: counters

Optional: pie charts, circles split into segments for children to shade given fractions, calendar

 In the eTextbook of this lesson, you will find interactive links to a selection of teaching tools.

Before you teach

• Are children secure in adding fractions?
• Are children secure in finding fractions of amounts? For example, $\frac{1}{6}$ of 30 = 5
• Do children understand the circle of the pie chart represents all of the results as a whole?

Discover

Fractions and pie charts ②

Discover

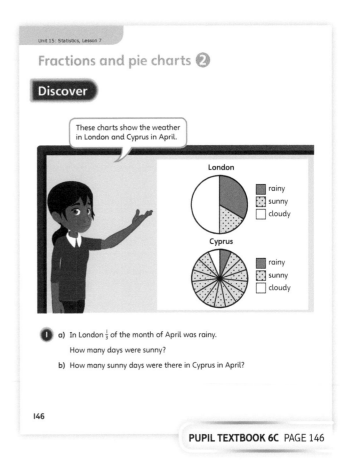

WAYS OF WORKING Pair work

ASK

- Question ① a): *How many days are there in April?*
- Question ① a): *How many days are there in $\frac{1}{3}$ of the month?*
- Question ① b): *How many segments are there in the pie chart for Cyprus?*
- Question ① b): *What information can you gather from the pie chart?*

IN FOCUS Question ① requires children to compare the fractions of two pie charts to identify how many days in April were sunny, cloudy or rainy. The pie charts have a different number of segments to make children consider that the category sections don't represent numbers but fractions of the whole. They will practise using fractions in a pie chart to calculate numbers in a category.

PRACTICAL TIPS Show children a calendar to remind them how many days there are in April (30). Provide children with counters of 3 different colours to represent the sunny, rainy and cloudy days in April.

ANSWERS

Question ① a): 5 days were sunny in London.

Question ① b): 26 days were sunny in Cyprus.

PUPIL TEXTBOOK 6C PAGE 146

Share

Share

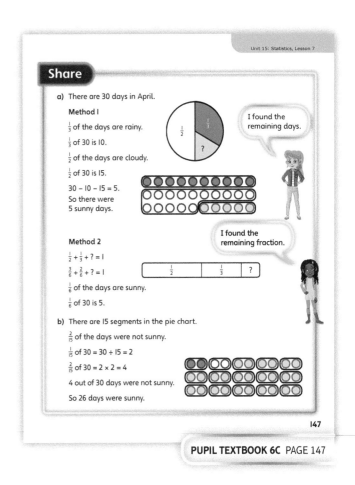

WAYS OF WORKING Whole class teacher led

ASK

- Question ① a): *Which method do you prefer and why?*
- Question ① b): *What does each section on the pie charts represent?*
- Question ① b): *What similarities are there between the pie charts?*

IN FOCUS Question ① a) shows two methods to work out the answer. Compare the two methods and discuss which method children prefer and why. Provide children with counters to model the first method. Encourage children to draw a bar model representing the problem. This is an opportunity for children to compare different methods of working out a problem and realise that they may find some methods are better than others for different problems.

PUPIL TEXTBOOK 6C PAGE 147

Think together

Whole class teacher led (I do, We do, You do)

ASK

• Question ❷: *What information do you have? How can you use this information to solve the problem?*
• Question ❸: *What do you notice in the pie charts (right angle)? How does that help you?*

IN FOCUS Question ❶ gives children the opportunity to recap how to find what fraction represents a category. They should realise that because they know how many children are represented by one segment, they can work out the fractions made by the different categories. Children are learning to use information they have about the pie chart to calculate further information.

STRENGTHEN For question ❶ remind children again that the fractions of a pie chart must add up to 1; for example, $\frac{1}{2} + \frac{1}{6} + \frac{2}{6} = 1$.

DEEPEN Provide children with a pie chart and challenge them to write their own questions about it. (They can use the question in question ❷ as a guide.)

ASSESSMENT CHECKPOINT Question ❶ will highlight whether children are confident about using information about a pie chart to calculate further information.

Question ❸ assesses whether children are confident at estimating fractions of a pie chart. Ask: *Do you recognise that a right angle means the fraction is $\frac{1}{4}$?*

ANSWERS

Question ❶: $\frac{1}{2}$ like fish fingers; $\frac{1}{6}$ like popcorn; $\frac{1}{8}$ like strawberries.

Question ❷: 36 students

Question ❸ a): Class 6 collected more paper.

Question ❸ b): Approximately 10·5 kg

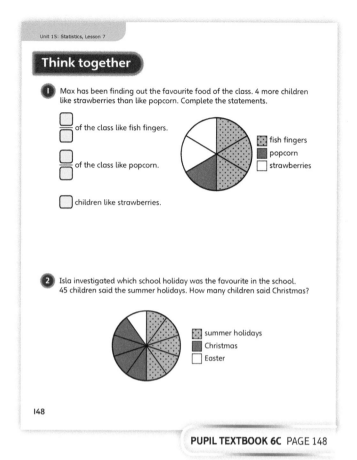

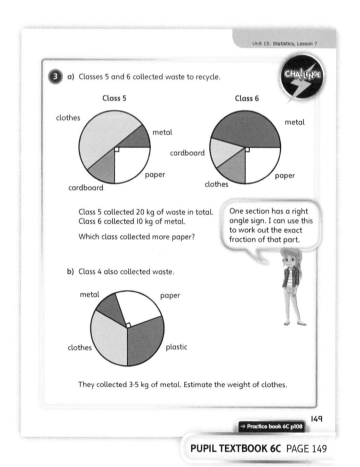

Practice

WAYS OF WORKING Independent thinking

IN FOCUS For question ① children are given a piece of information to calculate further information from a pie chart. Encourage children to identify what they know about the pie chart and consider how to use this information. Ask: *What else does it tell you?*

Question ③ gives children practice at reading information from a pie chart to work out whether statements about the categories are true or false. This requires them to calculate the numbers represented by fractions as well as vice versa. Do they see a step-by-step process for doing this? Ask: *What are the categories? Can you estimate the fractions? What information do you know? What do you need to find out?*

DEEPEN Challenge children to work in pairs and write a problem which gives the difference between two categories and requires their partner to calculate the total. They should sketch a pie chart to support the problem.

ASSESSMENT CHECKPOINT All questions test children's ability to interpret a pie chart.

Question ③ is a good question to use to check that children can use fractions of a pie chart to calculate totals or amounts in a category.

ANSWERS Answers to the **Practice** part of the lesson appear in a separate **Practice and Reflect answer guide**.

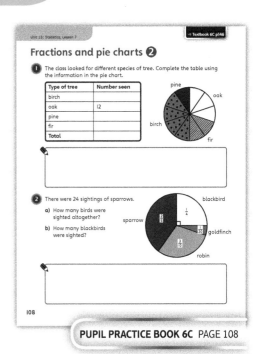

PUPIL PRACTICE BOOK 6C PAGE 108

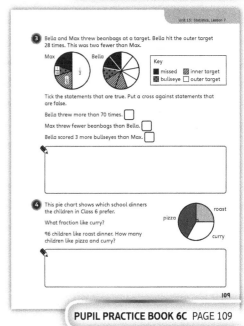

PUPIL PRACTICE BOOK 6C PAGE 109

Reflect

WAYS OF WORKING Independent thinking

IN FOCUS Children are challenged to write their own problem and sketch a pie chart to match.

ASSESSMENT CHECKPOINT This question will allow children to demonstrate that they understand how to use a fraction of a pie chart to calculate the total/whole.

ANSWERS Answers for the **Reflect** part of the lesson appear in the separate **Practice and Reflect answer book**.

After the lesson ⏸

- Are all children secure in using information about the pie chart to calculate further information?
- Are children confident with calculating and estimating fractions of a pie chart?

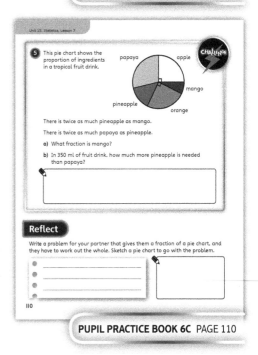

PUPIL PRACTICE BOOK 6C PAGE 110

Percentages and pie charts

Learning focus

In this lesson, children learn that the whole pie chart is represented by 100%. They compare and convert percentages of the pie chart to fractions. Children use percentages to calculate amounts of each category.

Small steps

→ Previous step: Fractions and pie charts (2)
→ **This step: Percentages and pie charts**
→ Next step: Interpreting line graphs

NATIONAL CURRICULUM LINKS

Year 6 Statistics

Interpret and construct pie charts and line graphs and use these to solve problems.

Year 6 Ratio and proportion

Solve problems involving the calculation of percentages [for example, of measures, and such as 15% of 360] and the use of percentages for comparison.

ASSESSING MASTERY

Children know that 100% represents the whole pie chart. They can compare percentages of the pie chart to fractions. Children use percentages to calculate amounts. They can use knowledge of fractions and angles and convert percentages into fractions and angles.

COMMON MISCONCEPTIONS

Some children may think degrees are the same as percentages. Remind them that the total degrees (or the whole) in a circle are 360, and the whole in percentages is 100%.

STRENGTHENING UNDERSTANDING

Children may need support converting percentages to fractions. Use bar models to support them. Recap percentages. Ask: *Can you find percentages of a given amount for example 70% of 150? 10% of 320?*

Practise converting percentages into fractions; for example: $50\% = \frac{1}{2}$, $25\% = \frac{1}{4}$, $20\% = \frac{1}{5}$.

Check children know the angles of a circle equal 360°.

GOING DEEPER

Explore the use of angles in pie charts. Ask: *Can you calculate the percentages of sections from given angles?*

KEY LANGUAGE

In lesson: percentage, pie chart, fraction, accurate, estimate, segment, half, degree

Other language to be used by the teacher: angle, data, tally chart, bar chart, part, whole, category, results, total, section

STRUCTURES AND REPRESENTATIONS

pie chart, bar model, tally chart

RESOURCES

Optional: counters, cubes, pie charts with degrees marked, circles split into segments for children to shade given percentages, individual whiteboards

 In the eTextbook of this lesson, you will find interactive links to a selection of teaching tools.

Before you teach ⏸

- Are children secure in calculating percentages?
- Can children convert percentages into fractions?
- Can children calculate angles in a circle?

Discover

WAYS OF WORKING Pair work

ASK

- Question **1** a): *What percentage of Mars's atmosphere is oxygen? How can you work it out?*
- Question **1** b): *What would $\frac{1}{5}$ of 100% be?*
- Question **1** b): *What information can you find in the pie chart?*

IN FOCUS Question **1** a) requires children to convert percentages to fractions to find what fractions of the atmosphere of Mars are nitrogen, argon and carbon dioxide. Ask: *What percentage of the atmosphere is carbon dioxide? How can you work this out?* Recap that a pie chart represents a whole and therefore the percentages in a pie chart add up to a total of 100%.

PRACTICAL TIPS Provide children with individual whiteboards or blackboards and encourage them to draw diagrams or bar models to help them work out the different percentages and fractions.

ANSWERS

Question **1** a): $\frac{1}{50}$ nitrogen, $\frac{1}{50}$ argon, $\frac{24}{25}$ carbon dioxide.

Question **1** b): Aki's estimate is just 1% too small, which is very accurate.

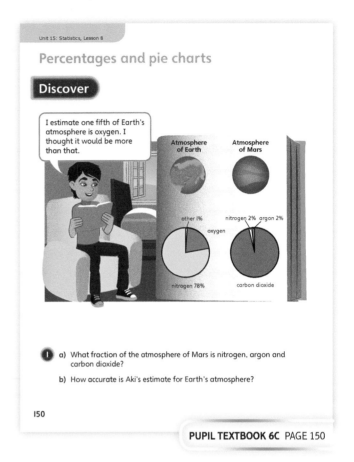

PUPIL TEXTBOOK 6C PAGE 150

Share

WAYS OF WORKING Whole class teacher led

ASK

- Question **1** a): *What do the percentages of a pie chart total? (100%)*
- Question **1** a): *Why is Flo checking using the percentages?*
- Question **1** b): *Do you find the bar model helpful?*

IN FOCUS Question **1** b) shows how to use a bar model to calculate the missing percentage. Children should know that the pie chart total is 100% and can use this to calculate missing data. Ask children to draw bar models to show the percentages of each planet's atmosphere to give a visual model.

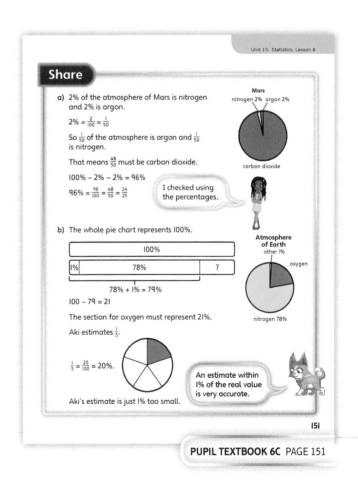

PUPIL TEXTBOOK 6C PAGE 151

Think together

Whole class teacher led (I do, We do, You do)

ASK

- Question ❶: *How many segments is the pie chart divided into? What fraction of the whole are they?*
- Question ❷: *What percentage is the whole? What are the percentages converted to fractions?*
- Question ❸: *How many degrees are there in a circle? What information do you have about the categories?*

IN FOCUS In question ❶ children are asked to work out percentages. This requires them to understand that the pie chart is divided into 10 segments (shown by the equally spaced marks around the outside). Each segment equals $\frac{1}{10}$ or 10% (100 ÷ 10 = 10).

In question ❷ children need to convert the percentages to fractions. You may want to point out that when calculating the fraction of fruit and vegetables in the pie chart, children should note that these two sections should be added together: 10% + 15% = 25% = $\frac{1}{4}$.

Question ❸ a) introduces the use of angles. There are 360° in a circle so 100% = 360°. If the children add up the given degrees they can calculate the missing information.

36° + 72° + 90° + ?° = 360°
198 + 162 = 360
162° = jogging

They then convert this to a percentage

162 ÷ 360 = 0·45 = 45%

STRENGTHEN Use bar models to show children how percentages equate to fractions.

Ask children to draw bar models to find $\frac{1}{5}, \frac{1}{2}, \frac{1}{3}, \frac{3}{4}$.

DEEPEN Explore the use of angles in pie charts. Give children more pie charts with degrees marked. Ask them to calculate the percentages of sections from the angles.

ASSESSMENT CHECKPOINT Question ❷ involves calculating percentages, fractions and numbers in a category. It provides a good opportunity to assess whether children have truly mastered pie charts.

ANSWERS

Question ❶: 70% salt water, 5% snow/ice, 5% mountain, 5% desert, 15% land that can be farmed.

Question ❷: Three statements match the pie chart. The third statement does not match. $\frac{1}{4}$ of his food is fruit and vegetables, not $\frac{1}{3}$.

Question ❸ a): 45% of people preferred jogging.

Question ❸ b): 192 people liked team sports.

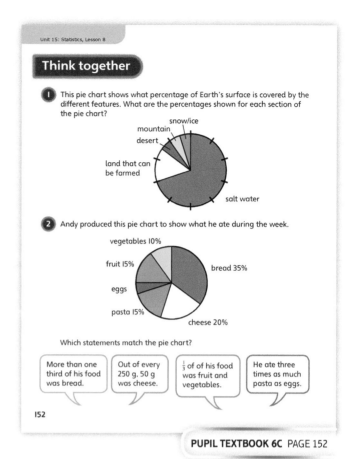

PUPIL TEXTBOOK 6C PAGE 152

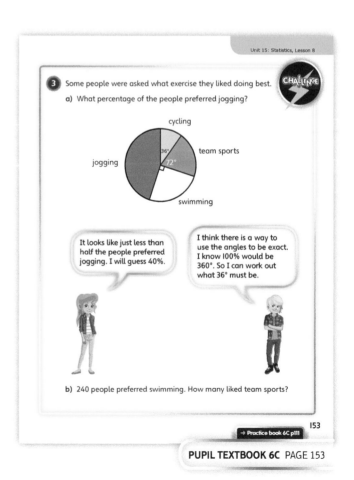

PUPIL TEXTBOOK 6C PAGE 153

Practice

WAYS OF WORKING Independent thinking

IN FOCUS In question **2** children must use percentages to work out how many people are in a category. This question includes a right angle. Children need to recognise that this means $\frac{1}{4}$ of the circle or 25% of the total.

In question **4**, the information for one team is supplied without a pie chart. Children may find it useful to draw a pie chart to represent this information to make it easier to compare the two teams.

STRENGTHEN If children are finding it a challenge to understand categories represented by degrees, remind them that there are 360° in a circle. So 180° = 50% = $\frac{1}{2}$; 90° = 25% = $\frac{1}{4}$. Suggest they draw bar models to show the equivalences.

DEEPEN Give children some information in percentages for them to draw pie charts. Challenge them to represent some of the percentages with degrees.

ASSESSMENT CHECKPOINT Question **3** tests children's understanding of how to work out what numbers percentages represent. Knowing that the three sections make up the whole, or 100%, and given the numbers for one category, children should be able to work out the numbers in the other categories.

ANSWERS Answers to the **Practice** part of the lesson appear in a separate **Practice and Reflect answer guide**.

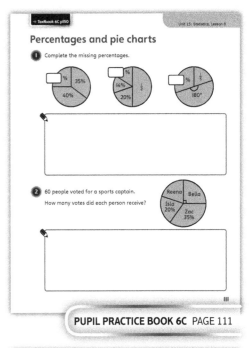

PUPIL PRACTICE BOOK 6C PAGE 111

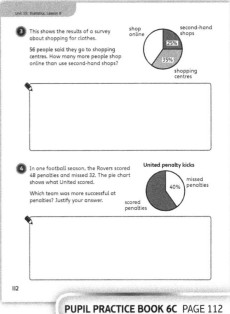

PUPIL PRACTICE BOOK 6C PAGE 112

Reflect

WAYS OF WORKING Independent thinking

IN FOCUS Children are challenged to draw a pie chart to show given percentages and a fraction. One percentage is missing so children calculate the missing percentage first: 25 ($\frac{1}{4}$) + 10 + 15 + ? = 100

ASSESSMENT CHECKPOINT The question contains a fraction and percentages. Children are asked to show how they know how to draw the pie chart and this will indicate whether they understand the concept of pie charts and the equivalence of fractions and percentages.

ANSWERS Answers for the **Reflect** part of the lesson appear in the separate **Practice and Reflect answer book**.

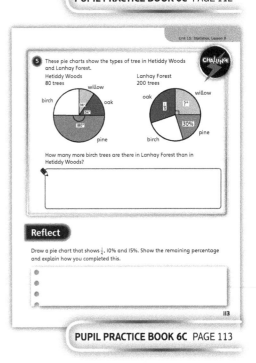

PUPIL PRACTICE BOOK 6C PAGE 113

After the lesson ⏸

- Can children apply their knowledge of fractions and angles?
- Do you need to give any children further help with degrees in pie charts?

Interpreting line graphs

Learning focus

In this lesson, children learn to read and understand line graphs. They learn to read amounts and times on the line graph and use this to solve problems.

Small steps

→ Previous step: Percentages and pie charts
→ **This step: Interpreting line graphs**
→ Next step: Constructing line graphs

NATIONAL CURRICULUM LINKS

Year 6 Statistics

Interpret and construct pie charts and line graphs and use these to solve problems.

ASSESSING MASTERY

Children can read amounts and times plotted on a curved or straight line graph and the amounts/times in between the plotted points. Children can solve problems by reading plotted points on a line graph.

Children can identify and describe changes in the line graphs, for example a pause or speed change.

Children know that a straight line shows a consistent and proportional increase or decrease and understand that the direction of a line or curve can show if something is increasing or decreasing.

Children can tell stories or describe what is happening to match a line graph for example someone walking to the bus stop, waiting for a bus, travelling on the bus.

COMMON MISCONCEPTIONS

Children may confuse the x-axis and y-axis on a line graph. Ask:
• *Which line is the x-axis and which is the y-axis?*

Children may read and interpret the scales used on a line graph incorrectly. Ask:
• *What is the scale on this line graph? What does each interval represent?*

STRENGTHENING UNDERSTANDING

Discuss the line graphs in detail with children and get them to practise reading simple points from graphs. Start with marked points and progress to unmarked points. Children need to be confident in reading graphs before using line graphs to solve problems and answer two-step questions.

GOING DEEPER

Explore different shaped line graphs with children (curved and straight). Ask children to create stories to explain what a line graph is showing, including why a curve flattens out or goes up more steeply.

KEY LANGUAGE

In lesson: interpret, line, graph, increase, above, below, zero (0), value, minus (−), estimate, accurate, between, fraction, percentage

Other language to be used by the teacher: plot, point, x-axis, y-axis, vertical, horizontal

STRUCTURES AND REPRESENTATIONS

line graphs

RESOURCES

Mandatory: graph paper

Optional: tracing paper, rulers

 In the eTextbook of this lesson, you will find interactive links to a selection of teaching tools.

 Before you teach

• Are children secure in interpreting the scale on a y-axis and x-axis?
• Are children secure in adding and subtracting negative numbers?

Discover

WAYS OF WORKING Pair work

ASK

- Question ❶ a): *What type of graph is this?*
- Question ❶ a): *Which is the y-axis and which is the x-axis? What scale is used on the y-axis and x-axis?*
- Question ❶ a): *Is the temperature increasing or decreasing? How do you know?*

IN FOCUS Question ❶ asks children to read a line graph to see what the temperature is at certain times of day. Children need to recognise that the y-axis is showing the temperature and the x-axis is showing the time. Ask: *Can you work out what the temperature was at 6 am and what the temperature was at 6.30 am to calculate the difference?*

PRACTICAL TIPS Provide children with tracing paper and rulers so they can draw lines over the graph; for example, from 1 °C on the y-axis to the plotted line and down to the x-axis.

ANSWERS

Question ❶ a): 3 °C

Question ❶ b): 7:10 am approximately

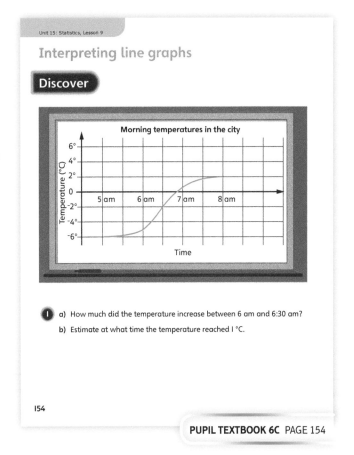

Share

WAYS OF WORKING Whole class teacher led

ASK

- Question ❶ a): *Did you read the temperatures for the times 6 am and 6:30 am correctly?*
- Question ❶ b): *What has been drawn to make it easier for you to read the line graph (dotted lines drawn on)? Does this help you?*
- Question ❶ b): *What shape is the line? Is it straight or curved? What direction is it going in? What does that mean?*

IN FOCUS Close ups of the graph show how drawing a dotted line can help with reading the temperature and time on the axes. The axes are like number lines. Discuss how to calculate the difference. This is shown with jumps, which will be familiar with children. Model how to use tracing paper and a dotted line to help read from the line graph.

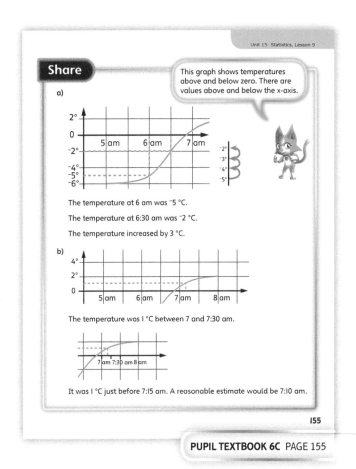

Think together

Whole class teacher led (I do, We do, You do)

ASK

- Question **1**: *What time did the balloon go above 500 m? What time did the balloon go below 500 m? Can you calculate the time in between?*
- Question **2**: *Could you use tracing paper and a ruler to help you find an unmarked point on the line graph?*
- Question **3**: *Can you describe the scale on the line graph? Why do you think it is flat in the middle?*

IN FOCUS For question **1** children need to identify the time the balloon went above 500 m (this is a marked point) and the time the balloon came back down below the 500 m (this is an unmarked point), then calculate the time in between. For question **2** children are asked to read the temperatures from the line graph. To do this they need to identify that 9 am is halfway between 6 am and 12 pm, both of which are marked on the x-axis. They then need to interpret the scale on the y-axis (every 0·5 degree). In question **3**, the challenge question, a line graph compares the time and distance travelled. Children need to interpret what is happening in the part of the graph in the middle where the distance remains the same (Aki is in the shop/not walking/Aki is resting/no distance has been covered during this time).

STRENGTHEN Discuss the line graphs in detail and practise reading simple points from the graph. Begin with marked points and progress to unmarked points. Children need to be confident in reading line graphs before using graphs to solve problems and answer two-step questions.

DEEPEN Ask children to create further questions about the line graphs for a partner to answer. Ask them to create a story to show on a line graph. Ask: *Can you use the line graph to predict further data?*

ASSESSMENT CHECKPOINT Question **1** assesses whether children can identify a point on a line graph and read its position on both axes.

In question **2** children must estimate an unmarked point on a line graph. Check that they are able to read intervals on the axes correctly in order to estimate accurately.

ANSWERS

Question **1**: The balloon goes above 500 m at 13:30 and it comes down below 500 m between 16:15 and 16:30 at approximately 16:20. The balloon was above 500 m for approximately 2 hours and 50 minutes.

Question **2**:

Time	9:00 – Day 1	9:00 – Day 2	9:00 – Day 3
Temperature	38·75	37·75	37·1

Question **3** a): It takes Aki 4 minutes to get to the shop. He stays in the shop for 10 minutes. The shop is 250 metres from his home.

Question **3** b): The graph is showing how far Aki has travelled, not how far from home he is.

Think together

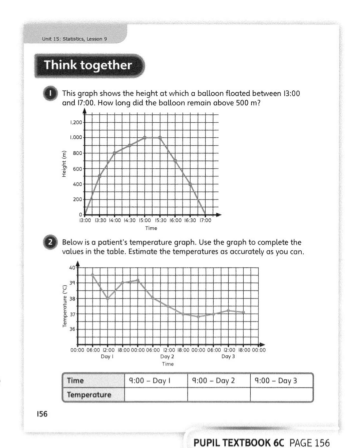

1 This graph shows the height at which a balloon floated between 13:00 and 17:00. How long did the balloon remain above 500 m?

2 Below is a patient's temperature graph. Use the graph to complete the values in the table. Estimate the temperatures as accurately as you can.

Time	9:00 – Day I	9:00 – Day 2	9:00 – Day 3
Temperature			

156

PUPIL TEXTBOOK 6C PAGE 156

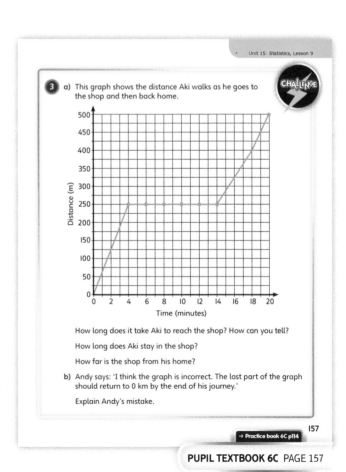

3 a) This graph shows the distance Aki walks as he goes to the shop and then back home.

CHALLENGE

How long does it take Aki to reach the shop? How can you tell?

How long does Aki stay in the shop?

How far is the shop from his home?

b) Andy says: 'I think the graph is incorrect. The last part of the graph should return to 0 km by the end of his journey.'

Explain Andy's mistake.

157

→ Practice book 6C p114

PUPIL TEXTBOOK 6C PAGE 157

Practice

WAYS OF WORKING Independent thinking

IN FOCUS In question ❶ a) children read and estimate plotted points on a line graph and estimate times in between the plotted points. In question ❶ b) they are asked to calculate the difference between two temperatures. Both require accurate reading of the x and y-axis.

Question ❸ asks children to read a line graph to complete sentences. This will necessitate them recognising what the changes in direction of the graph are showing them

STRENGTHEN Discuss the line graphs in detail. Consider the shape and direction of the line: is it curved or straight, does it show a temperature increasing or decreasing? Support children to interpret the scales. Provide tracing paper for children to draw lines and estimate amounts in between plotted points.

DEEPEN Look at line graphs linked to cross-curricular topics such as plants growing over time, shadow lengths in science.

ASSESSMENT CHECKPOINT Use question ❶ to check that children can read amounts and times plotted on a line graph and can read and estimate amounts and times in between plotted points.

Question ❸ provides the opportunity to assess whether children can identify and describe changes in a line graph such as a pause or change in speed.

ANSWERS Answers to the **Practice** part of the lesson appear in a separate **Practice and Reflect answer guide**.

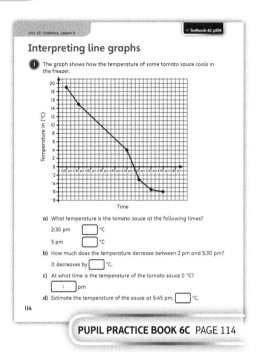

PUPIL PRACTICE BOOK 6C PAGE 114

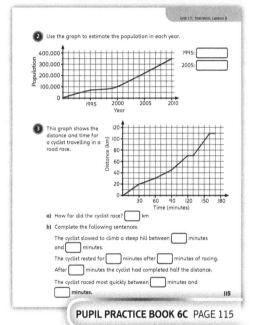

PUPIL PRACTICE BOOK 6C PAGE 115

Reflect

WAYS OF WORKING Independent thinking

IN FOCUS Children are asked to give tips on reading a line graph accurately. Encourage them to imagine they are explaining to someone how to interpret line graphs. Ask them to consider the shape of the curve and pauses in the line as well as plotted points. Suggest that they use bullet points to list the tips they have.

ASSESSMENT CHECKPOINT Look for tips that include ways to avoid mistakes in reading scales and identifying missing points. This will prove that children have really understood the lesson and can interpret line graphs with confidence.

ANSWERS Answers for the **Reflect** part of the lesson appear in the separate **Practice and Reflect answer book**.

After the lesson ⏸

- Can children describe what the line graph shows?
- How many children can confidently read and estimate amounts and times from the line graph?
- Do children understand what the x-axis and y-axis are for?

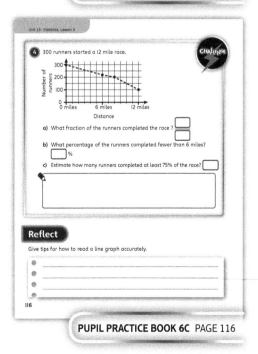

PUPIL PRACTICE BOOK 6C PAGE 116

Constructing line graphs

Learning focus

In this lesson, children learn to create and plot more complex line graphs building on skills from Year 5. They choose and draw an appropriate scale.

Small steps

→ Previous step: Interpreting line graphs
→ **This step: Constructing line graphs**

NATIONAL CURRICULUM LINKS

Year 6 Statistics

Interpret and construct pie charts and line graphs and use these to solve problems.

ASSESSING MASTERY

Children can decide on an appropriate scale to use for the *y*-axis and *x*-axis. They can plot points accurately onto a graph and draw an accurate line linking the points they have plotted. Children can use the line graph to identify and plot missing data.

COMMON MISCONCEPTIONS

Children may find it difficult to decide on an appropriate scale. Encourage them to consider the smallest point and the greatest point and the difference between these. Ensure children use regular intervals that are easy to interpret; for example: 2s, 5s, 10s and hourly, half hourly, every 10 minutes, etc.

STRENGTHENING UNDERSTANDING

Provide children with the *x*-axis and *y*-axis completed. Discuss the intervals and why these are appropriate. Once children are secure in plotting points onto a graph, support them to draw their own. Provide step-by-step guidance. Ask: *What does the y-axis need to go up to? What does the x-axis need to go up to? How close are the points to plot? What regular intervals can we use?*

GOING DEEPER

Ask children to investigate conversion graphs. Ask: *Can you explain why they are in a straight line? Do all conversion line graphs have a straight line?*

KEY LANGUAGE

In lesson: construct, line, graph, point, value, convert/conversion, straight, equivalent, predict, scale, axis/axes

Other language to be used by the teacher: curve, plot, point, *x*-axis, *y*-axis, vertical, horizontal

STRUCTURES AND REPRESENTATIONS

line graph

RESOURCES

Mandatory: graph paper

Optional: tracing paper, rulers

 In the eTextbook of this lesson, you will find interactive links to a selection of teaching tools.

Before you teach ⏸

- Are children secure in reading the scale on a *y*-axis and *x*-axis?
- Are children confident in interpreting tables of data?

Discover

Constructing line graphs

WAYS OF WORKING Pair work

ASK

- Question **1** a): *What are the points showing?*
- Question **1** a): *Where would the next points go?*

IN FOCUS This question introduces the use of a line graph to show a conversion. Encourage children to discuss and interpret the graph. Ask: *Do you recognise that the y-axis is showing the kilometres and the x-axis is showing the miles?* Discuss how children can use the data in the table to plot the next points and calculate how many kilometres there are in 20 miles.

PRACTICAL TIPS Provide children with tracing paper and rulers, to plot the missing points on to the graph.

ANSWERS

Question **1** a): 20 miles converts to 32 km, 25 miles converts to 40 km

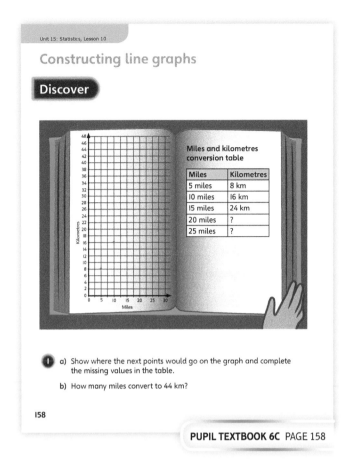

Discover

Miles and kilometres conversion table

Miles	Kilometres
5 miles	8 km
10 miles	16 km
15 miles	24 km
20 miles	?
25 miles	?

1 a) Show where the next points would go on the graph and complete the missing values in the table.

b) How many miles convert to 44 km?

158

PUPIL TEXTBOOK 6C PAGE 158

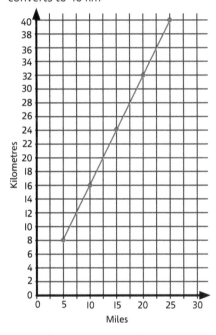

Question **1** b): 27·5 miles converts to 44 km

Share

WAYS OF WORKING Whole class teacher led

ASK

- Question **1** a): *Are the missing points plotted where you thought?*
- Question **1** a): *What did you need to do to complete the line graph? (Plot points and connect the points with a line)*
- Question **1** b): *Did anyone notice the line was straight? What does this tell us?*

IN FOCUS Recap the questions together. Check the plotted points together. How many children worked these out? Discuss the straight line. Ask: *Can you recognise and explain that this means the rate of change is consistent or proportional?*

Share

a) The next point on the graph shows that 15 miles convert to 24 km.

I noticed the points lie in a straight line.

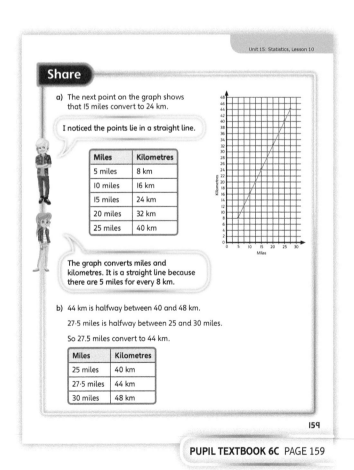

Miles	Kilometres
5 miles	8 km
10 miles	16 km
15 miles	24 km
20 miles	32 km
25 miles	40 km

The graph converts miles and kilometres. It is a straight line because there are 5 miles for every 8 km.

b) 44 km is halfway between 40 and 48 km.

27·5 miles is halfway between 25 and 30 miles.

So 27·5 miles convert to 44 km.

Miles	Kilometres
25 miles	40 km
27·5 miles	44 km
30 miles	48 km

159

PUPIL TEXTBOOK 6C PAGE 159

Think together

WAYS OF WORKING Whole class teacher led (I do, We do, You do)

ASK
- Question ❷: *Where should you plot the point for 8 pm?*
- Question ❸: *What scale would be appropriate to use and why?*
- Question ❸: *How can you use the graph to find out other data?*

IN FOCUS For question ❸ children have to draw a conversion line graph from data. Children should think about how they can use the graph specifically to answer the questions in the challenge question rather than calculate the conversions first using the data.

STRENGTHEN Discuss the line graphs in detail and support children to identify what scale to use on the axes. Practise plotting points on to the graph and joining the dots with a line. Discuss what each graph shows.

DEEPEN Challenge children to draw a line graph to match a story of a journey, for example: Lee leaves the house at 4:30 pm and arrives at 6.00 pm; Kate walks 1 km to the train station. She waits 10 minutes for the train. The train journey is 100 km and takes 70 minutes.

ASSESSMENT CHECKPOINT Question ❸ will show whether children can decide on an appropriate scale to use for the *y*-axis and *x*-axis.

All questions will show that children have understood the lessons on line graphs and are confident with identifying and plotting points and reading off information.

ANSWERS

Question ❶: 10 miles is equivalent to 16 km. 20 miles is equivalent to 32 km. There are 1,600 metres in 1 mile.

Question ❷: The shadow was 10 m long at approximately 8:15 am and exactly 4 pm. A reasonable estimate for the height of the shadow at 8 pm is around 20 m.

Question ❸: 40 inches = 1,016 mm; 50 inches = 1,270 mm

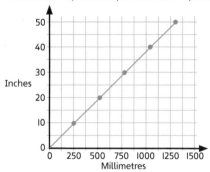

Answers will be approximate:
25 inches = 635 mm
800 mm = 30 inches
15 inches = 38 cm
1 m = 39 inches
6 ft = 1·8 m

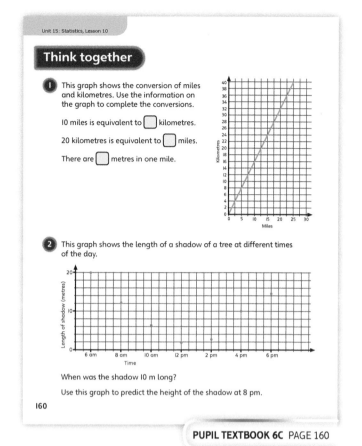

Think together

❶ This graph shows the conversion of miles and kilometres. Use the information on the graph to complete the conversions.

10 miles is equivalent to ☐ kilometres.

20 kilometres is equivalent to ☐ miles.

There are ☐ metres in one mile.

❷ This graph shows the length of a shadow of a tree at different times of the day.

When was the shadow 10 m long?

Use this graph to predict the height of the shadow at 8 pm.

160

PUPIL TEXTBOOK 6C PAGE 160

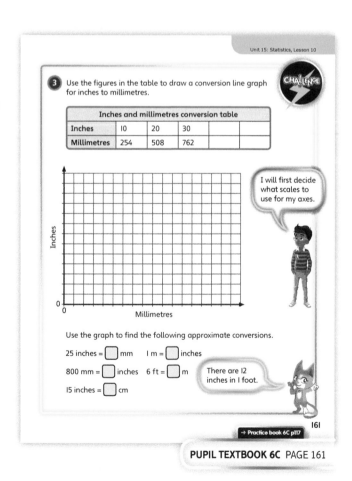

❸ Use the figures in the table to draw a conversion line graph for inches to millimetres.

Inches and millimetres conversion table				
Inches	10	20	30	
Millimetres	254	508	762	

I will first decide what scales to use for my axes.

Use the graph to find the following approximate conversions.

25 inches = ☐ mm   1 m = ☐ inches

800 mm = ☐ inches   6 ft = ☐ m

15 inches = ☐ cm

There are 12 inches in 1 foot.

→ Practice book 6C p117

161

PUPIL TEXTBOOK 6C PAGE 161

Practice

WAYS OF WORKING Independent thinking

IN FOCUS Children use the data in tables to plot points on to line graphs. They need to use the graphs to identify other data. Ensure the children use the graphs to read and identify unmarked points and add to the data listed in the table rather than calculating the further data.

STRENGTHEN Discuss the line graphs in detail and support children to identify the scale used on the axes. Discuss the shapes of each graph and what this tells you about the data. Look at the graph in question ❶ and ask: *Do you think a conversion graph will always be a straight line? Why?*

DEEPEN In question ❹ children need to draw a conversion line graph from an incomplete table. Children should think about how they can use the graph to complete both conversion tables, rather than calculating the conversions first and then plotting the graph. Remind children they will first need to choose an appropriate scale to label the axes.

ASSESSMENT CHECKPOINT All questions can be used to check that children can plot points accurately onto a graph, can draw an accurate line linking the points they have plotted and can use a line graph to identify and plot missing data.

ANSWERS Answers to the **Practice** part of the lesson appear in a separate **Practice and Reflect answer guide**.

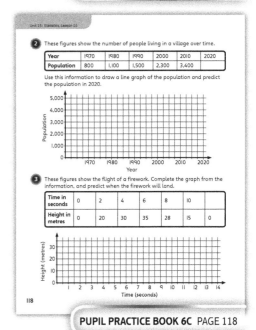

PUPIL PRACTICE BOOK 6C PAGE 117

PUPIL PRACTICE BOOK 6C PAGE 118

Reflect

WAYS OF WORKING Independent thinking

IN FOCUS Children need to explain how they would go about drawing a line graph to convert from metres to kilometres. Their explanation should include how to choose a scale for the axes as well as how to plot the points.

ASSESSMENT CHECKPOINT Writing an explanation of how to draw a line graph will show whether children are confident about constructing line graphs and whether there is anything they don't truly understand.

ANSWERS Answers for the **Reflect** part of the lesson appear in the separate **Practice and Reflect answer book**.

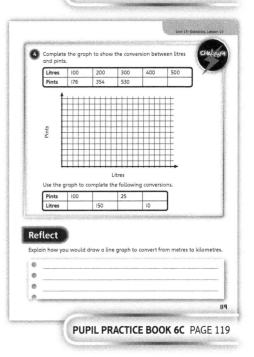

PUPIL PRACTICE BOOK 6C PAGE 119

After the lesson ⏸

- Can all children create a line graph accurately?
- Are all children confident about using a line graph to identify data?

End of unit check

> Don't forget the *Power Maths* unit assessment grid on p26.

WAYS OF WORKING Group work adult led

IN FOCUS

- Question **1** and question **2** focus on the mean. Children demonstrate they can calculate the mean of a set of data by adding the data to find the total and then dividing by the amount of numbers in the set.
- Questions **3** and **4** focus on pie charts. Children need to read and interpret the pie chart considering fractions and percentages.
- Question **5** focusses on line graphs. Children need to read two points on the graph and calculate the difference.

ANSWERS AND COMMENTARY Children calculate the mean from a set of data, demonstrate they can find missing data using the mean, read and interpret pie charts in terms of fractions and percentages and can interpret line graphs.

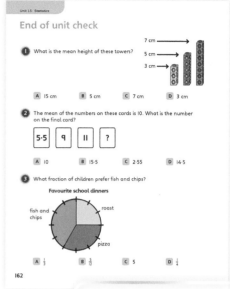

PUPIL TEXTBOOK 6C PAGE 162

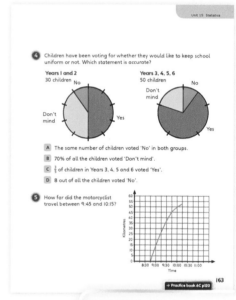

PUPIL TEXTBOOK 6C PAGE 163

Q	A	WRONG ANSWERS AND MISCONCEPTIONS	STRENGTHENING UNDERSTANDING
1	B	A suggests children have added the data but not divided.	Mean = total ÷ amount of numbers in a set
2	D	A suggests children have given the mean as the answer but have not understood the question properly. C suggests children have added the data and divided by the mean.	Give children sets of data and ask them to calculate the mean. Set 1: 3, 4, 5, 3 Set 2: 3·5, 5, 7·5 Set 3: 40, 30, 35, 25, 30
3	B	C suggests children have calculated how many of the segments represent fish and chips but not given the answer as a fraction.	Recap fractions and percentages of circles with the children. Provide circles and ask the children to shade $\frac{1}{2}, \frac{1}{4}, \frac{1}{3}, \frac{3}{4}$ etc. This will help the children to visualise the fractions.
4	D	B shows the children have miscalculated the percentage of children who don't mind. C shows the children have miscalculated the fraction of children who voted 'Yes'.	
5		The answer is 7·5 miles.	Practise reading plotted points and in between plotted points from a line graph.

My journal

WAYS OF WORKING Independent thinking

ANSWERS AND COMMENTARY

Question ❶ asks children to create a line graph. Children need to decide on an appropriate scale for the *x*-axis and *y*-axis and plot the points accurately before joining the dots with a line. Then the children need to demonstrate they are able to use the graph to find the value of $19 in £. Ensure the children use the graph to read the value of $19 rather than calculating from the data.

Question ❷ gives children the opportunity to really think about what they have learnt in this unit and formalise what they know about the advantages and disadvantages of different types of chart. Encourage them to look back at the lessons to help them remember what sort of things they might need to use a chart for.

Power check

WAYS OF WORKING Independent thinking

ASK

- *Can you calculate the mean of a set of numbers?*
- *Are you confident in reading pie charts?*
- *How confidently can you create a line graph?*
- *Could you explain how to use the graph to find information?*

Power play

WAYS OF WORKING Pair work

IN FOCUS The power play uses dice to generate data and then the children have to plot the points onto a line graph. Use the **Power play** to develop children's confidence in plotting data onto a line graph.

ANSWERS AND COMMENTARY Encourage children to check their partner is plotting the data correctly onto the line graph. They need to be sure that at the end of the game, the line is in the correct place because this determines the winner of the game!

After the unit ⏸

- Are children able to suggest what type of graph and chart is most appropriate for different types of data/situations?
- Do children know when using the mean is most useful?

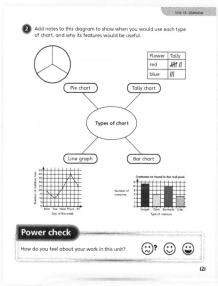

PUPIL PRACTICE BOOK 6C PAGE 120

PUPIL PRACTICE BOOK 6C PAGE 121

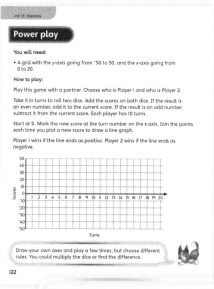

PUPIL PRACTICE BOOK 6C PAGE 122

Strengthen and **Deepen** activities for this unit can be found in the *Power Maths* online subscription.

Published by Pearson Education Limited, 80 Strand, London, WC2R 0RL.

www.pearsonschools.co.uk

Text © Pearson Education Limited 2018
Edited by Pearson, Little Grey Cells Publishing Services and Haremi Ltd
Designed and typeset by Kamae Design
Original illustrations © Pearson Education Limited 2018
Illustrated by Diego Diaz, Adam Linley and Nadene Naude at Beehive Illustration; and Kamae.
Cover design by Pearson Education Ltd
Back cover illustration © Diego Diaz and Nadene Naude at Beehive Illustration.

Series Editor: Tony Staneff
Consultants: Professor Liu Jian and Professor Zhang Dan

The rights of Liu, Jian, Josh Lury, Catherine Casey, Zhou, Da, Zhang Dan, Zhu, Dejiang, Emily Fox, Tim Handley, Wei, Huinv, Hou, Huiying, Zhang, Jing, Steph King, Huang, Lihua, Yin, Lili, Liu, Qimeng and Zhu, Yuhong to be identified as authors of this work have been asserted by them in accordance with the Copyright, Designs and Patents Act 1988.

First published 2018

22 21 20 19
10 9 8 7 6 5 4 3

British Library Cataloguing in Publication Data
A catalogue record for this book is available from the British Library

ISBN 978 0 435 19042 2

Printed in Great Britain by Ashford Colour Press Ltd.

www.activelearnprimary.co.uk

Note from the publisher
Pearson has robust editorial processes, including answer and fact checks, to ensure the accuracy of the content in this publication, and every effort is made to ensure this publication is free of errors. We are, however, only human, and occasionally errors do occur. Pearson is not liable for any misunderstandings that arise as a result of errors in this publication, but it is our priority to ensure that the content is accurate. If you spot an error, please do contact us at resourcescorrections@pearson.com so we can make sure it is corrected.